STERLING
Test Prep

AP
Physics 1
Practice Questions

2nd edition

www.Sterling-Prep.com

2 1

ISBN-13: 978-1-5142156-0-9

Sterling Test Prep products are available at special quantity discounts for sales, promotions, counseling offices and other educational purposes.

For more information contact our Sales Department at

Sterling Test Prep
6 Liberty Square #11
Boston, MA 02109

info@sterling-prep.com

Congratulations on choosing this book as part of your AP Physics 1 preparation!

Scoring high on AP exams is important for admission to college. To achieve a high score on AP Physics 1, you need to develop skills to properly apply the science knowledge you have to solving each question. To be able to do this, you must solve numerous practice questions, because understanding how to apply key physical relationships and formulas is more valuable on the test than simple memorization.

This book provides 679 physics practice questions that test your knowledge of all topics tested on the AP Physics 1 exam. It contains three diagnostic tests (with three more available online) to help you identify the topics you are not well prepared for. It also contains eight sections of topical practice questions, so you can selectively work with the topic you need to study and master. In the second part of the book, you will find answer keys and explanations for the problems in the diagnostic tests and topical practice questions.

The explanations provide step-by-step solutions for qualitative questions and detailed explanations for conceptual questions. The explanations include the foundations and important details needed to answer related questions on the AP Physics 1. By reading these explanations carefully and understanding how they apply to solving the question, you will learn important physical concepts and the relationships between them. This will prepare you for the exam and you will be able to maximize your score.

All the questions in this book are prepared by physics instructors with years of experience in applied physics, as well as in academic settings This team of physics experts analyzed the content of the test, released by the College Board, and designed practice questions that will help you build knowledge and develop the skills necessary for your success on the exam. The questions were reviewed for quality and effectiveness by our science editors who possess extensive credentials, are educated in top colleges and universities and have years of teaching and editorial experience.

We wish you great success in your future academic achievements and look forward to being an important part of your successful preparation for the AP Physics 1!

Sterling Test Prep Team   151125gdx

How to Use This Book

To extract the maximum benefit from this book, we recommend that you start by doing the first diagnostic test and use the answer key to identify the topics you need to spend more time on. Spend some time going through the explanations to this diagnostic test. Review all the explanations, not only those that you got right. After this, practice with the topical questions for those topics you identified as your weak areas – take your time and master those questions.

Next, take the second diagnostic test. You should see a dramatic improvement in your performance on the topics that you practiced prior to this. Analyze your performance on the second diagnostic test and find new topics that you can improve on. Work with the corresponding topical practice questions.

Finally, take the third diagnostic test. At this point, you should be very strong on all topics. If you still find weaknesses, spend extra time going through the solutions and do more practice. You may also find three additional diagnostic tests on our web site.

Ultimately, your goal should be to complete all three diagnostic tests, all topical practice questions and go through all the explanations.

Share your opinion

Your feedback is important because we strive to provide the highest quality prep materials. If you are satisfied with the content of this book, post your review on Amazon, so others can benefit from your experience.

If you have any questions or comments about the material, email us at info@sterling-prep.com and we will resolve any issues to your satisfaction.

To access these and other AP questions online at a special pricing go to page 308 for the web address

Table of Contents

Our Commitment to the Environment

Sterling Test Prep is committed to protecting our planet's resources by supporting environmental organizations with proven track records of conservation, environmental research and education and preservation of vital natural resources. A portion of our profits is donated to support these organizations so they can continue their important missions. These organizations include:

 Ocean Conservancy For over 40 years, Ocean Conservancy has been advocating for a healthy ocean by supporting sustainable solutions based on science and cleanup efforts. Among many environmental achievements, Ocean Conservancy laid the groundwork for an international moratorium on commercial whaling, played an instrumental role in protecting fur seals from overhunting and banning the international trade of sea turtles. The organization created national marine sanctuaries and served as the lead non-governmental organization in the designation of 10 of the 13 marine sanctuaries. In twenty five years of International Coastal Cleanups, volunteers of Ocean Conservancy have removed over 144 million pounds of trash from beaches. Ocean Conservancy mobilizes citizen advocates to facilitate change and protect the ocean for future generations.

 For 25 years, Rainforest Trust has been saving critical lands for conservation through land purchases and protected area designations. Rainforest Trust has played a central role in the creation of 73 new protected areas in 17 countries, including Falkland Islands, Costa Rica and Peru. Nearly 8 million acres have been saved thanks to Rainforest Trust's support of in-country partners across Latin America, with over 500,000 acres of critical lands purchased outright for reserves. Through partnerships and community engagement, Rainforest Trust empowers indigenous people to steward their own resources offering them education, training, and economic assistance.

 Since 1980, Pacific Whale Foundation has been saving whales from extinction and protecting our oceans through science and advocacy. As an international organization, with ongoing research projects in Hawaii, Australia and Ecuador, PWF is an active participant in global efforts to address threats to whales and other marine life. A pioneer in non-invasive whale research, PWF was an early leader in educating the public, from a scientific perspective, about whales and the need for ocean conservation. In addition to critically important whale education and research, PWF was instrumental in stopping the operation of a high-speed ferry in whale calving areas, prohibiting smoking and tobacco use at all Maui County beaches and parks, banning the display of captive whales and dolphins in Maui County, and supporting Maui County's ban on plastic grocery bags.

Thank you for choosing our products to achieve your educational goals.

With your purchase you support environmental causes around the world.

AP PHYSICS 1 EXAM

The AP Physics 1 Exam is 3 hours long and includes a multiple-choice section (90 minutes) and a free-response section (90 minutes). The multiple-choice section is divided into two parts, and the free-response section is divided into three parts, as shown in the table below. Student performance metrics on these four parts are compiled and weighted to determine an overall AP Exam score. Questions are answered filling in the appropriate oval on the answer sheet.

Section	Question Type	Number of Questions	Timing (minutes)	Percentage of Total Exam Score
I	Multiple-choice questions (single-select)	45	90	50%
	Multiple-choice questions (multi-select)	5		
II	Part A: Experimental-design question	1	90	50%
	Part B: Quantitative/qualitative-translation question	1		
	Part C: Short-answer questions	3		

Scientific or graphing calculators may be used by students throughout both sections of the exam. A list of approved graphing calculators can be located on the College Board website. Calculators should not be used to store data/text or to communicate between other calculators. Proctors will monitor activity to ensure compliance during the exam.

Students are not allowed to bring their own equation sheets. Rather, equation tables will be provided to students at the beginning of their exam.

Assessment of Student Learning

AP Physics 1 exam questions evaluate students' ability to:

- provide qualitative and quantitative explanations to physical phenomena based on physics principles and theories;

- mathematically and symbolically solve problems;

- design and describe experiments, analyze data and sources of error, draw conclusions based on evidence;

- develop and interpret conceptual models.

Topics Covered on AP Physics 1 Exam

- Kinematics

- Dynamics: Newton's laws

- Circular motion and universal law of gravitation

- Simple harmonic motion (simple pendulum and mass-springs systems)

- Impulse, linear momentum, and conservation of linear momentum (collisions)

- Work, energy, and conservation of energy

- Rotational motion (torque, rotational kinematics and energy, rotational dynamics, and conservation of angular momentum)

- Electrostatics (electric charge and electric force)

- DC circuits (resistors only)

- Mechanical waves and sound

Types of Questions

Multiple-Choice Questions

There are two types of multiple-choice questions featured on the AP Physics 1 exam, both of which include four possible answer choices per question. The first type, *single-select*, are questions requiring students to choose the one correct answer. The second type, *multi-select*, require students to choose the two correct answers.

Experimental-Design Questions

These questions require students to design and describe an investigation, analyze authentic lab data and observations to identify patterns or explain physical phenomena.

Qualitative/Quantitative Translation Questions

These questions require students to translate between quantitative and qualitative justification and reasoning.

Short-Answer Questions

These questions require a paragraph long coherent argument statement. Space is provided for students to show all their work in answering these questions.

TEST-TAKING STRATEGIES

The best way to do well on AP Physics 1 is to be really good at physics. There is no way around that. Prepare for the test as much as you can, so you can answer with confidence as many questions as possible. With that being said, there are strategies you should employ when you approach a question on the exam.

The task of pacing yourself will become easier if you are aware of the number of questions you need to answer to reach the score you want to get. Always strive for the highest score, but also be realistic about your level of preparation. It may be helpful if you research what counts as a good score for the colleges you are applying to. You can talk to admissions offices at colleges, research college guidebooks or specific college websites, or talk to your guidance counselor. You should find out which score would earn you a college placement credit and which score would be beneficial to your application without earning a credit.

Below are some test-taking strategies to help you maximize your score. Many of these strategies you already know and they may seem like common sense. However, when a student is feeling the pressure of a timed test, these common sense strategies might be forgotten.

Mental Attitude

If you psych yourself out, chances are you will do poorly on the test. To do well on the test, particularly physics, which calls for cool, systemic thinking, you must remain calm. If you start to panic, your mind won't be able to find correct solutions to the questions. Many steps can be taken before the test to increase your confidence level. Buying this book is a good start because you can begin to practice, learn the information you should know to master the topics and get used to answering physics questions. However, there are other things you should keep in mind:

Study in advance. The information will be more manageable, and you will feel more confident if you've studied at regular intervals during the weeks leading up to the test. Cramming the night before is not a successful tactic.

Be well rested. If you are up late the night before the test, chances are you will have a difficult time concentrating and focusing on the day of the test, as you will not feel fresh and alert.

Come up for air. The best way to take this three-hour-long test is not to keep your head down, concentrating intensely for the entire time. Even though you only have 1 minute and 48 seconds per question (on multiple-choice section) and there is no time to waste, it is recommended to take a few seconds between the questions to take a deep breath and relax your muscles.

Time Management

Aside from good preparation, time management is the most important strategy that you should know how to use on any test. You have an average time of 1 minute 48 seconds for each question on the multiple choice section. Even though, you will breeze through some in less than a minute, with others you may be stuck on for three minutes.

Don't dwell on any one question for too long. You should aim to look at every question on the test. It would be unfortunate to not earn the points for a question you could have easily answered just because you did not get a chance to look at it. If you are still in the first half of the test and find yourself spending more than a minute on one question and don't see yourself getting closer to solving it, it is better to move on. It will be more productive if you come back to this question with a fresh mind at the end of the test. You do not want to lose points because you were stuck on one or few questions and did not get a chance to work with other questions that are easy for you.

Nail the easy questions quickly. Each student has their strong and weak topics, and you might be a master on a certain type of questions that are normally considered difficult. Skip the questions you are struggling with and nail the easy ones.

Skip the unfamiliar. If you come across a question that is totally unfamiliar to you, skip it. Do not try to figure out what is going on or what they are trying to ask. At the end of the test, you can go back to these questions if you have time. If you are encountering a question that you have no clue about, most likely you won't be able to answer it through analysis. The better strategy is to leave such questions to the end and use the guessing strategy on them at the end of the test.

Understanding the Question

It is important that you know what the question is asking before you select your answer choice. This seems obvious, but it is surprising how many students don't read a question carefully because they rush through the test and select a wrong answer choice.

A successful student will not just read the question, but will take a moment to understand the question before even looking at the answer choices. This student will be able to separate the important information from distracters and will not get confused on the questions that are asking to identify a false statement (which is the correct answer). Once you've identified what you're dealing with and what is being asked, you should be able to spend less time on picking the right answer. If the question is asking for a general concept, try to answer the question before looking at the answer choices, then look at the choices. If you see a choice that matches the answer you thought of, most likely it is the correct choice.

Correct Way to Guess

Random guessing won't help you on the test, but educated guessing is the strategy you should use in certain situations if you can eliminate at least one (or even two) of the five possible choices.

If you just randomly entered responses for the first 20 questions, there is a 25% chance of guessing correctly on any given question. Therefore, the odds are you would guess right on 5 questions and wrong on 15 questions. However, if for each of the 20 questions you can eliminate one answer choice because you know it to be wrong (wrong order of magnitude, wrong units, etc.), you will have a 33% chance of being right and your odds would move to 7 questions right and 13 questions wrong. Correspondingly, if you can eliminate 2 wrong answers, you can increase your odds to 50%.

Guessing is not cheating and should not be viewed that way. Rather it is a form of "partial credit" because while you might not be sure of the correct answer, you do have relevant knowledge to identify one or two choices that are wrong.

AP Physics 1 Tips

Tip 1: Know the formulas

Since 70–80% of the test requires that you know how to use the formulas, it is imperative that you memorize and understand when to use each one. It is not permitted to bring any papers with notes to the test, but you will be given a sheet with formulas allowed by the College Board.

As you work with this book, you will learn the application of all the important physical formulas and will use them in many different question types.

Tip 2: Know how to manipulate the formulas

You must know how to apply the formulas in addition to just memorizing them. Questions will be worded in ways unfamiliar to you to test whether you can manipulate equations to calculate the correct answer. Knowing that $F = ma$ is not helpful without understanding that $a = F/m$ because it is very unlikely that a question will ask to calculate the force acting on an object with a given mass and acceleration. Rather you are likely to be asked to calculate the acceleration of an object of a given mass with the force acting on it.

Tip 3: Estimating

This tip is only helpful for quantitative questions. For example, estimating can help you choose the correct answer if you have a general sense of the order of magnitude. This is especially applicable to questions where all answer choices have different orders of magnitude and you can save time that you would have to spend on actual calculations.

Tip 4: Draw the question

Don't hesitate to write, draw or graph your thought process once you have read and understood the question. This can help you determine what kind of information you are dealing with. Draw the force and velocity vectors, ray/wave paths, or anything else that may be helpful. Even if a question does not require a graphic answer, drawing a graph (for example, a sketch of a particle's velocity) can allow a solution to become obvious.

Tip 5: Eliminating wrong answers

This tip utilizes the strategy of educated guessing. You can usually eliminate one or two answer choices right away in many questions. In addition, there are certain types of questions for which you can use a particular elimination method.

By using logical estimations for qualitative questions, you can eliminate the answer choices that are unreasonably high or unreasonably low.

Last helpful tip: fill in your answers carefully

This seems like a simple thing, but it is extremely important. Many test takers make mistakes when filling in answers whether it is a paper test or computer-based test. Make sure you pay attention and check off the answer choice you actually chose as correct.

COMMON PHYSICS FORMULAS & CONVERSIONS

Constants and Conversion Factors

1 unified atomic mass unit	$1\ u = 1.66 \times 10^{-27}\ kg$
	$1\ u = 931\ MeV/c^2$
Proton mass	$m_p = 1.67 \times 10^{-27}\ kg$
Neutron mass	$m_n = 1.67 \times 10^{-27}\ kg$
Electron mass	$m_e = 9.11 \times 10^{-31}\ kg$
Electron charge magnitude	$e = 1.60 \times 10^{-19}\ C$
Avogrado's number	$N_0 = 6.02 \times 10^{23}\ mol^{-1}$
Universal gas constant	$R = 8.31\ J/(mol \cdot K)$
Boltzmann's constant	$k_B = 1.38 \times 10^{-23}\ J/K$
Speed of light	$c = 3.00 \times 10^8\ m/s$
Planck's constant	$h = 6.63 \times 10^{-34}\ J \cdot s$
	$h = 4.14 \times 10^{-15}\ eV \cdot s$
	$hc = 1.99 \times 10^{-25}\ J \cdot m$
	$hc = 1.24 \times 10^3\ eV \cdot nm$
Vacuum permittivity	$\varepsilon_0 = 8.85 \times 10^{-12}\ C^2/N \cdot m^2$
Coulomb's law constant	$k = 1/4\pi\varepsilon_0 = 9.0 \times 10^9\ N \cdot m^2/C^2$
Vacuum permeability	$\mu_0 = 4\pi \times 10^{-7}\ (T \cdot m)/A$
Magnetic constant	$k' = \mu_0/4\pi = 10^{-7}\ (T \cdot m)/A$
Universal gravitational constant	$G = 6.67 \times 10^{-11}\ m^3/kg \cdot s^2$
Acceleration due to gravity at Earth's surface	$g = 9.8\ m/s^2$
1 atmosphere pressure	$1\ atm = 1.0 \times 10^5\ N/m^2$
	$1\ atm = 1.0 \times 10^5\ Pa$
1 electron volt	$1\ eV = 1.60 \times 10^{-19}\ J$
Balmer constant	$B = 3.645 \times 10^{-7}\ m$
Rydberg constant	$R = 1.097 \times 10^7\ m^{-1}$
Stefan constant	$\sigma = 5.67 \times 10^{-8}\ W/m^2 K^4$

Units			Prefixes		
Name	**Symbol**		**Factor**	**Prefix**	**Symbol**
meter	m		10^{12}	tera	T
kilogram	kg		10^{9}	giga	G
second	s		10^{6}	mega	M
ampere	A		10^{3}	kilo	k
kelvin	K		10^{-2}	centi	c
mole	mol		10^{-3}	mili	m
hertz	Hz		10^{-6}	micro	μ
newton	N		10^{-9}	nano	n
pascal	Pa		10^{-12}	pico	p
joule	J				
watt	W				
coulomb	C				
volt	V				
ohm	Ω				
henry	H				
farad	F				
tesla	T				
degree Celsius	°C				
electronvolt	eV				

Values of Trigonometric Functions for Common Angles

θ	$\sin \theta$	$\cos \theta$	$\tan \theta$
0°	0	1	0
30°	1/2	$\sqrt{3}/2$	$\sqrt{3}/3$
37°	3/5	4/5	3/4
45°	$\sqrt{2}/2$	$\sqrt{2}/2$	1
53°	4/5	3/5	4/3
60°	$\sqrt{3}/2$	1/2	$\sqrt{3}$
90°	1	0	∞

Newtonian Mechanics

		a = acceleration
	$v = v_0 + at$	A = amplitude
	$x = x_0 + v_0 t + \frac{1}{2} a t^2$	E = energy
Translational Motion		
	$v^2 = v_0^2 + 2a\Delta x$	F = force
	$\vec{a} = \dfrac{\sum \vec{F}}{m} = \dfrac{\vec{F}_{net}}{m}$	f = frequency
		h = height
	$\omega = \omega_0 + \alpha t$	I = rotational inertia
	$\theta = \theta_0 + \omega_0 t + \frac{1}{2} \alpha t^2$	J = impulse
Rotational Motion		K = kinetic energy
	$\omega^2 = \omega_0^2 + 2\alpha\Delta\theta$	k = spring constant
	$\vec{\alpha} = \dfrac{\sum \vec{\tau}}{I} = \dfrac{\vec{\tau}_{net}}{I}$	ℓ = length
		m = mass
Force of Friction	$\left|\vec{F}_f\right| \leq \mu\left|\vec{F}_n\right|$	N = normal force
Centripetal Acceleration	$a_c = \dfrac{v^2}{r}$	P = power
		p = momentum
Torque	$\tau = r_\perp F = rF \sin\theta$	L = angular momentum
		r = radius of distance
Momentum	$\Delta\vec{p} = m\vec{v}$	T = period
Impulse	$J = \Delta\vec{p} = \vec{F}\Delta t$	t = time
		U = potential energy
Kinetic Energy	$K = \frac{1}{2} m v^2$	v = velocity or speed
		W = work done on a
Potential Energy	$\Delta U_g = mg\Delta y$	system
Work	$\Delta E = W = F_\parallel d = Fd \cos\theta$	x = position
		y = height
Power	$P = \dfrac{\Delta E}{\Delta t} = \dfrac{\Delta W}{\Delta t}$	α = angular acceleration

Simple Harmonic Motion	$x = A\cos(\omega t) = A\cos(2\pi f t)$	
		μ = coefficient of friction
Center of Mass	$x_{cm} = \dfrac{\sum m_i x_i}{\sum m_i}$	
		θ = angle
Angular Momentum	$L = I\omega$	τ = torque
		ω = angular speed
Angular Impulse	$\Delta L = \tau \Delta t$	
Angular Kinetic Energy	$K = \dfrac{1}{2} I\omega^2$	
Work	$W = F\Delta r \cos\theta$	
Power	$P = Fv \sin\theta$	
Spring Force	$|\vec{F_s}| = k|\vec{x}|$	
Spring Potential Energy	$U_s = \dfrac{1}{2} kx^2$	
Period of Spring Oscillator	$T_s = 2\pi\sqrt{m/k}$	
Period of Simple Pendulum	$T_p = 2\pi\sqrt{\ell/g}$	
Period	$T = \dfrac{2\pi}{\omega} = \dfrac{1}{f}$	
Gravitational Body Force	$|\vec{F_g}| = G\dfrac{m_1 m_2}{r^2}$	
Potential Energy of Gravitational Body	$U_G = -\dfrac{Gm_1 m_2}{r}$	

Electricity and Magnetism

Electric Field Strength	$\vec{E} = \dfrac{\vec{F}_E}{q}$	A = area
		B = magnetic field
		C = capacitance
Electric Field Strength	$\|\vec{E}\| = \dfrac{1}{4\pi\varepsilon_0}\dfrac{\|q\|}{r^2}$	d = distance
		E = electric field
Electric Field Strength	$\|\vec{E}\| = \dfrac{\|\Delta V\|}{\|\Delta r\|}$	ϵ = emf
		F = force
Electric Field Force	$\|\vec{F}_E\| = \dfrac{1}{4\pi\varepsilon_0}\dfrac{\|q_1 q_2\|}{r^2}$	I = current
		l = length
Voltage	$V = \dfrac{1}{4\pi\varepsilon_0}\dfrac{q}{r}$	P = power
		Q = charge
Current	$I = \dfrac{\Delta Q}{\Delta t}$	q = point charge
		R = resistance
Resistance	$R = \dfrac{\rho l}{A}$	r = separation
		t = time
Power	$P = I\Delta V$	U = potential energy
		V = electric potential
Current	$I = \dfrac{\Delta V}{R}$	v = speed
		κ = dielectric constant
Resistors in Series	$R_s = \sum_i R_i$	ρ = resistivity
		θ = angle
Resistors in Parallel	$\dfrac{1}{R_p} = \sum_i \dfrac{1}{R_i}$	$\varPhi$ = flux

Sound

Standing Wave/ Open Pipe Harmonics	$\lambda = \dfrac{2L}{n}$	$f = frequency$
		$L = length$
Closed Pipe Harmonics	$\lambda = \dfrac{4L}{n}$	$m = mass$
		$M = molecular$ $mass$
Harmonic Frequencies	$f_n = n f_1$	$n = harmonic$ $number$
Speed of Sound in Ideal Gas	$v_{sound} = \sqrt{\dfrac{yRT}{M}}$	$R = gas\ constant$
		$T = tension$
Speed of Wave Through Wire	$v = \sqrt{\dfrac{T}{m/L}}$	$v = velocity$
		$y = adiabatic$ $constant$
Doppler Effect (Approaching)	$f_{observed} = \left(\dfrac{v}{v - v_{source}}\right) f_{source}$	$\lambda = wavelength$
Doppler Effect (Receding)	$f_{observed} = \left(\dfrac{v}{v + v_{source}}\right) f_{source}$	

Geometry and Trigonometry

Rectangle	$A = bh$	$A = area$
		$C = circumference$
Triangle	$A = \dfrac{1}{2}bh$	$V = volume$
		$S = surface\ area$
Circle	$A = \pi r^2$	$b = base$
	$C = 2\pi r$	$h = height$
Rectangular Solid	$V = lwh$	$l = length$
		$w = width$
Cylinder	$V = \pi r^2 l$	$r = radius$
	$S = 2\pi rl + 2\pi r^2$	$\theta = angle$
Sphere	$V = \dfrac{4}{3}\pi r^3$ $S = 4\pi r^2$	
Right Triangle	$a^2 + b^2 = c^2$ $\sin\theta = \dfrac{a}{c}$ $\cos\theta = \dfrac{b}{c}$ $\tan\theta = \dfrac{a}{b}$	

AP PHYSICS 1
DIAGNOSTIC TESTS

DIAGNOSTIC TEST #1

ANSWER SHEET

#	Answer:				Mark for review	#	Answer:				Mark for review
1:	A	B	C	D	____	26:	A	B	C	D	____
2:	A	B	C	D	____	27:	A	B	C	D	____
3:	A	B	C	D	____	28:	A	B	C	D	____
4:	A	B	C	D	____	29:	A	B	C	D	____
5:	A	B	C	D	____	30:	A	B	C	D	____
6:	A	B	C	D	____	31:	A	B	C	D	____
7:	A	B	C	D	____	32:	A	B	C	D	____
8:	A	B	C	D	____	33:	A	B	C	D	____
9:	A	B	C	D	____	34:	A	B	C	D	____
10:	A	B	C	D	____	35:	A	B	C	D	____
11:	A	B	C	D	____	36:	A	B	C	D	____
12:	A	B	C	D	____	37:	A	B	C	D	____
13:	A	B	C	D	____	38:	A	B	C	D	____
14:	A	B	C	D	____	39:	A	B	C	D	____
15:	A	B	C	D	____	40:	A	B	C	D	____
16:	A	B	C	D	____	41:	A	B	C	D	____
17:	A	B	C	D	____	42:	A	B	C	D	____
18:	A	B	C	D	____	43:	A	B	C	D	____
19:	A	B	C	D	____	44:	A	B	C	D	____
20:	A	B	C	D	____	45:	A	B	C	D	____
21:	A	B	C	D	____	46:	A	B	C	D	____
22:	A	B	C	D	____	47:	A	B	C	D	____
23:	A	B	C	D	____	48:	A	B	C	D	____
24:	A	B	C	D	____	49:	A	B	C	D	____
25:	A	B	C	D	____	50:	A	B	C	D	____

1. What property of matter determines an object's resistance to change in its state of motion?

      I. mass   II. density   III. volume

  A. I only   **B.** II only   **C.** III only   **D.** I and II only

2. Two forces of equal magnitude act on an object. If each force is 4.6 N and the angle between them is 40°, what is the magnitude and direction of a third force for the object to be in equilibrium?

  A. 2.3 N, to the right   **C.** 6.5 N, to the right

  B. 4.3 N, to the right   **D.** 8.6 N, to the right

3. How far from the heavier end must the fulcrum of a massless 10 m seesaw be if an 800 N father on one side is to balance his 200 N son at the other end?

  A. 0.5 m   **B.** 2 m   **C.** 1 m   **D.** 8 m

4. In the absence of friction, how much work would a boy do while pulling a 10 kg sled a distance of 3.5 m with a 20 N force?

  A. 57 J   **B.** 70 J   **C.** 1.8 J   **D.** 85 J

5. Total constructive interference is observed when two waves with the same frequency and wavelength are at a:

  A. 45° phase difference   **C.** 180° phase difference

  B. 90° phase difference   **D.** 0° phase difference

6. The Doppler shift occurs when the source of waves and a detector are moving relative to each other. There is an increase in the detected frequency when the source and detector are approaching each other, and a decrease in the detected frequency when they are moving away from each other. A commuter train is moving rapidly at 50 m/s towards Kevin who is standing still. The train sounds its horn at 420 Hz. The speed of sound is 350 m/s at a temperature of 29 °C. What frequency does Kevin hear after the train passes?

  A. 335 Hz   **B.** 368 Hz   **C.** 424 Hz   **D.** 446 Hz

7. What is the peak current for a 26 μF capacitor connected across a 120 V_{rms} 60 Hz source?

  A. 1.2 A   **B.** 7.3 A   **C.** 2.7 A   **D.** 0 A

8. Two charges, $Q_1 = 3.4 \times 10^{-10}$ C and $Q_2 = 6.8 \times 10^{-9}$ C, are separated by a distance of 1 cm. Let F_1 be the magnitude of the electrostatic force felt by Q_1 due to Q_2 and let F_2 be the magnitude of the electrostatic force felt by Q_2 due to Q_1. What is the ratio of F_1 / F_2?

A. 2   **B.** 1   **C.** 16   **D.** 8

9. Ignoring air resistance, how long does it take a coin to reach the ground when it is dropped from a 42 m building?   Use $g = 10$ m/s^2

A. 1.4 s   **B.** 2.9 s   **C.** 3.6 s   **D.** 5.4 s

10. Which of the following statements is TRUE regarding the acceleration experienced by a block moving down a frictionless plane that is inclined at a 20° angle?

A. It remains constant
B. It increases as the block moves down the plane
C. It increases at a rate proportional to the incline
D. It decreases at a rate proportional to the incline

11. A bullet shot from a gun with a longer barrel has a greater muzzle velocity because the bullet receives a greater:

    I. force   II. impulse   III. acceleration

A. I only   **B.** II only   **C.** III only   **D.** I and II only

12. A ball bounces on the floor three times, whereby it loses 20% of its energy with each bounce due to heating. How high is the third bounce, provided the ball was released 250 cm from the floor?

A. 115 cm   **B.** 150 cm   **C.** 75 cm   **D.** 128 cm

13. What is the period of a wave if its frequency is 10 Hz?

A. 0.1 s   **B.** 10 s   **C.** 100 s   **D.** 10 s

14. What is the frequency of a pressure wave with a wavelength of 2.5 m that is traveling at 1,600 m/s?

A. 640 Hz   **B.** 5.6 kHz   **C.** 0.64 Hz   **D.** 4 kHz

15. At terminal velocity, an object falling toward the surface of the Earth has a velocity that:

A. depends on the mass of the object   **C.** remains constant
B. depends on the weight of the object   **D.** increases

16. A box that weighs 40 N is on a rough horizontal surface. An external force F is applied horizontally to the box. A normal force and a friction force are also present. When force F equals 8.8 N, the box is in motion at a constant velocity. The box decelerates when force F is removed. What is the magnitude of the acceleration of the box? (Use acceleration due to gravity g = 10 m/s^2)

    A. 0.55 m/s^2　　　**B.** 1.1 m/s^2　　　**C.** 4.4 m/s^2　　　**D.** 2.2 m/s^2

17. Two friends are standing on opposite ends of a canoe which is initially at rest with respect to the lake. Steve is on the right when he throws a very massive ball to the left, and Mike, on the left, catches it. Ignoring friction between the canoe and the water, after the ball is caught, the canoe:

    A. moves to the right before reversing direction　　**C.** remains stationary
    B. moves to the left before reversing direction　　**D.** moves to the right

18. A 1,000 kg car is traveling at 30 m/s on a level road when the driver slams on the brakes, bringing the car to a stop. What is the change in kinetic energy during the braking, if the skid marks are 35 m long?

    A. -4.5×10^5 J　　　**B.** 0 J　　　**C.** -9×10^{10} J　　　**D.** 4.2×10^5 J

19. In a given medium with fixed boundaries, the longest wavelength that produces a standing wave is 4 m. What is the lowest possible frequency associated with a standing wave within this medium, if waves propagate through the medium at 8 m/s?

    A. 0.5 Hz　　　**B.** 1 Hz　　　**C.** 2 Hz　　　**D.** 6 Hz

20. Which of the following statements is FALSE?

    A. Waves from a vibrating string are transverse waves
    B. Sound travels much slower than light
    C. Sound waves are longitudinal pressure waves
    D. Sound can travel through a vacuum

21. The electric power of a lamp that carries 2 A at 120 V is:

    A. 24 W　　　**B.** 2 W　　　**C.** 60 W　　　**D.** 240 W

22. A 3 Ω and a 1.5 Ω resistor are connected in parallel within a circuit. If the voltage drop across the 3 Ω resistor is 2 V, what is the sum of the currents through these two resistors?

    A. 4/3 amps　　　**B.** 3/2 amps　　　**C.** 2 amps　　　**D.** 2/3 amps

23. A small boat is moving at a velocity of 3.35 m/s when it is accelerated by a river current perpendicular to the initial direction of motion. Relative to the initial direction of motion, what is the new velocity of the boat after 33.5 s if the current acceleration is 0.75 m/s²?

A. 62 m/s at 7.6°

B. 62 m/s at 82.4°

C. 25 m/s at 7.6°

D. 25 m/s at 82.4°

24. Lisa is standing in a moving truck, and she suddenly falls backward because the truck's:

A. speed remained the same

B. velocity decreased

C. acceleration remained the same

D. velocity increased

25. A machinist turns the power on for a stationary grinding wheel at time $t = 0$ s. The wheel accelerates uniformly for 10 s and reaches the operating angular velocity of 58 radians/s. The wheel is run at that angular velocity for 30 s before the power is shut off. The wheel slows down uniformly at 1.4 radians/s² until it stops. What is the approximate total number of revolutions for the wheel?

A. 460   **B.** 320   **C.** 380   **D.** 510

26. How much work is done on a crate if it is pushed 2 m with a force of 20 N?

A. 10 J   **B.** 20 J   **C.** 30 J   **D.** 40 J

27. The graph shows the position (x) as a function of time (t) for a system undergoing simple harmonic motion. Which of the following graphs represents the acceleration of this system as a function of time?

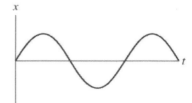

A.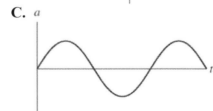

C.

B.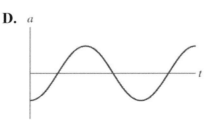

D.

28. Sound can undergo refraction in:

   I. air   II. water   III. a vacuum

   A. I only   **B.** II only   **C.** III only   **D.** I and II only

29. Ignoring air resistance, what is the speed of a rock as it hits the ground if it was dropped from a 50 m cliff? (Use acceleration due to gravity $g = 10$ m/s²)

   A. 21 m/s   **B.** 14 m/s   **C.** 32 m/s   **D.** 42 m/s

30. A 15 kg block on a table is connected by a string to a 60 kg mass, which is hanging over the edge of the table. Ignoring the frictional force, what is acceleration of the 15 kg block when the 60 kg block is released? (Use acceleration due to gravity $g = 10$ m/s²)

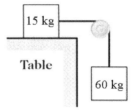

   A. 9.5 m/s²   **B.** 7.5 m/s²   **C.** 10.5 m/s²   **D.** 8 m/s²

31. If the speed of a moving object doubles, then what else doubles?

   I. Acceleration   II. Kinetic energy   III. Momentum

   A. I only   **B.** II only   **C.** III only   **D.** I and II only

32. Which statement is correct when a flower pot of mass m falls from rest to the ground for a distance h below?

   A. The speed of the pot when it hits the ground is proportional to m
   B. The KE of the pot when it hits the ground does not depend on h
   C. The KE of the pot when it hits the ground is proportional to h
   D. The speed of the pot when it hits the ground is proportional to h

33. Crests of an ocean wave pass a pier every 10 s. What is the wavelength of the ocean waves if the waves are moving at 4.6 m/s?

   A. 4.4 m   **B.** 0.46 m   **C.** 4.6 m   **D.** 46 m

34. Two speakers placed 3 m apart are producing in-phase sound waves with a wavelength of 1 m. A microphone is placed between the speakers to determine the intensity of the sound at various points. What kind of point exists exactly 0.5 m to the left of the speaker on the right? (Use speed of sound $v = 340$ m/s)

   A. Antinode   **C.** Node and antinode
   B. Node   **D.** Destructive interference

35. The resistance of an object equals:

A. length × resistivity × cross-sectional area

B. length / (resistivity × cross-sectional area)

C. current / voltage

D. voltage / current

36. What causes an object to become electrostatically charged?

A. Charge is created

B. Protons are transferred

C. Electrons are transferred

D. Protons and electrons are transferred

37. Determine both the distance traveled and the magnitude of the displacement when an object moves 16 m to the North and then moves 12 m to the South.

A. 4 m, 4 m   B. 28 m, 28 m   C. 28 m, 4 m   D. 4 m, 28 m

38. A potted plant of mass *M* is resting on a flat board. One end of the board is lifted slowly until the potted plant begins to slide. What does the angle θ that the board must make for sliding to occur depend on?

A. *M*

B. μ_s, static friction

C. μ_k, kinetic friction

D. *g*, acceleration due to gravity

39. A 1 kg chunk of putty moving at 1 m/s collides and sticks to a stationary 6 kg box. What is the total momentum of the box and putty? (Assume the box rests on a frictionless surface)

A. 0 kg·m/s   B. 1 kg·m/s   C. 2 kg·m/s   D. 3 kg·m/s

40. A 20 kg object is dropped from a height of 100 m. Ignoring air resistance, how much gravitational PE has the object lost when its speed is 30 m/s?

A. 2,050 J   B. 2,850 J   C. 9,000 J   D. 5,550 J

41. The total distance traveled by an object in one complete cycle of simple harmonic motion is how many times the amplitude?

A. one   B. two   C. three   D. four

42. With a total of four tuning forks, what is the greatest number of different beat frequencies that can be heard by striking the forks one pair at a time?

A. 2   B. 4   C. 6   D. 8

43. Which is a unit of measuring resistance to a change of motion?

A. N   B. ohm   C. $\sec^{-1}$ D. kg

44. At constant speed, an object following a straight-line path has:

A. decreasing acceleration   C. zero acceleration
B. no forces acting on it   D. increasing velocity

45. The masses of the blocks and the velocities before and after a collision are:

In this example, the collision is:

A. completely inelastic   C. characterized by an increase in KE
B. completely elastic   D. characterized by a decrease in momentum

46. Which statement correctly describes the situation when a 6 kg mass moving at 2 m/s and a 3 kg mass moving at 4 m/s are gliding over a horizontal frictionless surface? A horizontal force *F*, which directly opposes their motion, results in the objects coming to rest.

A. The 6 kg mass travels twice the distance of the 3 kg mass before stopping
B. The 3 kg mass travels farther, but less than twice the distance of the 6 kg mass before stopping
C. The 3 kg mass travels twice the distance of the 6 kg mass before stopping
D. The 6 kg mass loses four times more KE than the 3 kg mass before stopping

47. What is the approximate wavelength of a wave that has a speed of 360 m/s and a period of 4.2 s?

A. 0.15 m   B. 0.86 m   C. 1.5 m   D. 8.6 m

48. What is the effect on a system's mechanical energy if only the amplitude of a vibrating mass-and-spring system is doubled?

A. Increases by a factor of 2   C. Increases by a factor of 3
B. Increases by a factor of 4   D. Remains the same

49. What is the current through a 12 ohm resistor connected to a 120 V power supply?

A. 1 A   B. 8 A   C. 10 A   D. 20 A

50. If the distance between two electrostatic charges is doubled, how is the force between them affected?

A. Increases by 2   B. Increases by 4   C. Decreases by $\sqrt{2}$ D. Decreases by 4

DIAGNOSTIC TEST #2

ANSWER SHEET

#	Answer:				Mark for review	#	Answer:				Mark for review
1:	A	B	C	D	____	26:	A	B	C	D	____
2:	A	B	C	D	____	27:	A	B	C	D	____
3:	A	B	C	D	____	28:	A	B	C	D	____
4:	A	B	C	D	____	29:	A	B	C	D	____
5:	A	B	C	D	____	30:	A	B	C	D	____
6:	A	B	C	D	____	31:	A	B	C	D	____
7:	A	B	C	D	____	32:	A	B	C	D	____
8:	A	B	C	D	____	33:	A	B	C	D	____
9:	A	B	C	D	____	34:	A	B	C	D	____
10:	A	B	C	D	____	35:	A	B	C	D	____
11:	A	B	C	D	____	36:	A	B	C	D	____
12:	A	B	C	D	____	37:	A	B	C	D	____
13:	A	B	C	D	____	38:	A	B	C	D	____
14:	A	B	C	D	____	39:	A	B	C	D	____
15:	A	B	C	D	____	40:	A	B	C	D	____
16:	A	B	C	D	____	41:	A	B	C	D	____
17:	A	B	C	D	____	42:	A	B	C	D	____
18:	A	B	C	D	____	43:	A	B	C	D	____
19:	A	B	C	D	____	44:	A	B	C	D	____
20:	A	B	C	D	____	45:	A	B	C	D	____
21:	A	B	C	D	____	46:	A	B	C	D	____
22:	A	B	C	D	____	47:	A	B	C	D	____
23:	A	B	C	D	____	48:	A	B	C	D	____
24:	A	B	C	D	____	49:	A	B	C	D	____
25:	A	B	C	D	____	50:	A	B	C	D	____

1. A projectile is fired at time $t = 0$ s from point O of a ledge. It has initial velocity components of $v_{ox} = 30$ m/s and $v_{oy} = 300$ m/s with a time in flight of 75 s. The projectile lands at point P. What is the horizontal distance that the projectile travels?

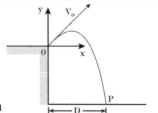

    A. 3,020 m   **B.** 2,880 m   **C.** 2,420 m   **D.** 2,250 m

2. A car of mass m is traveling along the roadway up a slight incline of angle θ to the horizontal when the driver sees a deer and suddenly applies the brakes. The car skids before coming to rest. Which expression gives the force of friction on the car if the coefficient of static friction between the tires and the road is μ_s, and the coefficient of kinetic friction is μ_k?

    A. $\mu_k N$ **B.** $\mu_s N$ **C.** mg **D.** $mg \sin \theta$

3. A torque of 14 N·m is applied to a solid, uniform disk with a radius of 0.6 m. What is the mass of the disk if it accelerates at 5.3 rad/s^2?

    A. 7.6 kg   **B.** 4.2 kg   **C.** 14.7 kg   **D.** 21.4 kg

4. Energy is the:

    I. ability to do work
    II. work that can be done by an object with potential or kinetic energy
    III. work needed to generate potential or kinetic energy

    A. I only   **B.** II only   **C.** III only   **D.** I, II and III

5. The displacement of a vibrating tuning fork and the resulting sound wave is related to:

    A. period   **B.** amplitude   **C.** resonance   **D.** frequency

6. The decibel level of sound is related to its:

    A. velocity   **B.** frequency   **C.** wavelength   **D.** intensity

7. What is the voltage across a 5.5 Ω resistor if the current through it is 10 A?

    A. 1 V   **B.** 5 V   **C.** 55 V   **D.** 5.5 V

8. A positive charge Q is held fixed at the origin. A positive charge z is let go from point p on the positive x-axis. Ignoring friction, which statement describes the velocity of z after it is released?

    A. Increases indefinitely   **C.** Increases, then decreases, but never reaches zero
    B. Decreases to zero   **D.** Increases, but never exceeds a certain limit

9. The slope of a line at a single point on a position vs. time graph gives:

A. average acceleration   **C.** instantaneous velocity

B. change in acceleration   **D.** average velocity

10. What is the net force on a 1,200 kg Alpha Romeo that is moving at a constant speed of 3.5 m/s and turning to the left on a curve of the road that has an effective radius of 4 m?

A. 1,550 N   **B.** 2,160 N   **C.** 3,600 N   **D.** 8,465 N

11. An irregularly-shaped object 10 m long is placed with each end on two nearby scales. If the scale on the right reads 94 N and the scale on the left reads 69 N, how far from the left is the object's center of gravity? (Use acceleration due to gravity $g = 9.8$ m/s^2)

A. 6.8 m   **B.** 6.3 m   **C.** 5.8 m   **D.** 8.1 m

12. Marshall drops a water balloon from the top of a building onto Peter on the sidewalk below. Ignoring air resistance, how tall is the building if the balloon is traveling at 29 m/s when it strikes Peter's head? (Use acceleration due to gravity $g = 10$ m/s^2 and the distant of Peter's head above the ground = 1 m)

A. 50.5 m   **B.** 37.5 m   **C.** 43 m   **D.** 26 m

13. Assuming no change in the system's mass m, increasing the spring constant k of a spring system causes what kind of change in the resonant frequency of the system?

A. No change   **C.** Decrease only if the ratio k/m is > 1

B. Increase   **D.** Increase only if the ratio k/m is $\geq$ 1

14. Assuming that all other factors remain constant, what happens to the velocity of sound as the temperature of the air increases?

A. Does not change because it is dependent only on the state of the substance

B. Increases when atmospheric pressure is high and decreases when the pressure is low

C. Increases

D. Decreases

15. How long does it take for a rock to reach the maximum height of its trajectory if a boy throws it with an initial velocity of 3.13 m/s at 30° above the horizontal? (Use acceleration due to gravity $g = 9.8$ m/s^2)

A. 0.16 s   **B.** 0.28 s   **C.** 0.333 s   **D.** 0.446 s

16. What is the reaction force if, as a ball falls, the action force is the pull of the Earth's mass on the ball?

    A. None present   **C.** The downward acceleration due to gravity

    B. The pull of the ball's mass on Earth   **D.** The air resistance acting against the ball

17. Shawn, with a mass of 105 kg, sits 5.5 m to the left of the center of a seesaw. Mark and John, each with a mass of 20 kg, are seated on the right side of the seesaw. If Mark sits 10 m to the right of the center, how far to the right from the center should John sit to balance the seesaw? (Use acceleration due to gravity $g = 10$ m/s^2)

    A. 5 m   **B.** 10 m   **C.** 19 m   **D.** 20 m

18. Is it possible for a system to have negative potential energy?

    A. Yes, because the choice of the zero for potential energy is arbitrary

    B. No, because this has no physical meaning

    C. Yes, if the kinetic energy is positive

    D. Yes, if the total energy is positive

19. What is the speed of 2 m long water waves as they pass by a floating piece of cork that bobs up and down for one complete cycle each second?

    A. 8 m/s   **B.** 0.5 m/s   **C.** 1 m/s   **D.** 2 m/s

20. A guitar has a 14 cm string and sounds a 440 Hz musical note when played without fingering. How far from the end of the string should Samantha place her fingers to play a 520 Hz note?

    A. 5.8 cm   **B.** 0.8 cm   **C.** 1.6 cm   **D.** 2.2 cm

21. What is the equivalent resistance of the circuits if each has a resistance of 600 Ω?

    A. 60 Ω   **B.** 1,200 Ω   **C.** 600 Ω   **D.** 175 Ω

22. A proton is traveling to the right and encounters region Y that contains an electric field where the proton speeds up. In what direction does the electric field in region Y point?

    A. To the left   **B.** To the right   **C.** Down into the page   **D.** Up from the page

23. What is the shape of the line on a position vs. time graph for constant linear acceleration?

    A. curve   **B.** sloped line   **C.** sinusoidal graph   **D.** horizontal line

24. What is true about the acceleration of an object that travels at constant speed in a circular path?

   A. It is equal to zero because the speed is constant
   B. It is not equal to zero and is always directed tangent to the path
   C. It is not equal to zero and is always directed behind the radius of the path
   D. It is not equal to zero and is always directed toward the center of the path

25. A steel ball A is thrown in the air with a speed of 4 m/s at an angle of 60° from the horizontal. It drops onto steel ball B which is 1.4 times the mass of A. If ball A comes to rest after the collision and ball B bounces, what is the horizontal component of ball B's velocity?

   A. 0.4 m/s   **B.** 0.6 m/s   **C.** 1.4 m/s   **D.** 1.8 m/s

26. Susan pulls on a wagon with a force of 70 N. What is the average power generated by Susan if the wagon moves a total of 45 m in 3 min?

   A. 18 W   **B.** 27 W   **C.** 14 W   **D.** 21 W

27. Simple harmonic motion (SMH) is characterized by acceleration that:

   A. is proportional to displacement   **C.** decreases linearly
   B. is proportional to velocity   **D.** is inversely proportional to displacement

28. An over-taut violin string was tuned with a tuning fork that produced an accurate pitch of 340 Hz. What is the period of vibration of the violin string if a beat frequency of 4 Hz is produced when the string and the fork are sounded together?

   A. 1/336 sec   **B.** 1/321 sec   **C.** 1/344 sec   **D.** 1/327 sec

29. A ball is projected horizontally with an initial speed of 5 m/s from an initial height of 50 m. Ignoring air resistance, how far has the ball traveled horizontally from its original position when it lands? (Use acceleration due to gravity $g = 10$ m/s^2)

   A. 11 m   **B.** 16 m   **C.** 20 m   **D.** 7 m

30. A 200 g hockey puck slides up a metal ramp that is inclined at a 30° angle. The coefficients of static and kinetic friction between the hockey puck and the metal ramp are $\mu_s = 0.4$ and $\mu_k = 0.3$, respectively. The initial speed of the hockey puck is 14 m/s. What vertical height does the puck reach above its starting point? (Use acceleration due to gravity $g = 9.8$ m/s^2)

   A. 11 m   **B.** 4.8 m   **C.** 8.6 m   **D.** 14 m

31. A 6.5 g bullet was fired horizontally into a 2 kg wooden block that is suspended on a 1.5 m string. The bullet becomes embedded in the block of wood, and immediately after that, the block and the bullet move at 2 m/s. The suspended wooden block with embedded bullet swings upward by height *h*. How high does the block with bullet swing before it comes to rest? (Use acceleration due to gravity $g = 9.8$ m/s^2)

  A. 5.5 cm   **B.** 20 cm   **C.** 12 cm   **D.** 44 cm

32. A hammer of mass *m* is dropped from a roof and falls a distance *h* before striking the ground. How does the maximum velocity of the hammer, just before it hits the ground, change if *h* is doubled? Assume no air resistance.

  A. It is multiplied by √2   **C.** It is increased by 200%
  B. It is multiplied by 2   **D.** It is multiplied by 4

33. A simple pendulum has a bob of mass *M* and a period T. If *M* is doubled, what is the new period?

  A. T/√2   **B.** T   **C.** T√2   **D.** 2T

34. Color depends on what characteristics of light?

     I. frequency   II. wavelength   III. amplitude

  A. I only   **B.** II only   **C.** III only   **D.** I and II only

35. What is the current through the 2 Ω resistor if the current through the 8 Ω resistor is 0.8 A?

  A. 4.4 A
  B. 16 A
  C. 1.5 A
  D. 6 A

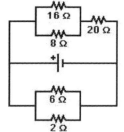

36. A 0.4 kg harmonic oscillator has a total oscillation energy of 10 J. What is the oscillation frequency if the oscillation amplitude is 20 cm? (Use 1 J = 1 N·m)

  A. 3 Hz   **B.** 4.3 Hz   **C.** 2.1 Hz   **D.** 5.6 Hz

37. An object starting from rest accelerates uniformly along a straight line until its final velocity is *v*, while traveling a distance *d*. What would be the distance traveled if the object accelerated uniformly from rest until its final velocity was 4*v*?

  A. 2*d*   **B.** 4*d*   **C.** 6*d*   **D.** 16*d*

38. Satellite #1 has mass *M,* which takes time T to orbit Earth. If satellite #2 has twice the mass, how long does it take for satellite #2 to orbit Earth?

A. T/2　　　　　**B.** T　　　　　　**C.** 2T　　　　　　**D.** 4T

39. Sonja is sitting on the outer edge of a carousel that is 18 m in diameter. What is the velocity of Sonja in m/s if the carousel makes 5 rev/min?

A. 3.3 m/s　　　　**B.** 0.8 m/s　　　　**C.** 8.8 m/s　　　　**D.** 4.7 m/s

40. Two identical arrows, one with twice the kinetic energy, are fired into a hay bale. Compared to the slower arrow, the faster arrow penetrates:

A. the same distance　　　　　**C.** four times as far

B. twice as far　　　　　　　　**D.** more than four times as far

41. The phenomena of compressions and rarefactions are characteristic of:

　　I. longitudinal waves　　　　II. transverse waves　　　　III. standing waves

A. I only　　　**B.** II only　　　**C.** III only　　　**D.** I and II only

42. What is the decibel level of a sound with an intensity of 10^{-7} W/m^2?

A. 10 dB　　　　**B.** 20 dB　　　　**C.** 30 dB　　　　**D.** 50 dB

43. A yacht moving initially at 10.7 m/s N, drifts due NE at the same speed. The captain, to correct the yacht's bearing, accelerates the engine and turns the rudder NW. How long does it take to cross the original line of longitude if the engine delivers a constant acceleration of 4.4 m/s^2?

A. 1.3 s　　　　**B.** 1.8 s　　　　**C.** 2.4 s　　　　**D.** 3.6 s

44. A 5.5 kg box slides down an inclined plane that makes an angle of 40° with the horizontal. At what rate does the box accelerate down the slope if the coefficient of kinetic friction μ_k is 0.19? (Use acceleration due to gravity $g = 9.8$ m/s^2)

A. 7.5 m/s^2　　　**B.** 6.4 m/s^2　　　**C.** 4.9 m/s^2　　　**D.** 5.9 m/s^2

45. An object is released from rest at a height *h* above the surface of the Earth, where *h* is much smaller than the radius of the Earth. The object's speed is *v* as it strikes the ground. Ignoring air resistance, at what height should the object be released from rest for it to strike the ground with a speed of 2*v*? (Use *g* = acceleration due to gravity)

A. 4*gh*　　　　**B.** 4*h*　　　　**C.** 2*gh*　　　　**D.** 2*h*

46. A projectile weighing 120 N is traveling horizontally with respect to the surface of the Earth at a constant velocity of 6 m/s. Ignoring air resistance, what is the power required to maintain this motion?

A. 0 W   **B.** 20 W   **C.** 120 W   **D.** 2 W

47. On the Moon, the acceleration of gravity is $g / 6$. If a pendulum has a period T on Earth, what will be the period on the Moon?

A. $T\sqrt{6}$ **B.** $T/6$ **C.** $T/\sqrt{6}$ **D.** $T/3$

48. Electromagnetic waves consist of:

A. particles of heat energy
B. high-frequency gravitational waves
C. compressions and rarefactions of electromagnetic pulses
D. oscillating electric and magnetic fields

49. A 9 V battery is connected to two resistors in a series. One resistance is 5 ohms and the other is 10 ohms. Which is true about the current for the locations (A, B, C, D) marked along the circuit?

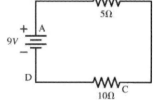

A. Current at A > current at B > current at C > current at D
B. Current at A > current at B = current at C = current at D
C. Current at A = current at B = current at C = current at D
D. Current at A = current at B = current at C > current at D

50. An object is traveling uniformly at a v of 5 m/s. What is its final velocity if it experiences a uniform acceleration of 2 m/s^2 for 6 s?

A. 12 m/s   **B.** 28 m/s   **C.** 17 m/s   **D.** 32 m/s

DIAGNOSTIC TEST #3

ANSWER SHEET

#	Answer:				Mark for review	#	Answer:				Mark for review
1:	A	B	C	D	___	26:	A	B	C	D	___
2:	A	B	C	D	___	27:	A	B	C	D	___
3:	A	B	C	D	___	28:	A	B	C	D	___
4:	A	B	C	D	___	29:	A	B	C	D	___
5:	A	B	C	D	___	30:	A	B	C	D	___
6:	A	B	C	D	___	31:	A	B	C	D	___
7:	A	B	C	D	___	32:	A	B	C	D	___
8:	A	B	C	D	___	33:	A	B	C	D	___
9:	A	B	C	D	___	34:	A	B	C	D	___
10:	A	B	C	D	___	35:	A	B	C	D	___
11:	A	B	C	D	___	36:	A	B	C	D	___
12:	A	B	C	D	___	37:	A	B	C	D	___
13:	A	B	C	D	___	38:	A	B	C	D	___
14:	A	B	C	D	___	39:	A	B	C	D	___
15:	A	B	C	D	___	40:	A	B	C	D	___
16:	A	B	C	D	___	41:	A	B	C	D	___
17:	A	B	C	D	___	42:	A	B	C	D	___
18:	A	B	C	D	___	43:	A	B	C	D	___
19:	A	B	C	D	___	44:	A	B	C	D	___
20:	A	B	C	D	___	45:	A	B	C	D	___
21:	A	B	C	D	___	46:	A	B	C	D	___
22:	A	B	C	D	___	47:	A	B	C	D	___
23:	A	B	C	D	___	48:	A	B	C	D	___
24:	A	B	C	D	___	49:	A	B	C	D	___
25:	A	B	C	D	___	50:	A	B	C	D	___

1. The slope of a tangent line at a given time value on a position vs. time graph indicates:

A. instantaneous acceleration

B. change in acceleration

C. instantaneous velocity

D. average velocity

2. Which statement must be true for an object moving with constant nonzero velocity?

A. The net force on the object is zero

B. The net force on the object is positive

C. A constant force is being applied to the object in the direction opposite of motion

D. A constant force is being applied to the object in the direction of motion

3. A 3 kg stone is dropped from a height of 5 m. Ignoring air resistance, what is its momentum on impact? (Use acceleration due to gravity $g = 10$ m/s^2)

A. 7.5 kg·m/s   B. 5 kg·m/s   C. 30 kg·m/s   D. 45 kg·m/s

4. An ideal, massless spring with a spring constant of 3 N/m has a 0.9 kg mass attached to one end and the other end is attached to a beam. If the system is initially at equilibrium and the mass is then down 18 cm below the equilibrium length and released, what is the magnitude of the net force on the mass just after its release? (Use acceleration due to gravity is $g = 10$ m/s^2)

A. 0.54 N   B. 0.75 N   C. 6 N   D. 0.35 N

5. A 30 N block is attached to the free end of an anchored spring and is allowed to slide back and forth on a frictionless table. Determine the frequency of motion if the spring constant. (Use spring constant $k = 40$ N/m and acceleration due to gravity $g = 9.8$ m/s^2)

A. 0.30 Hz   B. 0.57 Hz   C. 2.3 Hz   D. 3.6 Hz

6. A piano is tuned so that the frequency of the third harmonic of one string is 786.3 Hz. If the fundamental frequency of another string is 785.8 Hz then what is the beat frequency between the notes?

A. 0 Hz   B. 1 Hz   C. 0.5 Hz   D. 786.3 Hz

7. What quantity does the slope of this graph represent if the graph shows the power dissipated in a resistor as a function of the resistance?

A. Maximum power transferred across the resistor

B. Square of the current across resistor

C. Current across the resistor

D. Potential difference across the resistor

8. What is the unit of the product of amps × volts?

   A. Watt   **B.** Amp   **C.** Joule   **D.** Ohm

9. The graph shows the position of an object as a function of time. At which moment in time is the speed of the object equal to zero?

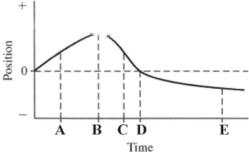

   A. A
   B. B
   C. C
   D. D

10. Why does it take more force to start moving a heavy bookcase across the carpet than to keep it moving?

   A. For objects in motion, kinetic friction is a force in the same direction as the motion
   B. The coefficient of static friction is greater than the forces of movement
   C. The coefficient of static friction is greater than the coefficient of kinetic friction
   D. The coefficient of kinetic friction is greater than the coefficient of static friction

11. A 1 kg chunk of putty moving at 1 m/s collides with and sticks to a 7 kg box that is initially at rest. What is the speed that the box and putty are then set in motion? (Assume the box rests on a frictionless surface)

   A. 1/8 m/s   **B.** 1/6 m/s   **C.** 1/4 m/s   **D.** 1/7 m/s

12. A 1,500 kg car moving at 45 km/h locks its brakes and skids 30 m. How far does the same car skid if it is traveling at 150 km/h?

   A. 230 m   **B.** 160 m   **C.** 445 m   **D.** 333 m

13. How does the frequency of vibration relate to the time it takes to complete one cycle?

   A. Inversely with the time   **C.** Directly with the time
   B. Inversely with the amplitude   **D.** Directly with the amplitude

14. A mosquito produces 1.5×10^{-11} W of sound energy. How many mosquitoes are needed to power a 30 W bulb if the sound energy could be used for this purpose?

   A. 6×10^{11} **B.** 2×10^{12} **C.** 2×10^{11} **D.** 6×10^{12}

15. If an object is accelerating, which values must change?

    I. Speed   II. Velocity   III. Direction

  A. I only   **B.** II only   **C.** III only   **D.** I and II only

16. Michelle takes off down a 50 m high, 10° slope on her jet-powered skis. The skis have a thrust of 260 N. The combined mass of the skis and Michelle is 50 kg. Michelle's speed at the bottom of the slope is 40 m/s. Assuming the mass of the fuel is negligible, what is the coefficient of kinetic friction of her skis on the snow? (Use acceleration due to gravity $g = 9.8$ m/s^2)

  A. 0.23   **B.** 0.53   **C.** 0.68   **D.** 0.42

17. Johnny is sitting on the outer edge of a carousel that is 18 m in diameter. What is the velocity of Johnny if the carousel makes 5.3 rev/min?

  A. 4.2 m/s   **B.** 5 m/s   **C.** 3.1 m/s   **D.** 9.8 m/s

18. A 4 kg mass is affixed to the end of a vertical spring with a spring constant of 10 N/m. When the mass comes to rest, how much has the spring stretched?

  A. 1 m   **B.** 4 m   **C.** 5 m   **D.** 0.1 m

19. In music, the 3rd harmonic corresponds to which overtone?

  A. 1st   **B.** 2nd   **C.** 3rd   **D.** 4th

20. What is the wavelength of the standing wave when a 12 m string, fixed at both ends, is resonating at a frequency that produces 4 nodes?

  A. 6 m   **B.** 8 m   **C.** 4 m   **D.** 24 m

21. Which statement is correct about the equivalent resistance when four unequal resistors are connected in parallel?

  A. It is the average of the largest and smallest resistance
  B. It is less than the smallest resistance
  C. It is more than the largest resistance
  D. It is the average of the four resistances

22. Two particles of like charge and equal mass are separated by a fixed distance. What is the effect on the repulsive force between the particles if the mass of one particle is doubled?

  A. Doubles   **C.** Increases by ½
  B. Quadruples   **D.** Remains the same

23. For constant linear acceleration, the velocity vs. time graph is a:

    A. sloped line   **B.** curve   **C.** horizontal line   **D.** cubic graph

24. A 40 kg runner is running around a track. The curved portions of the track are arcs of a circle that has a radius of 16 m. The runner is running at a constant speed of 4 m/s. What is the net force on the runner on the curved portion of the track?

    A. 150 N   **B.** 5 N   **C.** 40 N   **D.** 100 N

25. A solid cylinder with an 80 cm radius is positioned on a frictionless plane inclined at 30° above the horizontal. A force (F) is exerted by a string wrapped around the cylinder. The center of mass of the cylinder does not move when F has a certain critical value. What is the angular acceleration of the spool when F is at this critical value? (Use acceleration due to gravity $g = 10$ m/s^2)

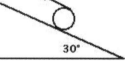

    A. 15.8 rad/s^2 **C.** 12.5 rad/s^2
    B. 23 rad/s^2 **D.** 18.6 rad/s^2

26. A stone of mass m is dropped from a height h toward the ground. Ignoring air resistance, which statement is true about the stone as it hits the ground?

    A. Its KE is proportional to h **C.** Its speed is proportional to h
    B. Its KE is proportional to h^2 **D.** Its speed is inversely proportional to h^2

27. When a light ray traveling in glass strikes an air boundary, which type of phase change occurs in the reflected ray?

    A. 45° phase change   **B.** 180° phase change   **C.** –45° phase change   **D.** No phase change

28. The tension in each of two strings is adjusted so that both vibrate at exactly 822 Hz. The tension in one string is then increased slightly. Five beats per second are then heard when both strings vibrate. What is a new frequency of the string that was tightened?

    A. 824 Hz   **B.** 816 Hz   **C.** 827 Hz   **D.** 818 Hz

29. A car and a truck are initially alongside each other at time $t = 0$. Their motions along a straight road are represented by the velocity vs. time graph. At time T, which statement is true for the vehicles?

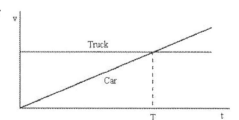

    A. The car traveled farther than the truck
    B. The truck traveled farther than the car
    C. They traveled the same distance
    D. The truck had a greater acceleration than the car

30. A hockey puck slides on a surface of frictionless ice. If the mass of the puck is 300 grams, and it moves in a straight line with a constant velocity of 5 m/s, what is the net force acting on the puck?

    A. 0 N   **B.** 1 N   **C.** 30 N   **D.** 750 N

31. A motor can provide a maximum of 120 N·m of torque. If all of this torque is used to accelerate a solid, uniform flywheel of mass 12 kg and radius 4 m, what is the time necessary for the flywheel to accelerate from rest to 7.35 rad/s?

    A. 4.4 s   **B.** 3.9 s   **C.** 1.1 s   **D.** 5.9 s

32. A 1.2 kg bowling ball is dropped from a height of 6 m. During its fall, it is constantly acted upon by air resistance, with a force of 3.4 N. Accounting for air resistance, what is the speed of the bowling ball as it hits the ground? (Use acceleration due to gravity $g = 10$ m/s^2)

    A. 9.2 m/s   **B.** 10.6 m/s   **C.** 11.3 m/s   **D.** 13.4 m/s

33. As a water wave passes, a floating leaf oscillates up and down completely for two cycles in 1 s. What is the wave's speed, if the wave's wavelength is 12 m?

    A. 1 m/s   **B.** 10 m/s   **C.** 6 m/s   **D.** 40 m/s

34. Sound intensity is defined as:

    A. power per unit time   **C.** energy passing through a unit of volume per unit time
    B. power per unit area   **D.** energy passing through a unit of area per unit time

35. When the current through a resistor is increased by a factor of 4, by what factor does the power dissipated by the resistor change?

    A. Increases by 16   **C.** Decreases by 4
    B. Increases by 4   **D.** Decreases by 16

36. A kilowatt-hour is a unit of:

    A. work   **B.** current   **C.** power   **D.** charge

37. When an object moves with constant acceleration, can its velocity change direction?

    A. Yes, a car that starts from rest, speeds up, slows to a stop, and then backs up is an example
    B. No, because it is always slowing down
    C. No, because it is always speeding up
    D. Yes, a Frisbee thrown straight up is an example

38. A car of mass m is driving up a road with a slight incline θ above the horizontal. The driver sees a road closure and skids to a stop. The coefficient of static friction between the tires and the road is μ_s, and the coefficient of kinetic friction is μ_k. What is the magnitude of the gravity component of the force parallel to the surface of the road?

A. $mg \sin \theta$ **B.** $mg \tan \theta$ **C.** mg **D.** $mg \cos \theta$

39. An object with a mass of 60 kg moves across a level surface with a constant speed of 13.5 m/s. If there is a frictional force, and the coefficient of kinetic friction is 0.8, which must be true about the forces acting on the object?

  A. There must be an unbalanced amount of vertical force acting on the object allowing it to move
  B. No forces are doing work on the object
  C. There must be some other horizontal force acting on the object
  D. The force exerted on the object by kinetic friction is negligible

40. What is the power output necessary for a 54 kg person to run at constant velocity up a 10 m hillside in 4 s, if the hillside is inclined at 30° above the horizontal? (Use acceleration due to gravity $g = 9.8$ m/s^2 and 1 hp = 745 W)

A. 1.92 hp   **B.** 1.12 hp   **C.** 0.89 hp   **D.** 3.94 hp

41. Some of a wave's energy dissipates as heat. In time, this reduces the wave's:

A. amplitude   **B.** frequency   **C.** speed   **D.** wavelength

42. A piano tuned with the frequency of the third harmonic of the C_3 string is 783 Hz. What is the frequency of the C_3 fundamental?

A. 473 Hz   **B.** 261 Hz   **C.** 387 Hz   **D.** 185 Hz

43. Describe the forces on a system which consists of a bicycle and a rider as the rider pedals at a constant speed in a straight line?

  A. Air resistance on the rider is greater than the applied force
  B. The resisting force of friction is greater than the applied forces
  C. The resisting force of friction is less than the applied forces
  D. All forces are balanced

44. In a binary star system, two stars revolve about their combined center of mass and are attracted to each other by the force of gravity. The force of gravity between the stars (masses M_1 and M_2) is F. If the mass of one of the stars is decreased by a factor of 2, how would this affect the force between them?

  A. Remains the same   **C.** Decreases by a factor of 4
  B. Increases by a factor of 2   **D.** Decreases by a factor of 2

45. For projectile motion with no air resistance, the vertical component of a projectile's acceleration:

A. is always positive
B. remains a nonzero constant

C. continuously increases
D. continuously decreases

46. The total mechanical energy of a system is:

A. either all kinetic energy or all potential energy, at any one instant
B. constant if there are only conservative forces acting
C. found through the product of potential energy and kinetic energy
D. equally divided between kinetic energy and potential energy in every instance

47. A 340 nm thick oil film floats on the surface of water. The surface of the oil is illuminated from above at normal incidence with white light. What are the two wavelengths of light that are in the 400 nm to 800 nm wavelength band, which are most strongly reflected? (Use the index of refraction for oil n = 1.5 and index of refraction for water n = 1.33)

A. 420 nm and 750 nm
B. 406 nm and 706 nm

C. 410 nm and 760 nm
D. 408 nm and 680 nm

48. A 1 m string is fixed at both ends and plucked. What is the wavelength corresponding to the fourth harmonic if the speed of the waves on this string is 4.2×10^4 m/s?

A. 1 m   **B.** 0.5 m   **C.** 4/3 m   **D.** 3/2 m

30. A suitcase of mass 80 kg is pushed in a straight line across a horizontal floor at a constant speed of 3 m/s. What is the net force on the suitcase? (Use coefficient of kinetic friction $\mu_k = 0.3$)

A. 0 N   **B.** 240 N   **C.** 800 N   **D.** 27 N

50. Two point charges of +18 μC and –6 μC are separated by a distance of 15 cm. What is the electric field E midway between the two charges? (Coulomb's constant $k = 9 \times 10^9$ N·m²·C⁻²)

A. 25.2×10^5 N/C toward the positive charge
B. 25.2×10^5 N/C toward the negative charge
C. 25.2×10^6 N/C toward the positive charge
D. 25.2×10^6 N/C toward the negative charge

AP PHYSICS 1
TOPICAL PRACTICE
QUESTIONS

KINEMATICS AND DYNAMICS

1. Starting from rest, how long does it take for a sports car to reach 60 mi/h, if it has an average acceleration of 13.1 mi/h·s?

    A. 6.6 s   **B.** 3.1 s   **C.** 4.5 s   **D.** 4.6 s

2. A cannon ball is fired with an initial speed of 20 m/s at a 30° angle with the horizontal. Ignoring air resistance, how long does it take the cannon ball to reach the top of its trajectory? (Use acceleration due to gravity $g = 10$ m/s^2)

    A. 0.5 s   **B.** 1 s   **C.** 1.5 s   **D.** 2 s

3. Darlene starts her car from rest and accelerates at a constant 2.5 m/s^2 for 9 s to get to her cruising speed. She then drives for 15 minutes at constant speed. She arrives at her destination, which is a straight-line distance of 31.5 km away, exactly 1.25 hours later. What is her average velocity during the interval of 1.25 hours?

    A. 3 m/s   **B.** 7 m/s   **C.** 18 m/s   **D.** 22.5 m/s

4. Which of the following cannot be negative?

    A. Instantaneous speed   **C.** Acceleration of gravity

    B. Instantaneous acceleration   **D.** Displacement

5. How far does a car travel while accelerating from 5 m/s to 21 m/s at a rate of 3 m/s^2?

    A. 15 m   **B.** 21 m   **C.** 69 m   **D.** 105 m

6. Acceleration is sometimes expressed in multiples of *g*, where *g* is the acceleration due to gravity. How many *g* are experienced, on average, by the driver in a car crash if the car's velocity changes from 30 m/s to 0 m/s in 0.15 s? (Use acceleration due to gravity $g = 9.8$ m/s^2)

    A. 22 *g*   **B.** 28 *g*   **C.** 20 *g*   **D.** 14 *g*

7. Ignoring air resistance, how many forces are acting on a bullet fired horizontally after it leaves the rifle?

    A. Two (one from the gunpowder explosion and one from gravity)
    B. One (from the motion of the bullet)
    C. One (from the gunpowder explosion)
    D. One (from the pull of gravity)

8. Suppose that a car traveling to the East begins to slow down as it approaches a traffic light. Which of the following statements about its acceleration is correct?

    A. The acceleration is towards the East

    B. The acceleration is towards the West

    C. Since the car is slowing, its acceleration is positive

    D. The acceleration is zero

9. On a planet where the acceleration due to gravity is 20 m/s^2, a freely falling object increases its speed each second by about:

    A. 20 m/s   **B.** 10 m/s   **C.** 30 m/s   **D.** 40 m/s

10. What is a car's acceleration if it accelerates uniformly in one dimension from 15 m/s to 40 m/s in 10 s?

    A. 1.75 m/s^2 **B.** 2.5 m/s^2 **C.** 3.5 m/s^2 **D.** 7.6 m/s^2

11. If the fastest a person can drive is 65 mi/h, what is the longest time she can stop for lunch if she wants to travel 540 mi in 9.8 h?

    A. 1 h   **B.** 2.4 h   **C.** 1.5 h   **D.** 2 h

12. What is a racecar's average velocity if it completes one lap around a 500 m track in 10 s?

    A. 10 m/s   **B.** 0 m/s   **C.** 5 m/s   **D.** 20 m/s

13. What is a ball's net displacement after 5 s if it is initially rolling up a slight incline at 0.2 m/s and decelerates uniformly at 0.05 m/s^2?

    A. 0.6 m   **B.** 0.3 m   **C.** 0.9 m   **D.** 1.2 m

14. What does the slope of a line connecting two points on a velocity vs. time graph represent?

    A. Change in acceleration   **C.** Average acceleration

    B. Instantaneous acceleration   **D.** Instantaneous velocity

15. An airplane needs to reach a speed of 210 km/h to take off. On a 1,800 m runway, what is the minimum acceleration necessary for the plane to reach this speed?

    A. 0.78 m/s^2 **B.** 0.94 m/s^2 **C.** 1.47 m/s^2 **D.** 1.1 m/s^2

16. A test rocket is fired straight up from rest with a net acceleration of 22 m/s^2. What maximum elevation does the rocket reach if the motor turns off after 4 s, but the rocket continues to coast upward? (Use acceleration due to gravity $g = 10$ m/s^2)

   A. 408 m   **B.** 320 m   **C.** 357 m   **D.** 563 m

17. Without any reference to direction, how fast an object moves refers to its:

   A. speed   **C.** momentum
   B. impulse   **D.** velocity

18. Ignoring air resistance, a 10 kg rock and a 20 kg rock are dropped at the same time. If the 10 kg rock falls with acceleration a, what is the acceleration of the 20 kg rock?

   A. $a / 2$ **B.** a **C.** $2a$ **D.** $4a$

19. As an object falls freely, its magnitude of:

      I. velocity increases   II. acceleration increases   III. displacement increases

   A. I only   **B.** I and II only   **C.** II and III only   **D.** I and III only

20. What forces are acting on the suitcase when Jack carries a 25 kg suitcase at a constant velocity of 1.7 m/s across a room for 12 s?

   A. Gravity pointing downward; normal force pointing upward; Jack's force pointing forward
   B. Gravity pointing downward and the normal force pointing upward
   C. Gravity pointing downward and Jack's force pointing upward
   D. Gravity pointing downward

21. A football kicker is attempting a field goal from 44 m away, and the ball just clears the lower bar with a time of flight of 2.9 s. What was the initial speed of the ball if the angle of the kick was 45° with the horizontal?

   A. 37 m/s   **B.** 2.5 m/s   **C.** 18.3 m/s   **D.** 21.4 m/s

22. Ignoring air resistance, if a rock, starting at rest, is dropped from a cliff and strikes the ground with an impact velocity of 14 m/s, from what height was it dropped? (Use acceleration due to gravity $g = 10$ m/s^2)

   A. 10 m   **B.** 30 m   **C.** 45 m   **D.** 70 m

23. An SUV is traveling at 20 m/s. Then Joseph steps on the accelerator pedal, accelerating at a constant 1.4 m/s^2 for 7 s. How far does he travel during these 7 s?

   A. 205 m   **B.** 177 m   **C.** 143 m   **D.** 158 m

24. Which of the following is NOT a scalar?

   A. temperature   **B.** distance   **C.** mass   **D.** force

25. Two identical balls (A and B) fall from rest from different heights to the ground. Ignoring air resistance, what is the ratio of the heights from which A and B fall if ball B takes twice as long as ball A to reach the ground?

   A. $1 : \sqrt{2}$ **B.** $1 : 4$ **C.** $1 : 2$ **D.** $1 : 8$

26. How far does a car travel in 10 s when it accelerates uniformly in one direction from 5 m/s to 30 m/s?

   A. 175 m   **B.** 25 m   **C.** 250 m   **D.** 650 m

27. Which graph represents an acceleration of zero?

   A. I only   **C.** I and II only
   B. II only   **D.** II and III only

28. Doubling the distance between an orbiting satellite and the Earth results in what change in the gravitational attraction between the two?

   A. Twice as much   **C.** One half as much
   B. Four times as much   **D.** One fourth as much

29. When is the average velocity of an object equal to the instantaneous velocity?

   A. Average velocity is always equal to the instantaneous velocity
   B. Only when velocity is constant
   C. Only when velocity is decreasing at a constant rate
   D. Only when velocity is increasing at a constant rate

30. A freely falling object on Earth, 10 s after starting from rest, has a speed of about: (Use acceleration due to gravity $g = 10$ m/s^2)

   A. 10 m/s   **B.** 20 m/s   **C.** 100 m/s   **D.** 150 m/s

31. A truck travels a certain distance at a constant velocity v for time t. If the truck travels three times as fast, covering the same distance, then by what factor does the time of travel in relation to t change?

   A. Increases by 3   **B.** Decreases by 3   **C.** Decreases by $\sqrt{3}$ **D.** Increases by 9

32. Assuming equal rates of acceleration, how much farther would Steve travel if he braked from 58 mi/h to rest than from 29 mi/h to rest?

    A. 2 times farther   **C.** 4 times farther

    B. 16 times farther   **D.** 3.2 times farther

33. What is the average speed of a racehorse if the horse makes one lap around a 400 m track in 20 s?

    A. 0 m/s   **B.** 7.5 m/s   **C.** 15 m/s   **D.** 20 m/s

34. What was a car's initial velocity if the car is traveling up a slight slope while decelerating at 0.1 m/s^2 and comes to a stop after 5 s?

    A. 0.5 m/s   **B.** 0.25 m/s   **C.** 2 m/s   **D.** 1.5 m/s

35. Average velocity equals the average of an object's initial and final velocity when acceleration is:

    A. constantly decreasing   **C.** constant

    B. constantly increasing   **D.** equal to zero

36. Ignoring air resistance, compared to a rock dropped from the same point, how much earlier does a thrown rock strike the ground, if it is thrown downward with an initial velocity of 10 m/s from the top of a 300 m building? (Use acceleration due to gravity $g = 9.8 \text{ m/s}^2$)

    A. 0.75 s   **B.** 0.33 s   **C.** 0.66 s   **D.** 0.95 s

37. With all other factors equal, what happens to the acceleration if the unbalanced force on an object of a given mass is doubled?

    A. Increased by one fourth   **C.** Increased fourfold

    B. Increased by one half   **D.** Doubled

38. How fast an object is changing speed or direction of travel is a property of motion known as:

    A. velocity   **B.** acceleration   **C.** speed   **D.** flow

39. Which statement concerning a car's acceleration must be correct if a car traveling to the North ($+y$ direction) begins to slow down as it approaches a stop sign?

    A. Acceleration is positive   **C.** Acceleration is negative

    B. Acceleration is zero   **D.** Acceleration decreases in magnitude as the car slows

40. For the velocity vs. time graph of a basketball player traveling up and down the court in a straight-line path, what is the total distance run by the player in the 10 s?

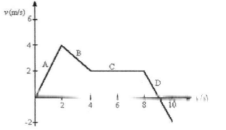

A. 20 m   C. 14 m

B. 22 m   D. 18 m

41. At the same time that a bullet is dropped into a river from a high bridge, another bullet is fired from a gun, straight down towards the water. Ignoring air resistance, the acceleration just before striking the water:

A. is greater for the dropped bullet   C. is the same for each bullet

B. is greater for the fired bullet   D. depends on how high the bullets started

42. Sarah starts her car from rest and accelerates at a constant 2.5 m/s^2 for 9 s to get to her cruising speed. What was her final velocity?

A. 22.5 m/s   B. 12.3 m/s   C. 4.6 m/s   D. 8.5 m/s

43. A bat hits a baseball, and the baseball's direction is completely reversed and its speed is doubled. If the actual time of contact with the bat is 0.45 s, what is the ratio of the acceleration to the original velocity?

A. -2.5 s^{-1} : 1   C. -9.8 s^{-1} : 1

B. -0.15 s^{-1} : 1   D. -6.7 s^{-1} : 1

44. A 2 kg weight is thrown vertically upward from the surface of the Moon at a speed of 3.2 m/s and it returns to its starting point in 4 s. What is the magnitude of acceleration due to gravity on the Moon?

A. 0.8 m/s^2 B. 1.6 m/s^2 C. 3.7 m/s^2 D. 8.4 m/s^2

45. What is the change in velocity for a bird that is cruising at 1.5 m/s and then accelerates at a constant 0.3 m/s^2 for 3 s?

A. 0.9 m/s   B. 0.6 m/s   C. 1.6 m/s   D. 0.3 m/s

46. All of the following are vectors, except:

A. velocity   B. displacement   C. acceleration   D. mass

Questions **47-49** are based on the following:

A toy rocket is launched vertically from ground level where $y = 0$ m, at time $t = 0$ s. The rocket engine provides constant upward acceleration during the burn phase. At the instant of engine burnout, the rocket has risen to 64 m and acquired a velocity of 60 m/s. The rocket continues to rise in unpowered flight, reaches maximum height and then falls back to the ground. (Use acceleration due to gravity $g = 9.8$ m/s^2)

47. What is the maximum height reached by the rocket?

    A. 274 m   **B.** 248 m   **C.** 223 m   **D.** 120 m

48. What is the upward acceleration of the rocket during the burn phase?

    A. 9.9 m/s^2 **B.** 4.8 m/s^2 **C.** 28 m/s^2 **D.** 11.8 m/s^2

49. What is the time interval during which the rocket engine provides upward acceleration?

    A. 1.5 s   **B.** 1.9 s   **C.** 2.3 s   **D.** 2.1 s

50. A car accelerates uniformly from rest along a straight track that has markers spaced at equal distances along it. As it passes Marker 2, the car reaches a speed of 140 km/h. Where on the track is the car when it is traveling at 70 km/h?

    A. Close to Marker 2   **C.** Before Marker 1
    B. Between Marker 1 and Marker 2   **D.** Close to the starting point

51. What are the two measurements necessary for calculating average speed?

    A. Distance and time   **C.** Velocity and time
    B. Distance and acceleration   **D.** Velocity and acceleration

52. A pedestrian traveling at speed v covers a distance x during a time interval t. If a bicycle travels at speed $3v$, how much time does it take the bicycle to travel the same distance?

    A. $t / 3$ **B.** $t - 3$ **C.** $t + 3^2$ **D.** $3t$

53. Ignoring air resistance, how much time passes before a ball strikes the ground if it is thrown straight upward with a velocity of 39 m/s? (Use acceleration due to gravity $g = 9.8$ m/s^2)

    A. 2.2 s   **B.** 8 s   **C.** 12 s   **D.** 4 s

54. A particle travels to the right along a horizontal axis with a constantly decreasing speed. Which one of the following describes the direction of the particle's acceleration?

    A. ↑   **B.** ↓   **C.** →   **D.** ←

55. Larry is carrying a 25 kg package at a constant velocity of 1.8 m/s across a room for 12 s. What is the work done by Larry on the package during the 12 s? (Use acceleration due to gravity $g = 10$ m/s^2)

    A. 0 J   **B.** 280 J   **C.** 860 J   **D.** 2,200 J

56. What does the slope of a tangent line at a time value on a velocity vs. time graph represent?

    A. Instantaneous acceleration   **C.** Instantaneous velocity
    B. Average acceleration   **D.** Position

57. A car is traveling North at 17.7 m/s. After 12 s, its velocity is 14.1 m/s in the same direction. What is the magnitude and direction of the car's average acceleration?

    A. 0.3 m/s^2, North   **B.** 2.7 m/s^2, North   **C.** 0.3 m/s^2, South   **D.** 3.6 m/s^2, South

58. The graph below shows the position of an object as a function of time. The letters A –E represent particular moments in time. At which moment in time is the speed of the object the highest?

    A. A   **B.** B   **C.** C   **D.** D

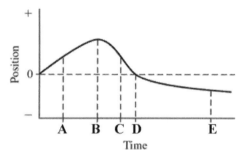

59. Ignoring air resistance, at a speed less than terminal velocity, what is happening to the speed of an object falling towards the surface of the Earth?

    A. Increasing at a decreasing rate   **C.** Decreasing
    B. Increasing   **D.** Constant

60. How far does a car travel if it starts from rest and accelerates at a constant 2 m/s^2 for 10 s, then travels with the constant speed it has achieved for another 10 s and finally slows to a stop with constant deceleration of magnitude 2 m/s^2?

    A. 150 m   **B.** 200 m   **C.** 350 m   **D.** 400 m

61. While a car travels around a circular track at constant speed, its:

    I. acceleration changes   II. acceleration is zero   III. velocity is zero

    A. I only   **B.** II only   **C.** III only   **D.** I and III only

62. How long does it take a ball to fall if it is dropped from a height of 10 m to the ground and experiences a constant downward acceleration of 9.8 m/s²?

A. 1.1 s   **B.** 1.4 s   **C.** 2.4 s   **D.** 3.1 s

63. A car travels 95 km North at 70 km/h, then turns around and travels 21.9 km at 80 km/h. What is the difference between the average speed and the average velocity on this trip?

A. 58 km/h   **B.** 37 km/h   **C.** 19 km/h   **D.** 27 km/h

64. What is the acceleration of a car that accelerates uniformly from 0 to 60 mi/h in 6 s?

A. 10 mi·h⁻¹·s⁻¹   **B.** 10 m/h²   **C.** 10 mi/h   **D.** 10 m/s²

65. What is a car's average velocity when it accelerates uniformly in one dimension from 5 m/s to 30 m/s in 10 s?

A. 4.5 m/s   **B.** 15 m/s   **C.** 17.5 m/s   **D.** 7.5 m/s

66. Which graph represents a constant non-zero velocity?

I.    II.    III. v
0 ⊢———— t

A. I only   **B.** II only   **C.** III only   **D.** I and II only

67. A train starts from rest and accelerates uniformly, until it has traveled 5.6 km and has acquired a velocity of 42 m/s. The train then moves at a constant velocity of 42 m/s for 420 s. The train then slows down uniformly at 0.065 m/s², until it stops moving. What is the acceleration during the first 5.6 km of travel?

A. 0.29 m/s²   **B.** 0.23 m/s²   **C.** 0.16 m/s²   **D.** 0.12 m/s²

68. A cannon ball is fired straight up at 50 m/s. Ignoring air resistance, what is the velocity at the highest point it reaches before starting to return towards Earth?

A. 0 m/s   **B.** 25 m/s   **C.** √50 m/s   **D.** 50 m/s

69. The tendency of a moving object to remain in unchanging motion in the absence of an unbalanced force is:

A. impulse   **B.** acceleration   **C.** free fall   **D.** inertia

70. Which statement is correct when an object that is moving in the +*x* direction undergoes an acceleration of 2 m/s²?

A. It travels at 2 m/s

B. It travels at 2 m/s²

C. It decreases its velocity by 2 m/s every second

D. It increases its velocity by 2 m/s every second

71. What is the increase in speed each second for a freely falling object?

A. 0 m/s

B. 9.8 m/s²

C. 9.8 m/s

D. 19.6 m/s

72. A marble is initially rolling up a slight incline at 0.2 m/s and starting at *t* = 0 s, decelerates uniformly at 0.05 m/s². At what time does the marble come to a stop?

A. 2 s

B. 4 s

C. 8 s

D. 12 s

73. An 8.7 hour trip is made at an average speed of 73 km/h. If the first third of the journey was driven at 96.5 km/h, what was the average speed for the rest of the trip?

A. 54 km/hr

B. 46 km/hr

C. 28 km/hr

D. 62 km/hr

74. The lightning flash and the thunder are not observed simultaneously because light travels much faster than sound, therefore it can be assumed as instantaneous when the lightning occurs. What is the distance from the lightning bolt to the observer, if the delay between the sound and lightning flash is 6 s? (Use speed of sound in air *v* = 340 m/s)

A. 2,040 m

B. 880 m

C. 2,360 m

D. 2,820 m

75. If a cat jumps at a 60° angle off the ground with an initial velocity of 2.74 m/s, what is the highest point of the cat's trajectory? (Use acceleration due to gravity *g* = 9.8 m/s²)

A. 9.46 m

B. 0.69 m

C. 5.75 m

D. 0.29 m

76. What is the resultant vector AB when vector A = 6 m and points 30° North of East, while vector B = 4 m and points 30° South of West?

A. 8 m at an angle 45° East of North

B. 8 m at an angle 30° North of East

C. 2 m at an angle 30° North of East

D. 2 m at an angle 45° North of East

77. How much farther would an intoxicated driver's car travel before he hits the brakes than a sober driver's car if both cars are initially traveling at 49 mi/h, and the sober driver takes 0.33 s to hit the brakes while the intoxicated driver takes 1 s to hit the brakes?

A. 38 ft

B. 52 ft

C. 32 ft

D. 48 ft

FORCE, MOTION, GRAVITATION

1. A boy attaches a weight to a string, which he swings counter-clockwise in a horizontal circle. Which path does the weight follow when the string breaks at point P?

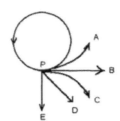

    A. path A   **C.** path C

    B. path B   **D.** path D

2. A garment bag hangs from a clothesline. The tension in the clothesline is 10 N on the right side of the garment bag and 10 N on the left side of the garment bag. What is the mass of the garment bag?

    A. 0.5 kg   **B.** 8 kg   **C.** 4 kg   **D.** 1 kg

3. A sheet of paper can be withdrawn from under a milk carton without toppling the carton if the paper is jerked away quickly. This demonstrates that:

    A. the milk carton has enough inertia

    B. gravity tends to hold the milk carton secure

    C. there is an action-reaction pair of forces

    D. the milk carton has no acceleration

4. A car of mass m is going up a shallow slope with an angle θ to the horizontal when the driver suddenly applies the brakes. The car skids as it comes to a stop. The coefficient of static friction between the tires and the road is μ_s, and the coefficient of kinetic friction is μ_k. Which expression represents the normal force on the car?

    A. $mg \tan \theta$ **B.** $mg \sin \theta$ **C.** $mg \cos \theta$ **D.** mg

5. A 27 kg object is accelerated at a rate of 1.7 m/s^2. How much force does the object experience?

    A. 62 N   **B.** 74 N   **C.** 7 N   **D.** 46 N

6. How are two identical masses moving if they are attached by a light string that passes over a small pulley? Assume that the table and the pulley are frictionless.

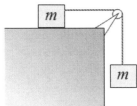

    A. With an acceleration equal to g

    B. With an acceleration greater than g

    C. At a constant speed

    D. With an acceleration less than g

7. An object is moving to the right in a straight line. The net force acting on the object is also directed to the right, but the magnitude of the force is decreasing with time. What happens to the object?

    A. Continues to move to the right with its speed increasing with time

    B. Continues to move to the right with a constant speed

    C. Continues to move to the right with its speed decreasing with time

    D. Continues to move to the right, slowing quickly to a stop

8. A crate is sliding down an inclined ramp at a constant speed of 0.55 m/s. Where does the vector sum of all the forces acting on this crate point?

    A. Perpendicular to the ramp   **C.** Vertically upward

    B. Vertically downward   **D.** None of the above

9. Consider an inclined plane that makes an angle θ with the horizontal. What is the relationship between the length of the ramp L and the vertical height of the ramp h?

    A. $h = L \sin \theta$ **C.** $L = h \sin \theta$

    B. $h = L \tan \theta$ **D.** $h = L \cos \theta$

10. Why is it just as difficult to accelerate a car on the Moon as it is to accelerate the same car on Earth?

        I. Moon and Earth have the same gravity

        II. weight of the car is independent of gravity

        III. mass of the car is independent of gravity

    A. I only   **B.** II only   **C.** III only   **D.** I and II only

11. Sean is pulling his son in a toy wagon. His son and the wagon together are 60 kg. For 3 s Sean exerts a force which uniformly accelerates the wagon from 1.5 m/s to 3.5 m/s. What is the acceleration of the wagon with his son?

    A. 0.67 m/s^2 **B.** 0.84 m/s^2 **C.** 1.66 m/s^2 **D.** 15.32 m/s^2

12. When an object moves in uniform circular motion, the direction of its acceleration is:

    A. directed away from the center of its circular path

    B. dependent on its speed

    C. in the opposite direction of its velocity vector

    D. directed toward the center of its circular path

13. What happens to a moving object in the absence of an external force?

   A. Gradually accelerates until it reaches its terminal velocity, at which point it continues at a constant velocity

   B. Moves with constant velocity

   C. Stops immediately

   D. Slows and eventually stops

14. A force of 1 N causes a 1 kg mass to have an acceleration of 1 m/s^2. From this information, a force of 9 N applied to a 9 kg mass would have what magnitude of acceleration?

   A. 18 m/s^2 **B.** 9 m/s^2 **C.** 1 m/s^2 **D.** 3 m/s^2

15. Which of the following statements is true about an object in two-dimensional projectile motion with no air resistance?

   A. The acceleration of the object is zero at its highest point

   B. The horizontal acceleration is always positive, regardless of the vertical acceleration

   C. The velocity is always in the same direction as the acceleration

   D. The horizontal acceleration is always zero, and the vertical acceleration is always a nonzero constant downward

16. A can of paint with a mass of 10 kg hangs from a rope. If the can is to be pulled up to a rooftop with a constant velocity of 0.5 m/s, what must the tension on the rope be? (Use acceleration due to gravity g = 10 m/s^2)

   A. 100 N   **B.** 40 N   **C.** 0 N   **D.** 120 N

17. What is the magnitude of the force exerted on a 1,000 kg object that accelerates at 2 m/s^2?

   A. 500 N   **B.** 1,000 N   **C.** 1,200 N   **D.** 2,000 N

18. A 1,300 kg car is driven at a constant speed of 4 m/s and turns to the right on a curve on the road, which has an effective radius of 4 m. What is the acceleration of the car?

   A. 0 m/s^2 **B.** 3 m/s^2 **C.** 4 m/s^2 **D.** 9.8 m/s^2

19. A block of mass m is resting on a 20° slope. The block has coefficients of friction μ_s = 0.55 and μ_k = 0.45 with the surface. Block m is connected via a massless string over a massless, frictionless pulley to a hanging 2 kg block. What is the minimum mass of block m so that it does not slip? (Use acceleration due to gravity g = 9.8 m/s^2)

   A. 0.8 kg   **B.** 1.3 kg   **C.** 3.7 kg   **D.** 2.3 kg

20. As shown in the figure to the right, two identical masses, attached by a light cord passing over a massless, frictionless pulley on an Atwood's machine, are hanging at different heights. If the two masses are suddenly released, then the:

    A. lower mass moves down   **C.** higher mass moves down
    B. masses remain stationary   **D.** motion is unpredictable

21. When Victoria jumps up in the air, which of the following statements is the most accurate?

    A. The ground cannot exert the upward force necessary to lift her into the air, because the ground is stationary. Rather, Victoria is propelled into the air by the internal force of her muscles acting on her body

    B. When Victoria pushes down on the Earth with a force greater than her weight, the Earth pushes back with the same magnitude force and propels her into the air

    C. Victoria is propelled up by the upward force exerted by the ground, but this force cannot be greater than her weight

    D. The Earth exerts an upward force on Victoria that is stronger than the downward force she exerts on the Earth, therefore Victoria is able to spring up

22. If a feather is pounded with a hammer, which experiences a greater force?

    A. The magnitude of the force is always the same on both
    B. If the feather moves, then it felt the greater force
    C. Depends on the force with which the hammer strikes the feather
    D. Always the hammer

23. A block is moving down a slope of a frictionless inclined plane. Compared to the weight of the block, what is the force parallel to the surface of the plane experienced by the block?

    A. Greater   **B.** Unrelated   **C.** Less than   **D.** Equal

24. A package falls off a truck that is moving at 30 m/s. Ignoring air resistance, the horizontal speed of the package just before it hits the ground is:

    A. 0 m/s   **B.** 15 m/s   **C.** $\sqrt{60}$ m/s   **D.** 30 m/s

25. A carousel with the radius r is turning counterclockwise at a frequency f. How does the velocity of a seat on the carousel change when f is doubled?

    A. Increases by a factor of $2r$ **C.** Remains unchanged
    B. Increases by a factor of r **D.** Doubles

26. What is the mass of a car if it takes 4,500 N to accelerate it at a rate of 5 m/s^2?

   A. 900 kg   **B.** 1,320 kg   **C.** 620 kg   **D.** 460 kg

27. Steve is standing facing forward in a moving bus. What force causes Steve to suddenly move forward when the bus comes to an abrupt stop?

   A. Force due to the air pressure inside the previously moving bus
   B. Force due to kinetic friction between Steve and the floor of the bus
   C. Force due to stored kinetic energy
   D. No forces were responsible for Steve's movement

28. A plastic ball in a liquid is acted upon by its weight and a buoyant force. The weight of the ball is 4.4 N. The buoyant force of 8.4 N acts vertically upward. An external force acting on the ball maintains it in a state of rest. What is the external force?

   A. 4 N, upward   **B.** 8.4 N, downward   **C.** 4.4 N, upward   **D.** 4 N, downward

29. A passenger on a train traveling on a horizontal track notices that a piece of luggage starts to slide directly toward the front of the train. From this, it can be concluded that the train is:

   A. slowing down   **C.** moving at a constant velocity forward
   B. speeding up   **D.** changing direction

30. An object has a mass of 36 kg and weighs 360 N at the surface of the Earth. If this object is transported to an altitude that is twice the Earth's radius, what is the object's mass and weight, respectively?

   A. 9 kg and 90 N   **B.** 36 kg and 90 N   **C.** 4 kg and 90 N   **D.** 36 kg and 40 N

31. A truck is moving at constant velocity. Inside the storage compartment, a rock is dropped from the midpoint of the ceiling and strikes the floor below. The rock hits the floor:

   A. just behind the midpoint of the ceiling
   B. exactly halfway between the midpoint and the front of the truck
   C. exactly below the midpoint of the ceiling
   D. just ahead of the midpoint of the ceiling

32. Jason takes off across level water on his jet-powered skis. The combined mass of Jason and his skis is 75 kg (the mass of the fuel is negligible). The skis have a thrust of 200 N and a coefficient of kinetic friction on water of 0.1. If the skis run out of fuel after only 67 s, how far has Jason traveled before he stops?

   A. 5,428 m   **B.** 3,793 m   **C.** 8,224 m   **D.** 10,331 m

33. A 200 g hockey puck is launched up a metal ramp that is inclined at a 30° angle. The puck's initial speed is 63 m/s. What vertical height does the puck reach above its starting point? (Use acceleration due to gravity $g = 9.8$ m/s^2, the coefficient of static friction $\mu_s = 0.40$ and kinetic friction $\mu_k = 0.30$ between the hockey puck and the metal ramp)

    A. 66 m   **B.** 200 m   **C.** 170 m   **D.** 130 m

34. When a 4 kg mass and a 10 kg mass are pushed from rest with equal force:

    A. 4 kg mass accelerates 2.5 times faster than the 10 kg mass
    B. 10 kg mass accelerates 10 times faster than the 4 kg mass
    C. 4 kg mass accelerates at the same rate as the 10 kg mass
    D. 10 kg mass accelerates 2.5 times faster than the 4 kg mass

35. If a person were to move into outer space far from any stars or planets, her:

    A. weight and mass decrease   **C.** weight remains the same but her mass changes
    B. weight and mass remain the same   **D.** weight changes, but her mass remains the same

36. Which of the following statements must be true when a 20 ton truck collides with a 1,500 lb car?

    A. During the collision, the force on the truck is equal to the force on the car
    B. The truck did not slow down during the collision, but the car did
    C. During the collision, the force on the truck is greater than the force on the car
    D. During the collision, the force on the truck is smaller than the force on the car

37. A block is on a frictionless table on Earth. The block accelerates at 3 m/s^2 when a 20 N horizontal force is applied to it. The block and table are then transported to the Moon. What is the weight of the block on the Moon? (Use acceleration due to gravity at the surface of the Moon = 1.62 m/s^2)

    A. 5.8 N   **B.** 14.2 N   **C.** 8.5 N   **D.** 11 N

38. What is the weight of a 0.4 kg bottle of wine? (Use acceleration due to gravity $g = 9.8$ m/s^2)

    A. 0.4 N   **B.** 4 N   **C.** 40 N   **D.** 20 N

39. Car A starts from rest and accelerates uniformly for time t to travel a distance of d. Car B, which has four times the mass of car A, starts from rest and also accelerates uniformly. If the magnitudes of the forces accelerating car A and car B are the same, how long does it take car B to travel the same distance d?

    A. t **B.** $2t$ **C.** $t/2$ **D.** $16t$

40. A 1,100 kg vehicle is traveling at 27 m/s when it starts to decelerate. What is the average braking force acting on the vehicle, if after 578 m it comes to a complete stop?

    A. −440 N   **B.** −740 N   **C.** −690 N   **D.** −540 N

41. An ornament of mass M, is suspended by a string from the ceiling inside an elevator. What is the tension in the string holding the ornament when the elevator is traveling upward with a constant speed?

    A. Equal to Mg **B.** Less than Mg **C.** Greater than Mg **D.** Equal to M / g

42. An object that weighs 75 N is pulled on a horizontal surface by a force of 50 N to the right. The friction force on this object is 30 N to the left. What is the acceleration of the object? (Use acceleration due to gravity $g = 9.8$ m/s^2)

    A. 0.46 m/s^2 **B.** 1.7 m/s^2 **C.** 2.6 m/s^2 **D.** 10.3 m/s^2

43. While flying horizontally in an airplane, a string attached from the overhead luggage compartment hangs at rest 15° away from the vertical toward the front of the plane. From this observation, it can be concluded that the airplane is:

    A. accelerating forward   **C.** accelerating upward at 15° from horizontal
    B. accelerating backward   **D.** moving backward

44. An object slides down an inclined ramp with a constant speed. If the ramp's incline angle is θ, what is the coefficient of kinetic friction (μ_k) between the object and the ramp?

    A. $\mu_k = 1$ **B.** $\mu_k = \cos\theta / \sin\theta$ **C.** $\mu_k = \sin\theta / \cos\theta$ **D.** $\mu_k = \sin\theta$

45. What is the magnitude of the net force on a 1 N apple when it is in free fall?

    A. 1 N   **B.** 0.1 N   **C.** 0.01 N   **D.** 10 N

46. What is the acceleration of a 105 kg tiger that accelerates uniformly from rest to 20 m/s in 10 s?

    A. 4.7 m/s^2 **B.** 1.5 m/s^2 **C.** 2 m/s^2 **D.** 3.4 m/s^2

47. Yania tries to pull an object by tugging on a rope attached to the object with a force of F. If the object does not move, what does this imply?

    A. The object has reached its natural state of rest and can no longer be set into motion
    B. The rope is not transmitting the force to the object
    C. There are no other forces acting on the object
    D. There are one or more other forces that act on the object with a sum of $-F$

48. If a force F is exerted on an object, the force which the object exerts back:

    A. depends on the mass of the object   **C.** depends on if the object is moving

    B. depends on the density of the object   **D.** equals $-F$

49. What is the mass of an object that experiences a gravitational force of 685 N near Earth's surface? (Use acceleration due to gravity $g = 9.8$ m/s^2)

    A. 76 kg   **B.** 62 kg   **C.** 70 kg   **D.** 81 kg

50. Sarah and her father Bob (who weighs four times as much) are standing on identical skateboards (with frictionless ball bearings), initially at rest. For a short time, Bob pushes Sarah on the skateboard. When Bob stops pushing:

    A. Sarah and Bob move away from each other, and Sarah's speed is four times that of Bob's

    B. Sarah and Bob move away from each other, and Sarah's speed is one fourth of Bob's

    C. Sarah and Bob move away from each other with equal speeds

    D. Sarah moves away from Bob, and Bob is stationary

51. Which best describes the motion of an object along a surface when considering friction?

    A. Less force is required to start than to keep the object in motion at a constant velocity

    B. The same force is required to start as to keep the object in motion at a constant velocity

    C. More force is required to start than to keep the object in motion at a constant velocity

    D. Once the object is set in motion, no force is required to keep it in motion at constant velocity

52. On the surface of Jupiter, the acceleration due to gravity is about three times that as on Earth. What is the weight of a 100 kg rock when it is taken from Earth to Jupiter? (Use acceleration due to gravity $g = 10$ m/s^2)

    A. 1,800 N   **B.** 3,000 N   **C.** 3,300 N   **D.** 4,000 N

53. Joe and Bill are playing tug-of-war. Joe is pulling with a force of 200 N, while Bill is simply holding onto the rope. What is the tension of the rope if neither person is moving?

    A. 75 N   **B.** 0 N   **C.** 100 N   **D.** 200 N

54. A 4 kg wooden block A slides on a frictionless table pulled by a hanging 5 kg block B via a massless string and pulley system as shown. What is the acceleration of block A as it slides? (Use acceleration due to gravity $g = 9.8$ m/s^2)

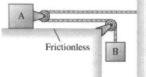

    A. 2.8 m/s^2 **B.** 1.6 m/s^2 **C.** 3.4 m/s^2 **D.** 4.1 m/s^2

55. Which of the following best describes the direction in which the force of kinetic friction acts relative to the interface between the interacting bodies?

    A. Parallel to the interface and in the same direction as the relative velocity

    B. Parallel to the interface and in the opposite direction of the relative velocity

    C. Perpendicular to the interface and in the same direction as the relative velocity

    D. Perpendicular to the interface and in the opposite direction of the relative velocity

56. A person who normally weighs 600 N is standing on a scale in an elevator. The elevator is initially moving upwards at a constant speed of 8 m/s and starts to slow down at a rate of 6 m/s^2. What is the reading of the person's weight on the scale in the elevator during the slowdown? (Use acceleration due to gravity $g = 9.8$ m/s^2)

    A. 600 N   **B.** 588 N   **C.** 98 N   **D.** 231 N

57. Which object feels the greater force when a satellite is in orbit around the Moon?

    A. It depends on the distance of the satellite from the Moon

    B. The Moon and the satellite feel exactly the same force

    C. The Moon because the satellite has a smaller mass

    D. The satellite because the Moon is much more massive

58. What is the acceleration of a 40 kg crate that is being pulled along a frictionless surface by a force of 140 N that makes an angle of 30° with the surface?

    A. 1.5 m/s^2 **B.** 2 m/s^2 **C.** 2.5 m/s^2 **D.** 3 m/s^2

59. A force is a vector quantity because it has both:

    I. action and reaction counterparts

    II. mass and acceleration

    III. magnitude and direction

    A. I only   **B.** II only   **C.** III only   **D.** I and II only

Questions **60-61** are based on the following:

Alice pulls her daughter on a sled by a rope on level snow. Alice is 70 kg and her daughter is 20 kg. The sled has a mass of 10 kg, which slides along the snow with a coefficient of kinetic friction of 0.09. The tension in the rope is 30 N, making an angle of 30° with the ground. They are moving at a constant 2.5 m/s for 4 s. (Use acceleration due to gravity $g = 10$ m/s^2)

60. What is the work done by the force of gravity on the sled?

    A. −3,000 J   **B.** 0 J   **C.** 1,000 J   **D.** 3,000 J

61. What is the work done by the rope on the sled?

A. 0 J   **B.** 130 J   **C.** 65 J   **D.** 260 J

62. What is the net force acting at the top of the path for an arrow that is shot upwards?

A. Greater than its weight   **C.** Instantaneously equal to zero
B. Equal to its weight   **D.** Greater than zero, but less than its weight

63. If an object weighs 740 N on Earth and 5,180 N on the surface of a nearby planet, what is the acceleration due to gravity on that planet? (Use acceleration due to gravity $g = 10 \text{ m/s}^2$)

A. 82 m/s²   **B.** 62 m/s²   **C.** 54 m/s²   **D.** 70 m/s²

64. Susan pushes on box G that is next to box H, causing both boxes to slide along the floor, as shown. The reaction force of Susan's push is the:

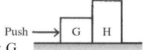

A. upward force of the floor on box G   **C.** push of box H on box G
B. push of box G against Susan   **D.** push of box G on box H

65. Two bodies of different masses are subjected to identical forces. Compared to the body with a smaller mass, the body with a greater mass experiences:

A. less acceleration, because the ratio of force to mass is smaller
B. greater acceleration, because the ratio of force to mass is greater
C. less acceleration, because the product of mass and acceleration is smaller
D. greater acceleration, because the product of mass and acceleration is greater

66. An object is propelled along a straight-line path by a force. If the net force were doubled, the object's acceleration would:

A. halve   **B.** stay the same   **C.** double   **D.** quadruple

67. A 500 kg rocket ship is firing two jets at once. The two jets are at right angles to each other with one firing with a force of 500 N and the other with a force of 1,200 N. What is the magnitude of the acceleration of the rocket ship?

A. 1.4 m/s²   **B.** 2.6 m/s²   **C.** 3.4 m/s²   **D.** 5.6 m/s²

68. Assume the strings and pulleys in the diagram below have negligible masses and the coefficient of kinetic friction between the 2 kg block and the table is 0.25. What is the acceleration of the 2 kg block? (Use acceleration due to gravity $g = 9.8 \text{ m/s}^2$)

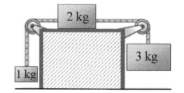

A. 3.2 m/s²   **B.** 4 m/s²   **C.** 0.3 m/s²   **D.** 2.5 m/s²

69. Which of the following statements must be true for an object moving with constant velocity in a straight line?

   A. The net force on the object is zero
   B. There are no forces acting on the object
   C. A constant force is being applied in the direction opposite of motion
   D. A constant force is being applied in the direction of motion

70. A person gives a shopping cart an initial push along a horizontal floor to get it moving and then releases the cart. The cart travels forward along the floor, gradually slowing as it moves. Consider the horizontal force on the cart while it is moving forward and slowing. Which of the following statements is correct?

   A. Only a forward force is acting, which diminishes with time
   B. Only a backward force is acting, no forward force is acting
   C. Both a forward and a backward force are acting on the cart, but the forward force is larger
   D. Both a forward and a backward force are acting on the cart, but the backward force is larger

71. A truck is using a hook to tow a car whose mass is one quarter that of the truck. If the force exerted by the truck on the car is 6,000 N, then the force exerted by the car on the truck is:

   A. 1,500 N   **B.** 24,000 N   **C.** 6,000 N   **D.** 12,000 N

72. How large is the force of friction impeding the motion of a bureau when the 120 N bureau is being pulled across the sidewalk at a constant speed by a force of 30 N?

   A. 0 N   **B.** 30 N   **C.** 120 N   **D.** 3 N

73. An object maintains its state of motion because it has:

   A. mass   **B.** acceleration   **C.** speed   **D.** weight

74. The Earth and the Moon attract each other with the force of gravity. The Earth's radius is 3.7 times that of the Moon, and the Earth's mass is 80 times greater than the Moon's. The acceleration due to gravity on the surface of the Moon is 1/6 the acceleration due to gravity on the Earth's surface. If the distance between the Earth and the Moon decreases by a factor of 4, how would the force of gravity between the Earth and the Moon change?

   A. Remain the same   **C.** Decrease by a factor of 16
   B. Increase by a factor of 16   **D.** Decrease by a factor of 4

75. Two forces acting on an object have magnitudes $F_1 = -6.6$ N and $F_2 = 2.2$ N. Which third force causes the object to be in equilibrium?

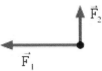

    A. 4.4 N at 162° counterclockwise from F_1
    B. 4 4 N at 108° counterclockwise from F_1
    C. 7 N at 162° counterclockwise from F_1
    D. 7 N at 108° counterclockwise from F_1

76. What are the readings on the spring scales when a 17 kg fish is weighed with two spring scales, if each scale has negligible weight?

    A. The top scale reads 17 kg, and the bottom scale reads 0 kg
    B. Each scale reads greater than 0 kg and less than 17 kg, but the sum of the scales is 17 kg
    C. The bottom scale reads 17 kg, and the top scale reads 0 kg
    D. The sum of the two scales is 34 kg

77. Two forces of equal magnitude are acting on an object as shown. If the magnitude of each force is 2.3 N and the angle between them is 40°, which third force causes the object to be in equilibrium?

    A. 1.8 N pointing to the right   **C.** 3.5 N pointing to the right
    B. 2.2 N pointing to the right   **D.** 4.3 N pointing to the right

78. An object at rest on an inclined plane starts to slide when the incline is increased to 17°. What is the coefficient of static friction between the object and the plane? (Use acceleration due to gravity $g = 9.8$ m/s^2)

    A. 0.37   **B.** 0.43   **C.** 0.24   **D.** 0.31

79. What is the force exerted by the table on a 2 kg book resting on it? (Use acceleration due to gravity $g = 10$ m/s^2)

    A. 100 N   **B.** 20 N   **C.** 10 N   **D.** 0 N

EQUILIBRIUM AND MOMENTUM

1. When is the angular momentum of a system constant?

    A. When no net external torque acts on the system
    B. When the linear momentum and the energy are constant
    C. When no net external force acts on the system
    D. When the total kinetic energy is positive

2. When a rock rolls down a mountainside at 7 m/s, the horizontal component of its velocity vector is 1.8 m/s. What was the angle of the mountain surface above the horizontal?

    A. 15°   **B.** 63°   **C.** 40°   **D.** 75°

3. A 200 N sled slides down a frictionless hill at an angle of 37° to the horizontal. What is the magnitude of the force that the hill exerts on the sled parallel to the surface of the hill?

    A. 170 N   **B.** 200 N   **C.** 74 N   **D.** 0 N

4. Water causes a water wheel to turn as it passes by. The force of the water is 300 N, and the radius of the wheel is 10 m. What is the torque around the center of the wheel?

    A. 0 N·m   **B.** 300 N·m **C.** 3,000 N·m   **D.** 3 N·m

5. Through what angle, in degrees, does a 33 rpm record turn in 0.32 s?

    A. 44°   **B.** 94°   **C.** 113°   **D.** 63°

6. A freight train rolls along a track with considerable momentum. What is its momentum if it rolls at the same speed but has twice the mass?

    A. Zero   **B.** Doubled   **C.** Quadrupled   **D.** Unchanged

---

Questions **7-9** are based on the following:

Three carts run along a level, frictionless one-dimensional track. Furthest to the left is a 1 kg cart I, moving at 0.5 m/s to the right. In the middle is a 1.5 kg cart II moving at 0.3 m/s to the left. Furthest to the right is a 3.5 kg cart III moving at 0.5 m/s to the left. Consider the three carts as a system because they collide and stick together. Use the direction to the right as positive.

7. What is the total momentum of the system before the collision?

    A. −2.6 kg·m/s   **B.** 1.4 kg·m/s   **C.** 0.6 kg·m/s   **D.** −1.7 kg·m/s

---

8. Assuming cart I and cart II collide first and cart III is still independent, what is the total momentum of the system just after cart I and cart II collide?

    A. −1.7 kg·m/s   **B.** 0.1 kg·m/s   **C.** 0.9 kg·m/s   **D.** −0.9 kg·m/s

9. What is the final velocity of the three carts?

    A. −0.35 m/s   **B.** −0.28 m/s   **C.** −0.87 m/s   **D.** 0.35 m/s

10. A 480 kg car is moving at 14.4 m/s when it collides with another car that is moving at 13.3 m/s in the same direction. If the second car has a mass of 570 kg and a new velocity of 17.9 m/s after the collision, what is the velocity of the first car after the collision?

    A. 19 m/s   **B.** −9 m/s   **C.** 9 m/s   **D.** 14 m/s

11. An 8 g bullet is shot into a 4 kg block at rest on a frictionless horizontal surface. The bullet remains lodged in the block. The block moves into a spring and compresses it by 8.9 cm. After the block comes to a stop, the spring fully decompresses and sends the block in the opposite direction. What is the magnitude of the impulse of the block (including the bullet), due to the spring, during the entire time interval in which the block and spring are in contact? (Use the spring constant = 1,400 N/m)

    A. 11 N·s   **B.** 8.3 N·s   **C.** 6.4 N·s   **D.** 13 N·s

12. An ice skater performs a fast spin by pulling in her outstretched arms close to her body. What happens to her rotational kinetic energy about the axis of rotation?

    A. Decreases   **C.** Increases

    B. Remains the same   **D.** It changes, but it depends on her body mass

13. A toy car is traveling in a circular path. If the velocity of the object is doubled without changing the path, what is the force required to maintain the object's motion?

    A. 2*F*   **B.** *F*   **C.** ½*F*   **D.** 4*F*

14. Which of the following is units of momentum?

    A. kg·m/s^2 **B.** J·s/m   **C.** N·m   **D.** kg·s

15. The impulse on an apple hitting the ground depends on:

    I. the speed of the apple just before it hits

    II. whether or not the apple bounces

    III. the time of impact with the ground

    A. I only   **B.** II only   **C.** III only   **D.** I, II and III

16. A 55 kg girl throws a 0.8 kg ball against a wall. The ball strikes the wall horizontally with a speed of 25 m/s and bounces back with the same speed. The ball is in contact with the wall for 0.05 s. What is the average force exerted on the wall by the ball?

    A. 27,500 N   **B.** 55,000 N   **C.** 400 N   **D.** 800 N

17. Three objects are moving along a straight line as shown. If the positive direction is to the right, what is the total momentum of this system?

    A. −70 kg·m/s   **C.** +86 kg·m/s

    B. +70 kg·m/s   **D.** −86 kg·m/s

6 m/s   3 m/s   2 m/s

7 kg   12 kg   4 kg

Questions **18-19** are based on the following:

Two ice skaters, Vladimir (60 kg) and Olga (40 kg) collide in midair. Just before the collision, Vladimir was going North at 0.5 m/s and Olga was going West at 1 m/s. Right after the collision and well before they land on the ground, they stick together. Assume they have no vertical velocity.

18. What is the magnitude of their velocity just after the collision?

    A. 0.1 m/s   **B.** 1.8 m/s   **C.** 0.9 m/s   **D.** 0.5 m/s

19. What is the magnitude of the total momentum just after the collision?

    A. 25 kg·m/s   **B.** 50 kg·m/s   **C.** 65 kg·m/s   **D.** 80 kg·m/s

20. A horse is running in a straight line. If both the mass and the speed of the horse are doubled, by what factor does its momentum increase?

    A. $\sqrt{2}$ **B.** 2   **C.** 4   **D.** 8

21. The mass of box P is greater than the mass of box Q. Both boxes are on a frictionless horizontal surface and connected by a light cord. A horizontal force F is applied to box Q, accelerating the boxes to the right. What is the magnitude of the force exerted by the connecting cord on box P?

    A. equal to F **C.** zero

    B. equal to $2F$ **D.** less than F but > 0

P   Q   → F

---

22. Which of the following is true when Melissa and her friend Samantha are riding on a merry-go-round, as viewed from above?

A. They have the same speed, but different angular velocity
B. They have different speeds, but the same angular velocity
C. They have the same speed and the same angular velocity
D. They have different speeds and different angular velocities

23. The relationship between impulse and impact force involves the:

A. time the force acts   **C.** difference between acceleration and velocity
B. distance the force acts   **D.** mass and its effect on resisting a change in velocity

24. Angular momentum cannot be conserved if the:

A. moment of inertia changes   **C.** angular velocity changes
B. system is experiencing a net force   **D.** system has a net torque

25. A 6.8 kg block of mass m is moving on a frictionless surface with a speed of $v_i = 5.4$ m/s and makes a perfectly elastic collision with a stationary block of mass M. After the collision, the 6.8 kg block recoils with a speed of $v_f = 3.2$ m/s. What is the magnitude of the average force on the 6.8 kg block while the two blocks are in contact for 2 s?

A. 4.4 N   **B.** 47.6 N   **C.** 32.6 N   **D.** 29.2 N

Questions **26-27** are based on the following:

A 4 kg rifle imparts a high velocity to a small 10 g bullet by exploding a charge that causes the bullet to leave the barrel at 300 m/s. Take the system as the combination of the rifle and bullet. Normally, the rifle is fired with the butt of the gun pressed against the shooter's shoulder. Ignore the force of the shoulder on the rifle.

26. What is the momentum of the system just after the bullet leaves the barrel?

A. 0 kg·m/s   **B.** 3 kg·m/s   **C.** 9 kg·m/s   **D.** 30 kg·m/s

27. What is the recoil velocity of the rifle (i.e. the velocity of the rifle just after firing)?

A. 23 m/s   **B.** 1.5 m/s   **C.** 5.6 m/s   **D.** 0.75 m/s

28. A ball thrown horizontally from a point 24 m above the ground strikes the ground after traveling horizontally a distance of 18 m. With what speed was it thrown, assuming negligible air resistance? (Use acceleration due to gravity $g = 9.8$ m/s^2)

A. 6.8 m/s   **B.** 7.5 m/s   **C.** 8.2 m/s   **D.** 8.6 m/s

29. An object is moving in a circle at constant speed. Its acceleration vector is directed:

A. toward the center of the circle
B. away from the center of the circle
C. tangent to the circle and in the direction of the motion
D. behind the normal and toward the center of the circle

30. Impulse is equal to the:

   I. force multiplied by the distance over which the force acts
   II. change in momentum
   III. momentum

A. I only   **B.** II only   **C.** III only   **D.** I and II only

31. A 4 kg object is at a height of 10 m above the Earth's surface. Ignoring air resistance, what is its kinetic energy immediately before impacting the ground if it is thrown straight downward with an initial speed of 20 m/s? (Use acceleration due to gravity $g = 10$ m/s^2)

A. 150 J   **B.** 300 J   **C.** 1,200 J   **D.** 900 J

32. A car traveling along the highway needs a certain amount of force exerted on it to stop. More stopping force may be required when the car has:

   I. less stopping distance   II. more momentum   III. more mass

A. I only   **B.** II only   **C.** III only   **D.** I, II and III

33. A table tennis ball moving East at a speed of 4 m/s collides with a stationary bowling ball. The table tennis ball bounces back to the West, and the bowling ball moves very slowly to the East. Which ball experiences the greater magnitude of impulse during the collision?

A. Bowling ball
B. Table tennis ball
C. Neither because both experience the same magnitude of impulse
D. It is not possible to determine since the velocities after the collision are unknown

34. Assume that a massless bar of 5 m is suspended from a rope and that the rope is attached to the bar at a distance x from the bar's left end. If a 30 kg mass hangs from the right side of the bar and a 6 kg mass hangs from the left side of the bar, what value of x results in equilibrium? (Use acceleration due to gravity $g = 9.8$ m/s^2)

A. 2.8 m **B.** 4.2 m **C.** 3.2 m **D.** 1.6 m

35. A block of mass m sits at rest on a rough inclined ramp that makes an angle θ with the horizontal. What must be true about the force of static friction (f) on the block?

A. $f > mg \sin \theta$ **C.** $f = mg$
B. $f = mg \cos \theta$ **D.** $f = mg \sin \theta$

36. A 30 kg block is pushed in a straight line across a horizontal surface. What is the coefficient of kinetic friction μ_k between the block and the surface if a constant force of 45 N must be applied to the block in order to maintain a constant velocity of 3 m/s? (Use acceleration due to gravity $g = 10$ m/s^2)

A. 0.1 **B.** 0.33 **C.** 0.15 **D.** 0.5

37. The impulse-momentum relationship is a direct result of:

I. Newton's First Law   II. Newton's Second Law   III. Newton's Third Law

A. I only   **B.** II only   **C.** III only   **D.** I and II only

---

Questions **38-40** are based on the following:

A 0.5 m by 0.6 m rectangular piece of metal is hinged ($\otimes$) (as shown) in the upper left corner, hanging so that the long edge is vertical. A 25 N force (Y) acts to the left at the lower left corner. A 15 N force (X) acts down at the lower right corner. A 30 N force (Z) acts to the right at the upper right corner. Each force vector is in the plane of the metal. Use counterclockwise as the positive direction.

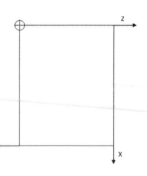

38. What is the torque of force X about the pivot?

A. 5 N·m **B.** 3 N·m **C.** −7.5 N·m **D.** 0 N·m

39. What is the torque of force Z about the pivot?

A. −10 N·m **B.** −4.5 N·m **C.** 4.5 N·m **D.** 0 N·m

---

40. What is the torque of force Y about the pivot?

A. −15 N·m   **B.** −3 N·m   **C.** 0 N·m   **D.** 3 N·m

41. A 50 g weight is tied to the end of a string and whirled at 20 m/s in a horizontal circle with a radius of 2 m. Ignoring the force of gravity, what is the tension in the string?

A. 5 N   **B.** 10 N   **C.** 50 N   **D.** 150 N

42. A small car collides with a large truck in a head-on collision. Which of the following statements concerning the magnitude of the average force during the collision is correct?

A. The small car and the truck experience the same average force
B. The force experienced by each one is inversely proportional to its velocity
C. The truck experiences the greater average force
D. The small car experiences the greater average force

43. A 10 kg bar that is 2 m long extends perpendicularly from a vertical wall. The free end of the bar is attached to a point on the wall by a light cable, which makes an angle of 30º with the bar. What is the tension in the cable? (Use acceleration due to gravity $g = 10$ m/s^2)

A. 75 N   **B.** 150 N   **C.** 100 N   **D.** 125 N

44. Object A has the same size and shape as object B, but is twice as heavy. When objects A and B are dropped simultaneously from a tower, they reach the ground at the same time. Object A has greater:

   I. speed   II. momentum   III. acceleration

A. I only   **B.** II only   **C.** III only   **D.** I and II only

45. Two vehicles approach a right angle intersection and then collide. After the collision, they become entangled. If their mass ratio was 1 : 4 and their respective speeds as they approached were both 12 m/s, what is the magnitude of the velocity immediately following the collision?

A. 16.4 m/s   **B.** 11.9 m/s   **C.** 13.4 m/s   **D.** 9.9 m/s

46. A fisherman is on a boat that is stationary on the water. He throws the anchor off his boat at an angle of 5° above the horizontal. With reference to the water, if the anchor weighs twice as much as he does and the boat reacts by moving with a speed of 2.9 m/s during the throw, how fast did he throw the anchor? (Assume the mass of the boat is negligible)

A. 2.2 m/s   **B.** 0.2 m/s   **C.** 1.5 m/s   **D.** 0.8 m/s

47. Ignoring the forces of friction, what horizontal force must be applied to an object with a weight of 98 N to give it a horizontal acceleration of 10 m/s²? (Use acceleration due to gravity $g = 9.8$ m/s²)

A. 9.8 N   **B.** 100 N   **C.** 79 N   **D.** 125 N

48. Consider a winch that pulls a cart at constant speed up an incline. Point A is at the bottom of the incline and point B is at the top. Which of the following statements is/are true from point A to B?

     I. The KE of the cart is conserved
     II. The PE of the cart is conserved
     III. The sum of the KE and PE of the cart is conserved

A. I only   **B.** II only   **C.** III only   **D.** I and II only

49. A high speed dart is shot from ground level with a speed of 140 m/s at an angle of 35° above the horizontal. What is the vertical component of its velocity after 4 s if air resistance is ignored? (Use acceleration due to gravity $g = 9.8$ m/s²)

A. 59 m/s   **B.** 75 m/s   **C.** 42 m/s   **D.** 36 m/s

50. What does the area under the curve of a force vs. time graph represent for a diver as she leaves the platform during her approach to the water below?

A. Work   **C.** Impulse
B. Momentum   **D.** Displacement

51. A rifle of mass 2 kg is suspended by strings. The rifle fires a bullet of mass 0.01 kg at a speed of 220 m/s. What is the recoil velocity of the rifle?

A. 0.001 m/s   **B.** 0.01 m/s   **C.** 0.1 m/s   **D.** 1.1 m/s

52. How do automobile air bags reduce injury during a collision?

A. They reduce the kinetic energy transferred to the passenger
B. They reduce the momentum exerted upon the passenger
C. They reduce the acceleration of the automobile
D. They reduce the forces exerted upon the passenger

Questions **53-55** are based on the following:

Tim nails a meter stick to a board at the meter stick's 0 m mark. Force I acts at the 0.5 m mark perpendicular to the meter stick with a force of 10 N, as shown in the figure. Force II acts at the end of the meter stick with a force of 5 N, making a 35° angle. Force III acts at the same point with a force of 20 N, providing tension but no shear. Use counterclockwise as the positive direction.

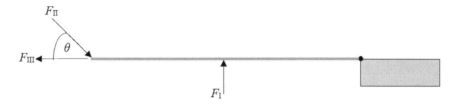

53. What is the torque of Force I about the fixed point?

    A. −5 N·m   **B.** 0 N·m   **C.** 5 N·m   **D.** 10 N·m

54. What is the torque of Force II about the fixed point?

    A. −4.8 N·m   **B.** −2.9 N·m   **C.** 4.8 N·m   **D.** 2.9 N·m

55. What is the torque of Force III about the fixed point?

    A. −20 N·m   **B.** 0 N·m   **C.** 10 N·m   **D.** 20 N·m

56. Two equal mass balls (one yellow and the other red) are dropped from the same height, and rebound off the floor. The yellow ball rebounds to a higher position. Which ball is subjected to the greater magnitude of impulse during its collision with the floor?

    A. Both balls were subjected to the same magnitude of impulse
    B. Red ball
    C. Yellow ball
    D. Requires the time intervals and forces

57. Calculate the impulse associated with a force of 4.5 N that lasts for 1.4 s:

    A. 5.4 kg·m/s   **B.** 6.8 kg·m/s   **C.** 4.6 kg·m/s   **D.** 6.3 kg·m/s

58. A heavy truck and a small truck roll down a hill. Ignoring friction, at the bottom of the hill, the heavy truck has greater:

    I. momentum   II. acceleration   III. speed

    A. I only   **B.** II only   **C.** III only   **D.** I and II only

59. A 78 g steel ball is released from rest and falls vertically onto a rigid surface. The ball strikes the surface and is in contact with it for 0.5 ms. The ball rebounds elastically, and returns to its original height during a round trip of 4 s. Assume that the surface does not deform during contact. What is the maximum elastic energy stored by the ball? (Use acceleration due to gravity $g = 9.8$ m/s²)

A. 23 J   **B.** 43 J   **C.** 11 J   **D.** 15 J

60. Cart A is 5 kg and cart B is 10 kg, and they are initially stationary on a frictionless horizontal surface. A force of 3 N to the right acts on cart A for 2 s. Subsequently, it hits cart B and the two carts stick together. What is the final velocity of the two carts?

A. 1 m/s   **B.** 0.67 m/s   **C.** 0.8 m/s   **D.** 1.5 m/s

61. A 0.12 kg baseball is thrown with a velocity of 23 m/s. It is struck with a bat with an average force of 5,000 N, which results in a velocity of 34 m/s in the opposite direction. How long were the bat and ball in contact?

A. 3.4×10^{-2} s   **C.** 1.4×10^{-3} s
B. 4.3×10^{-3} s   **D.** 2.3×10^{-2} s

62. Which of the following represents the kinetic energy for a sailboat of mass m that is moving with a momentum of p?

A. p^2 / m **B.** $\frac{1}{2}mp^2$ **C.** mp **D.** $p^2 / 2m$

63. A 2.2 kg block of mass m is moving on frictionless surface with a speed of $v_i = 9.2$ m/s, and it makes a perfectly elastic collision with a stationary block of mass M. After the collision, the 2.2 kg block recoils with a speed of $v_f = 2.5$ m/s. What is the mass of M?

A. 5.4 kg   **B.** 8.4 kg   **C.** 2.9 kg   **D.** 3.8 kg

64. Carts I and II are on a level, frictionless one-dimensional track. Cart I is 1 kg and is initially going right at 7 m/s, and cart II is 3 kg and is initially going left at 2 m/s when they collide. Cart I recoils with a speed of 3 m/s. What is the velocity of cart II after the collision?

A. 2.5 m/s to the right   **C.** 1.3 m/s to the right
B. 3.5 m/s to the right   **D.** 2.5 m/s to the left

65. Two boxes, A and B, are connected by a horizontal string S on a horizontal floor. A light wire pulls horizontally on box B, as shown, with a force of 100 N. The reaction force of this pull is the:

A. pull that string S exerts on box A **C.** pull that box B exerts on string S
B. pull of box B on the wire **D.** pull that string S exerts on box B

66. A uniform rod of mass *M* sticks out from a vertical wall and points toward the floor. The smaller angle it makes with the wall is θ, and the rod's end is attached to the ceiling by a string parallel to the wall. What is the tension in the supporting string?

A. $Mg \sin \theta$ **B.** Mg **C.** $Mg \sin \theta / 2$ **D.** $Mg / 2$

67. A moving object with no forces acting on it continues to move with constant non-zero:

   I. momentum   II. impulse   III. acceleration

A. I only   **B.** II only   **C.** III only   **D.** I and II only

68. Ignoring air resistance, the horizontal component of a projectile's velocity:

A. remains zero
B. first decreases and then increases
C. is always the same sign as the vertical component of velocity
D. remains a nonzero constant

69. A 3.3 kg object moving at 6.9 m/s makes a perfectly inelastic collision with a 3.6 kg object that is initially at rest. What percentage of the initial kinetic energy of the system is lost during the collision?

A. 66%   **B.** 59%   **C.** 71%   **D.** 52%

70. Two children are riding on a carousel. Lisa is at a greater distance from the axis of rotation than Katie is. Which girl has the larger angular displacement?

A. Lisa
B. Katie
C. Depends on the mass of each child
D. They have the same nonzero angular displacement

71. A 1,200 kg ore cart is rolling at 10 m/s across a flat surface. A crane dumps 800 kg of ore (vertically) into the cart. Ignoring the frictional force, how fast does the cart move after being loaded with ore?

A. 8.6 m/s **B.** 7.8 m/s **C.** 6 m/s **D.** 4 m/s

72. A small car crashes with a large truck in a head-on collision. Which of the following statements is correct regarding the magnitude of the momentum change during the collision?

A. The car and the truck experience the same change in momentum
B. The change in momentum experienced by each is inversely proportional to its mass
C. The truck experiences the greater change in momentum
D. The car experiences the greater change in momentum

73. A massless pulley is suspended from a cable that is attached to the beam of a building 10 m above the ground. A massless rope is slung over the pulley, and one end is attached to a bucket of bricks weighing 750 N. The free end of the rope is pulled, and the bucket is raised above the ground. The free end is then tied to a fixed point. What is the approximate downward force exerted by the cable attaching the pulley to the beam?

A. 750 N **B.** 375 N **C.** 1,000 N **D.** 1,500 N

74. A cannon recoils after firing a cannon ball. Why is the speed of the cannon's recoil smaller than that of the cannonball?

I. momentum of the cannon is smaller
II. cannon has more mass than the ball
III. momentum is mainly concentrated in the ball

A. I only **B.** II only **C.** III only **D.** I and II only

75. A 1.2 kg asteroid is traveling toward the Orion Nebula at a speed of 2.8 m/s. Another 4.1 kg asteroid is traveling at 2.3 m/s in a perpendicular direction. The two asteroids collide and stick together. What is the change in momentum from before to after the collision?

A. 0 kg·m/s **B.** 2.1 kg·m/s **C.** 9.4 kg·m/s **D.** 12 kg·m/s

76. A 1,120 kg car experiences an impulse of 30,000 N·s during a collision with a wall. If the collision takes 0.43 s, what was the speed of the car just before the collision?

A. 12 m/s **B.** 64 m/s **C.** 42 m/s **D.** 27 m/s

77. Does the centripetal force acting on an object do work on the object?

   A. No, because the force and the displacement of the object are perpendicular
   B. Yes, since a force acts and the object moves, and work is force times distance
   C. Yes, since it takes energy to turn an object
   D. No, because the object has constant speed

78. Cars with padded dashboards are safer in an accident than cars without padded dashboards, because a passenger hitting the dashboard has:

      I. increased time of impact
      II. decreased impulse
      III. decreased impact force

   A. I only   **B.** II only   **C.** III only   **D.** I and III only

79. The acceleration due to gravity on the Moon is only one-sixth of that on Earth, and the Moon has no atmosphere. If a person hit a baseball on the Moon with the same effort (and therefore at the same speed and angle) as on Earth, how far would the ball travel on the Moon compared to on Earth? (Ignore air resistance on Earth)

   A. The same distance as on Earth   **C.** 1/6 as far as on Earth
   B. 6 times as far as on Earth   **D.** 36 times as far as on Earth

80. A uniform meter stick weighing 20 N has a weight of 50 N attached to its left end and a weight of 30 N attached to its right end. The meter stick is hung from a rope. What is the tension in the rope and how far from the left end of the meter stick should the rope be attached so that the meter stick remains level?

   A. 100 N placed 37.5 cm from the left end of the meter stick
   B. 50 N placed 40 cm from the left end of the meter stick
   C. 80 N placed 37.5 cm from the left end of the meter stick
   D. 100 N placed 40 cm from the left end of the meter stick

81. To catch a ball, a baseball player extends her hand forward before impact with the ball and then lets it ride backward in the direction of the ball's motion upon impact. Doing this reduces the force of impact on the player's hand principally because the:

   A. time of impact is decreased   **C.** relative velocity is less
   B. time of impact is increased   **D.** force of impact is reduced by $\sqrt{2}$

82. A 1,200 kg car, moving at 15.6 m/s, collides with a stationary 1,500 kg car. If the two vehicles lock together, what is their combined velocity immediately after the collision?

A. 12.4 m/s   **B.** 5.4 m/s   **C.** 6.9 m/s   **D.** 7.6 m/s

83. A 0.05 kg golf ball, initially at rest, has a velocity of 100 m/s immediately after being struck by a golf club. If the club and ball were in contact for 0.8 ms, what is the average force exerted on the ball?

A. 5.5 kN   **B.** 4.9 kN   **C.** 11.8 kN   **D.** 6.3 kN

84. Which of the following is an accurate statement for a rigid body that is rotating?

A. All points on the body are moving with the same angular velocity
B. Its center of rotation is its center of gravity
C. Its center of rotation is at rest and therefore not moving
D. Its center of rotation must be moving with a constant velocity

85. Cart 1 (2 kg) and Cart 2 (2.5 kg) run along a frictionless, level, one-dimensional track. Cart 2 is initially at rest, and Cart 1 is traveling 0.6 m/s toward the right when it encounters Cart 2. After the collision, Cart 1 is at rest. Which of the following is true concerning the collision?

A. The collision is completely elastic   **C.** Momentum is conserved
B. Kinetic energy is conserved   **D.** Total momentum is decreased

86. What is the reason for using a long barrel in a gun?

A. Allows the force of the expanding gases from the gunpowder to act for a longer time
B. Increases the force exerted on the bullet due to the expanding gases from the gunpowder
C. Exerts a larger force on the shells
D. Reduces frictional losses

WORK AND ENERGY

1. Consider the following ways that a girl might throw a stone from a bridge. The speed of the stone as it leaves her hand is the same in each of the three cases.

      I. Thrown straight up
      II. Thrown straight down
      III. Thrown straight out horizontally

Ignoring air resistance, in which case is the vertical speed of the stone the greatest when it hits the water below?

    A. I only   **B.** II only   **C.** III only   **D.** I and II only

2. A package is being pulled along the ground by a 5 N force *F* directed 45° above the horizontal. Approximately how much work is exerted when the force pulls the package 10 m?

    A. 14 J   **B.** 35 J   **C.** 70 J   **D.** 46 J

3. Which quantity has the greatest influence on the amount of kinetic energy that a large truck has while moving down the highway?

    A. Velocity   **B.** Mass   **C.** Density   **D.** Direction

4. No work is done by gravity on a bowling ball that rolls along the floor of a bowling alley because:

    A. no potential energy is being converted to kinetic energy
    B. the force on the ball is at a right angle to the ball's motion
    C. its velocity is constant
    D. the total force on the ball is zero

5. A 5 kg toy car is rolling along level ground. At a given time, it is traveling at a speed of 2 m/s and accelerating at 3 m/s^2. What is the cart's kinetic energy at this time?

    A. 20 J   **B.** 8 J   **C.** 10 J   **D.** 4 J

6. A tree house is 8 m above the ground. If Peter does 360 J of work while pulling a box from the ground up to his tree house with a rope, what is the mass of a box? (Use acceleration due to gravity *g* = 10 m/s^2)

    A. 4.5 kg   **B.** 3.5 kg   **C.** 5.8 kg   **D.** 2.5 kg

7. For an ideal elastic spring, what does the slope of the curve represent for a displacement (*x*) vs. applied force (*F*) graph?

    A. The acceleration of gravity   **C.** The spring constant
    B. The square root of the spring constant   **D.** The reciprocal of the spring constant

---

8. A spring with a spring constant of 22 N/m is stretched from equilibrium to 3 m. How much work is done in the process?

A. 33 J   B. 66 J   C. 99 J   D. 198 J

9. A baseball is thrown straight up. Compare the sign of the work done by gravity while the ball goes up with the sign of the work done by gravity while it goes down:

A. negative on the way up and positive on the way down
B. negative on the way up and negative on the way down
C. positive on the way up and positive on the way down
D. positive on the way up and negative on the way down

10. Let A_1 represent the magnitude of the work done by gravity as mass A's gravitational energy increases by 400 J. Let B_1 represent the total amount of work necessary to increase mass B's kinetic energy by 400 J. How do A_1 and B_1 compare?

A. $A_1 > B_1$ C. $A_1 < B_1$
B. $A_1 = B_1$ D. $A_1 = 400 B_1$

11. According to the definition of work, pushing on a rock accomplishes no work unless there is:

A. an applied force equal to the rock's weight
B. movement perpendicular to the force
C. an applied force greater than the rock's weight
D. movement parallel to the force

12. A job is done slowly, while an identical job is done quickly. Both jobs require the same amount of work, but different amounts of:

I. energy   II. power   III. torque

A. I only   B. II only   C. I and II only   D. I and III only

13. On a force (F) vs. distance (d) graph, what represents the work done by the force F?

A. The area under the curve   C. The slope of the curve
B. A line connecting two points on the curve   D. The length of the curve

14. A 3 kg cat leaps from a tree to the ground, which is a distance of 4 m. What is its kinetic energy just before the cat reaches the ground? (Use acceleration due to gravity $g = 10$ m/s^2)

A. 0 J   B. 9 J   C. 120 J   D. 60 J

15. Work done by static friction is always:

A. greater than the forces opposing motion   C. along the surface
B. less than the forces opposing motion   D. zero

16. 350 J of work are required to fully drive a stake into the ground. If the average resistive force on the stake by the ground is 900 N, how long is the stake?

A. 2.3 m   **B.** 0.23 m   **C.** 3 m   **D.** 0.39 m

17. A lightweight object and a very heavy object are sliding with equal speeds along a level, frictionless surface. They both slide up the same frictionless hill with no air resistance. Which object rises to a greater height?

A. They both slide to exactly the same height
B. The heavy object, because it has more kinetic energy to carry it up the hill
C. The heavy object, because it has greater potential energy
D. The lightweight object, because it has more kinetic energy to carry it up the hill

18. If Investigator II does 3 times the work of Investigator I in one third the time, the power output of Investigator II is:

A. 9 times greater   **C.** 1/3 times greater
B. 3 times greater   **D.** the same

19. A diver who weighs 450 N steps off a diving board that is 9 m above the water. What is the kinetic energy when the diver strikes the water? (Use acceleration due to gravity $g = 10$ m/s^2)

A. 160 J   **B.** 540 J   **C.** 45 J   **D.** 4,050 J

20. A vertical, hanging spring stretches by 23 cm when a 160 N object is attached. What is the weight of a hanging plant that stretches the spring by 34 cm?

A. 237 N   **B.** 167 N   **C.** 158 N   **D.** 309 N

21. A mule pulls with a horizontal force F on a covered wagon of mass M. The mule and covered wagon are traveling at a constant speed v on level ground. How much work is done by the mule on the covered wagon during time Δt? (Use acceleration due to gravity $g = 10$ m/s^2)

A. $-Fv\Delta t$ **B.** $Fv\Delta t$ **C.** 0 J   **D.** $-F\sqrt{v}\Delta t$

22. Jane pulls on the strap of a sled at an angle of 32° above the horizontal. If 540 J of work are done by the strap while moving the suitcase a horizontal distance of 18 m, what is the tension in the strap?

A. 86 N   **B.** 112 N   **C.** 24 N   **D.** 35 N

23. A spring stretches 6 cm when a 120 g mass is attached to one of its ends. If an additional 100 g mass is added to the spring, what is the potential energy of the spring?

A. the same   **C.** 2 times greater
B. 4 times greater   **D.** $\sqrt{2}$ times greater

24. A Ferrari, Maserati and Lamborghini are moving with the same speed and each driver slams on his brakes. The most massive is the Ferrari, and the least massive is the Lamborghini. If the tires of all three cars have identical coefficients of kinetic friction with the road surface, which car experiences the greatest amount of work done by friction?

A. Maserati

B. Lamborghini

C. Ferrari

D. The amount is the same

25. A hammer does the work of driving a nail into a wooden board. Compared to the moment before the hammer strikes the nail, after it impacts the nail, the hammer's mechanical energy is:

A. the same

B. less, because work has been done on the hammer

C. greater, because the hammer has done work

D. less, because the hammer has done work

26. A 1,500 kg car is traveling at 25 m/s on a level road and the driver slams on the brakes. The skid marks are 10 m long. What is the work done by the road on the car?

A. -4.7×10^{-5} J　　　B. 0 J　　　C. 2×10^5 J　　　D. 3.5×10^5 J

27. A 1,000 kg car is traveling at 17 km/h. If a 2,000 kg truck has 20 times the kinetic energy of the car, how fast is the truck traveling?

A. 92 km/h　　　B. 64 km/h　　　C. 70 km/h　　　D. 54 km/h

28. A 1,500 kg car is traveling at 25 m/s on a level road and the driver slams on the brakes. The skid marks are 30 m long. What forces are acting on the car while it is coming to a stop?

A. Gravity down, normal force up, and a frictional force forwards

B. Gravity down, normal force up, and the engine force forwards

C. Gravity down, normal force up, and a frictional force backwards

D. Gravity down, normal force forward, and the engine force backwards

29. A 6,000 N piano is being raised via a pulley. For every 1 m that the rope is pulled down, the piano rises 0.15 m. In this pulley system, what is the force needed to lift the piano?

A. 60 N　　　B. 900 N　　　C. 600 N　　　D. 300 N

30. What does the area under the curve on a force vs. position graph represent?

A. Kinetic energy　　B. Momentum　　C. Work　　D. Displacement

31. What is the form in which most energy comes to and leaves the Earth?

A. Kinetic　　　B. Radiant　　　C. Chemical　　　D. Light

32. A driver abruptly slams on the brakes in her car, and the car skids a certain distance on a straight level road. If she had been traveling twice as fast, what distance would the car have skid, under the same conditions?

A. 1.4 times farther   **C.** 4 times farther
B. ½ as far   **D.** 2 times farther

33. A crane hoists an object weighing 2,000 N to the top of a building. The crane raises the object straight upward at a constant rate. Ignoring the forces of friction, at what rate is energy consumed by the electric motor of the crane if it takes 60 s to lift the mass 320 m?

A. 2.5 kW   **B.** 6.9 kW   **C.** 3.50 kW   **D.** 10.7 kW

34. A barbell with a mass of 25 kg is raised 3 m in 3 s before it reaches constant velocity. What is the power expended in this time? (Use acceleration due to gravity $g = 9.8$ m/s²)

A. 262 J   **B.** 34 J   **C.** 67 J   **D.** 98 J

35. Susan carried a 6.5 kg bag of groceries 1.4 m above the ground at constant velocity for 2.4 m across the kitchen. How much work did Susan do on the bag in the process? (Use acceleration due to gravity $g = 10$ m/s²)

A. 52 J   **B.** 0 J   **C.** 164 J   **D.** 138 J

36. A 1,000 kg car experiences a net force of 9,600 N while decelerating from 30 m/s to 22 m/s. How far does it travel while slowing down?

A. 17 m   **B.** 22 m   **C.** 12 m   **D.** 34 m

37. What is the power output in relation to the work W if a person exerts 100 J in 50 s?

A. ¼ W   **B.** ½ W   **C.** 2 W   **D.** 4 W

38. If a ball is released from a cliff ledge 58 m above the ground, how fast is the ball traveling when it reaches the ground? (Use acceleration due to gravity $g = 10$ m/s²)

A. 68 m/s   **B.** 16 m/s   **C.** 44 m/s   **D.** 34 m/s

39. A stone is held at a height *h* above the ground. A second stone with four times the mass is held at the same height. What is the gravitational potential energy of the second stone compared to that of the first stone?

A. Four times as much   **C.** One fourth as much
B. The same   **D.** One half as much

40. A 1.3 kg coconut falls off a coconut tree, landing on the ground 600 cm below. How much work is done on the coconut by the gravitational force? (Use acceleration due to gravity $g = 10$ m/s²)

A. 6 J   **B.** 78 J   **C.** 168 J   **D.** 340 J

41. Potential energy of an object is due to its:

A. location

B. momentum

C. acceleration

D. kinetic energy

42. A spring has a spring constant of 65 N/m. One end of the spring is fixed at point P, while the other end is connected to a 7 kg mass m. The fixed end and the mass sit on a horizontal, frictionless surface, so that the mass and the spring are able to rotate about P. The mass moves in a circle of radius $r = 4$ m, and the centripetal force of the mass is 15 N. What is the potential energy stored in the spring?

A. 1.7 J   B. 2.8 J   C. 3.7 J   D. 7.5 J

43. If electricity costs 8.16 cents/kW·h, how much would it cost you to run a 120 W stereo system 3.5 hours per day for 5 weeks?

A. $1.11   B. $1.46   C. $1.20   D. $0.34

44. A boy does 120 J of work to pull his sister back on a swing that has a 5.1 m chain, until the swing makes an angle of 32° with the vertical. What is the mass of his sister? (Use acceleration due to gravity $g = 9.8$ m/s^2)

A. 18 kg   B. 15.8 kg   C. 13.6 kg   D. 11.8 kg

45. What is the value of the spring constant if 111 J of work are needed to stretch a spring from 1.4 m to 2.9 m, if the spring starts at equilibrium?

A. 58 N/m   B. 53 N/m   C. 67 N/m   D. 34 N/m

46. The metric unit of a joule (J) is a unit of:

I. potential energy   II. kinetic energy   III. work

A. I only   B. II only   C. III only   D. I, II and III

47. A horizontal spring-mass system oscillates on a frictionless table. Find the maximum extension of the spring if the ratio of the mass to the spring constant is 0.038 kg·m/N, and the maximum speed of the mass is 18 m/s?

A. 3.4 m   B. 0.67 m   C. 3.4 cm   D. 67 cm

48. A truck weighs twice as much as a car, and is moving at twice the speed of the car. Which statement is true about the truck's kinetic energy compared to that of the car?

A. The truck has 8 times the KE

B. The truck has twice the KE

C. The truck has √2 times the KE

D. The truck has 4 times the KE

49. When a car brakes to a stop, its kinetic energy is transformed into:

 A. energy of rest   **C.** heat

 B. energy of momentum   **D.** stopping energy

50. A 30 kg block hangs from a spring with a spring constant of 900 N/m. How far does the spring stretch from its equilibrium position? (Use acceleration due to gravity $g = 10$ m/s^2)

 A. 12 cm   **B.** 33 cm   **C.** 50 cm   **D.** 0.5 cm

51. What is the kinetic energy of a 0.33 kg baseball thrown at a velocity of 40 m/s?

 A. 426 J   **B.** 574 J   **C.** 318 J   **D.** 264 J

52. An object is acted upon by a force as represented by the force vs. position graph below. What is the work done as the object moves from 0 m to 4 m?

 A. 10 J   **C.** 20 J

 B. 50 J   **D.** 30 J

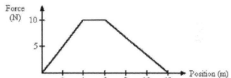

53. James and Bob throw identical balls vertically upward. James throws his ball with an initial speed twice that of Bob's. Assuming no air resistance, what is the maximum height of James's ball compared with that of Bob's ball?

 A. Equal   **C.** Four times

 B. Eight times   **D.** Two times

54. The graphs show the magnitude of the force (F) exerted by a spring as a function of the distance (x) the spring has been stretched. Which of the graphs shows a spring that obeys Hooke's Law?

A.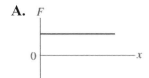

C.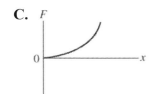

B.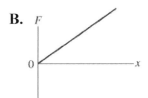

D.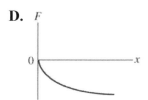

---

55. If a rocket travels through the air, it loses some of its kinetic energy due to air resistance. Some of this transferred energy:

A. decreases the temperature of the air around the rocket

B. is found in increased KE of the rocket

C. is found in increased KE of the air molecules

D. decreases the temperature of the rocket

56. A car moves four times as fast as an identical car. Compared to the slower car, the faster car has how much more kinetic energy?

A. 4 times   B. 8 times   C. $\sqrt{2}$ times   D. 16 times

57. A massless, ideal spring with spring constant k is connected to a wall on one end and to a massless plate on the other end. A mass m is sitting on a frictionless floor. The mass m is slid against the plate and pushed back a distance x. After release, it achieves a maximum speed v_1. In a second experiment, the same mass is pushed back a distance $4x$. After its release, it reaches a maximum speed v_2. How does v_2 compare with v_1?

A. $v_2 = v_1$ B. $v_2 = 2v_1$ C. $v_2 = 4v_1$ D. $v_2 = 16v_1$

58. A N·m/s is a unit of:

I. work   II. force   III. power

A. I only   B. II only   C. III only   D. I and II only

59. For the work energy theorem, which statement is accurate regarding the net work done?

A. The net work done plus the initial KE is the final KE

B. Final KE plus the net work done is the initial KE

C. The net work done minus the final KE is the initial KE

D. The net work done is equal to the initial KE plus the final KE

60. A 1,320 kg car climbs a 5° slope at a constant velocity of 70 km/h. Ignoring all resistance, at what rate must the engine deliver energy to drive the car? (Use acceleration due to gravity $g = 9.8$ m/s^2)

A. 45.1 kW   B. 18.7 kW   C. 38.3 kW   D. 22.6 kW

61. When a pebble is dropped from height h, it reaches the ground with kinetic energy. Ignoring air resistance, from what height should the pebble be dropped to reach the ground with twice the KE?

A. $\sqrt{2}h$ B. $2h$ C. $4h$ D. $8h$

62. Which of the following situations requires the greatest power?

    A. 50 J of work in 20 minutes   **C.** 10 J of work in 5 minutes

    B. 200 J of work in 30 minutes   **D.** 100 J of work in 10 minutes

63. The kilowatt-hour is a unit of:

    I. work   II. force   III. power

    A. I only   **B.** II only   **C.** III only   **D.** I and II only

64. A hydraulic press (like a simple lever), properly arranged, is capable of:

    I. multiplying energy input

    II. multiplying energy output

    III. exerting force only vertically

    A. I only   **B.** II only   **C.** III only   **D.** I and II only

65. 4.5×10^5 J of work are done on a 1,150 kg car while it accelerates from 10 m/s to some final velocity. What is this final velocity? (Use acceleration due to gravity $g = 10$ m/s^2)

    A. 30 m/s   **B.** 37 m/s   **C.** 12 m/s   **D.** 19 m/s

66. Which of the following is not a unit of work?

    A. N·m   **B.** kw·h   **C.** J   **D.** kg·m/s

67. The law of conservation of energy states that:

    I. the total amount of energy is constant

    II. energy cannot be used faster than it is created

    III. energy cannot change forms

    A. I only   **B.** II only   **C.** III only   **D.** I and II only

68. A crane lifts a 300 kg steel beam vertically upward a distance of 110 m. Ignoring frictional forces, how much work does the crane do on the beam if the beam accelerates upward at 1.4 m/s^2? (Use acceleration due to gravity $g = 9.8$ m/s^2)

    A. 2.4×10^3 J   **C.** 3.7×10^5 J

    B. 4.6×10^4 J   **D.** 6.2×10^5 J

69. Steve pushes twice as hard against a stationary brick wall as Charles. Which of the following statements is correct?

A. Both do the same amount of positive work

B. Both do positive work, but Steve does one-half the work of Charles

C. Both do positive work, but Steve does four times the work of Charles

D. Both do zero work

70. What is the change in the gravitational potential energy of an object if the height of the object above the Earth is doubled?

A. Quadruple   B. Doubled   C. Unchanged   D. Halved

71. If 1 N is exerted for a distance of 1 m in 1 s, the amount of power delivered is:

A. 3 W   B. 1/3 W   C. 2 W   D. 1 W

72. A brick is dropped from a roof and falls a distance h to the ground. If h were doubled, how does the maximal KE of the brick, just before it hits the ground, change?

A. It doubles   C. It remains the same

B. It increases by $\sqrt{2}$ D. It increases by 200

73. A helicopter with a single landing gear, descends vertically to land with a speed of 4.5 m/s. The helicopter's shock absorbers have an initial length of 0.6 m. They compress to 77% of their original length and the air in the tires absorbs 23% of the initial energy as heat. What is the ratio of the spring constant to the helicopter's mass?

A. 0.11 kN/kg·m   C. 0.8 kN/kg·m

B. 1.1 N/kg·m   D. 11 N/kg·m

74. A 21 ton airplane is observed to be a vertical distance of 2.6 km from its takeoff point. What is the gravitational potential energy of the plane with respect to the ground? (Use acceleration due to gravity $g = 9.8$ m/s^2)

A. 582 J   B. 384 J   C. 535 MJ   D. 414 MJ

75. A tennis ball bounces on the floor. During each bounce, it loses 31% of its energy due to heating. How high does the ball reach after the third bounce, if it is initially released 4 m from the floor?

A. 55 cm   B. 171 mm   C. 106 cm   D. 131 cm

WAVES AND PERIODIC MOTION

1. A simple harmonic oscillator oscillates with frequency *f* when its amplitude is A. What is the new frequency if the amplitude is doubled to 2A?

  A. $f/2$ **B.** f **C.** $4f$ **D.** $2f$

2. Springs A and B are attached in series with the free end of spring B attached to a wall. Spring A, which has a spring constant k_A, is then pulled a distance L_A from its rest position. If the connection point between Spring A and Spring B is pulled a distance L_B from its rest position by Spring A, what is the expression for the spring constant k_B of Spring B?

  A. L_B/k_A **B.** k_A^2 **C.** $k_A L_B$ **D.** $(k_A L_A)/L_B$

3. What is the source of all wave motion?

  A. Regions of variable high and low pressure   **C.** Harmonic particles
  B. Vibrating particles   **D.** Wave patterns

4. If a wave has a wavelength of 25 cm and a frequency of 1.68 kHz, what is its speed?

  A. 44 m/s   **B.** 160 m/s   **C.** 420 m/s   **D.** 314 m/s

5. The total energy stored in simple harmonic motion (SHM) is proportional to the:

  A. amplitude^2 **B.** spring constant   **C.** spring constant^2 **D.** amplitude

6. A 11 kg mass *m* is attached to a spring and allowed to hang in the Earth's gravitational field. The spring stretches 3 cm before reaching its equilibrium position. If the spring were allowed to oscillate, what would be its frequency? (Use acceleration due to gravity $g = 9.8$ m/s^2)

  A. 0.7 Hz   **B.** 1.8 Hz   **C.** 4.1 Hz   **D.** 2.9 Hz

7. The time required for one cycle of any repeating event is the:

  A. amplitude   **B.** frequency   **C.** period   **D.** rotation

8. A pendulum of length *L* is suspended from the ceiling of an elevator. When the elevator is at rest, the period of the pendulum is T. How does T change when the elevator moves upward with a constant velocity?

  A. Decreases only if the upward acceleration is less than ½g   **C.** Increases
  B. Decreases   **D.** Remains the same

9. What is the period of a transverse wave with a frequency of 100 Hz?

  A. 0.01 s   **B.** 0.05 s   **C.** 0.2 s   **D.** 20 s

---

10. Two radio antennae are located on a seacoast 10 km apart on a North-South axis. The antennas broadcast identical in-phase AM radio waves at a frequency of 4.7 MHz. 200 km offshore, a steamship travels North at 15 km/h passing East of the antennae with a radio tuned to the broadcast frequency. From the moment of the maximum reception of the radio signal on the ship, what is the time interval until the next occurrence of maximum reception? (Use the speed of radio waves equals the speed of light $c = 3 \times 10^8$ m/s and the path difference $= 1 \lambda$)

A. 7.7 min   **B.** 5.1 min   **C.** 3.8 min   **D.** 8.9 min

11. A 2.31 kg rope is stretched between supports 10.4 m apart. If one end of the rope is tweaked, how long will it take for the resulting disturbance to reach the other end? Assume that the tension in the rope is 74.4 N.

A. 0.33 s   **B.** 0.74 s   **C.** 0.65 s   **D.** 0.57 s

12. Simple pendulum A swings back and forth at twice the frequency of simple pendulum B. Which statement is correct?

A. Pendulum B is ¼ as long as A   **C.** Pendulum A is ½ as long as B
B. Pendulum A is twice as massive as B   **D.** Pendulum B is twice as massive as A

13. A weight attached to the free end of an anchored spring is allowed to slide back and forth in simple harmonic motion on a frictionless table. How many times greater is the spring's restoring force at $x = 5$ cm compared to $x = 1$ cm (measured from equilibrium)?

A. 2.5   **B.** 5   **C.** 7.5   **D.** 15

14. A massless, ideal spring projects horizontally from a wall and is connected to a 1 kg mass. The mass is oscillating in one dimension, such that it moves 0.5 m from one end of its oscillation to the other. It undergoes 10 complete oscillations in 60 s. What is the period of the oscillation?

A. 9 s   **B.** 3 s   **C.** 6 s   **D.** 12 s

15. The total mechanical energy of a simple harmonic oscillating system is:

A. a nonzero constant
B. maximum when it reaches the maximum displacement
C. zero when it reaches the maximum displacement
D. zero as it passes the equilibrium point

16. What is the frequency of the oscillations when a vibrating spring moves from its position of maximum elongation to its position of maximum compression in 1 s?

A. 0.75 Hz   **B.** 0.5 Hz   **C.** 1 Hz   **D.** 2.5 Hz

17. Which of the following is not a transverse wave?

    I. Radio   II. Light   III. Sound

A. I only   **B.** II only   **C.** III only   **D.** I and II only

18. If a wave has a speed of 362 m/s and a period of 4 ms, its wavelength is closest to:

A. 8.6 m   **B.** 1.5 m   **C.** 0.86 m   **D.** 15 m

19. Simple harmonic motion is characterized by:

A. acceleration that is proportional to negative displacement
B. acceleration that is proportional to velocity
C. constant positive acceleration
D. acceleration that is inversely proportional to negative displacement

20. If the frequency of a harmonic oscillator doubles, by what factor does the maximum value of acceleration change?

A. $2/\pi$ **B.** $\sqrt{2}$ **C.** 2   **D.** 4

21. An object that hangs from the ceiling of a stationary elevator by an ideal spring oscillates with a period T. If the elevator were to accelerate upwards with an acceleration of 2g, what is the period of oscillation of the object?

A. T/2   **B.** T   **C.** 2T   **D.** 4T

22. Which of the following changes made to a transverse wave must result in an increase in wavelength?

A. An increase in frequency and a decrease in speed
B. The wavelength is only affected by a change in amplitude
C. A decrease in frequency and an increase in speed
D. A decrease in frequency and a decrease in speed

23. If a wave travels 30 m in 1 s, making 60 vibrations per second, what are its frequency and speed, respectively?

A. 30 Hz and 60 m/s   **C.** 30 Hz and 30 m/s
B. 60 Hz and 30 m/s   **D.** 60 Hz and 15 m/s

24. Transverse waves propagate at 40 m/s in a string that is subjected to a tension of 60 N. If the string is 16 m long, what is its mass?

A. 0.6 kg   **B.** 0.9 kg   **C.** 0.2 kg   **D.** 9 kg

25. Doubling only the amplitude of a vibrating mass-on-spring system, changes the system frequency by what factor?

    A. Increases by 3   **C.** Increases by 5

    B. Increases by 2   **D.** Remains the same

26. A leaky faucet drips 60 times in 40 s. What is the frequency of the dripping?

    A. 0.75 Hz   **B.** 0.67 Hz   **C.** 1.5 Hz   **D.** 12 Hz

27. Particles of a material that move up and down perpendicular to the direction that the wave is moving are in what type of wave?

    A. torsional   **C.** longitudinal

    B. mechanical   **D.** transverse

28. The figure shows a graph of the velocity *v* as a function of time *t* for a system undergoing simple harmonic motion. Which one of the following graphs represents the acceleration of this system as a function of time?

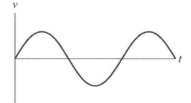

    A. *a*

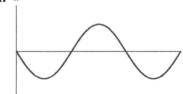

    C. *a*

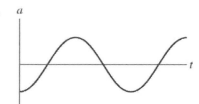

    B. *a*

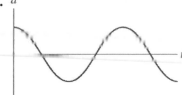

    D. *a*

29. When compared, a transverse wave and a longitudinal wave are found to have amplitudes of equal magnitude. Which statement is true about their speeds?

    A. The waves have the same speeds

    B. The transverse wave has exactly twice the speed of the longitudinal wave

    C. The speeds of the two waves are unrelated to their amplitudes

    D. The longitudinal wave has a slower speed

30. What is the frequency when a weight on the end of a spring bobs up and down and completes one cycle every 2 s?

A. 0.5 Hz   **B.** 1 Hz   **C.** 2 Hz   **D.** 2.5 Hz

31. The velocity of a given longitudinal sound wave in an ideal gas is $v = 340$ m/s at constant pressure and constant volume. Assuming an ideal gas, what is the wavelength for a 2,100 Hz sound wave?

A. 0.08 m   **B.** 0.16 m   **C.** 1.6 m   **D.** 7.3 m

32. When the mass of a simple pendulum is quadrupled, how does the time t required for one complete oscillation change?

A. Decreases to ¼t **B.** Decreases to ¾t **C.** Increases to 4t **D.** Remains the same

33. An object undergoing simple harmonic motion has an amplitude of 2.5 m. If the maximum velocity of the object is 15 m/s, what is the object's angular frequency (ω)?

A. 6.0 rad/s   **B.** 3.6 rad/s   **C.** 37.5 rad/s   **D.** 8.8 rad/s

34. Unpolarized light is incident upon two polarization filters that do not have their transmission axes aligned. If 14% of the light passes through, what is the measure of the angle between the transmission axes of the filters?

A. 73°   **B.** 81°   **C.** 43°   **D.** 58°

35. A mass on a spring undergoes simple harmonic motion. Which of the statements is true when the mass is at its maximum distance from the equilibrium position?

A. KE is nonzero   **C.** Speed is zero
B. Acceleration is at a minimum   **D.** Acceleration is maximum

36. What is the frequency if the speed of a sound wave is 240 m/s and its wavelength is 10 cm?

A. 2.4 Hz   **B.** 24 Hz   **C.** 240 Hz   **D.** 2,400 Hz

37. Unlike a transverse wave, a longitudinal wave has no:

A. wavelength   **B.** crests or troughs   **C.** amplitude   **D.** frequency

38. The density of aluminum is 2,700 kg/m^3. If transverse waves propagate at 36 m/s in a 4.6 mm diameter aluminum wire, what is the tension in the wire?

A. 43 N   **B.** 68 N   **C.** 58 N   **D.** 35 N

39. When a wave obliquely crosses a boundary into another medium, it is:

A. always slowed down   **B.** reflected   **C.** diffracted   **D.** refracted

40. A floating leaf oscillates up and down two complete cycles each second as a water wave passes by. What is the wave's frequency?

A. 0.5 Hz   **B.** 1 Hz   **C.** 2 Hz   **D.** 3 Hz

41. A higher pitch for a sound wave means the wave has a greater:

A. frequency   **B.** wavelength   **C.** amplitude   **D.** period

42. An object is attached to a vertical spring and bobs up and down between points A and B. Where is the object located when its kinetic energy is at a maximum?

A. One fourth of the way between A and B   **C.** Midway between A and B
B. One third of the way between A and B   **D.** At either A or B

43. A pendulum consists of a 0.5 kg mass attached to the end of a 1 m rod of negligible mass. What is the magnitude of the torque τ about the pivot when the rod makes an angle θ of 60° with the vertical? (Use acceleration due to gravity $g = 10$ m/s^2)

A. 2.7 N·m   **B.** 4.4 N·m   **C.** 5.2 N·m   **D.** 10.6 N·m

44. The Doppler effect is characteristic of:

     I. light waves   II. sound waves   III. water waves

A. I only   **B.** II only   **C.** III only   **D.** I, II and III

45. A crane lifts a 2,500 kg cement block using a steel cable which has a mass per unit length of 0.65 kg/m. What is the speed of the transverse waves on this cable? (Use acceleration due to gravity $g = 10$ m/s^2)

A. 196 m/s   **B.** 1,162 m/s   **C.** 322 m/s   **D.** 558 m/s

46. A simple pendulum consists of a mass M attached to a weightless string of length L. Which statement about the frequency f is accurate for this system when it experiences small oscillations?

A. The f is directly proportional to the period
B. The f is independent of the mass M
C. The f is inversely proportional to the amplitude
D. The f is independent of the length L

47. A child on a swing set swings back and forth. If the length of the supporting cables for the swing is 3.3 m, what is the period of oscillation? (Use acceleration due to gravity $g = 10$ m/s^2)

A. 3.6 s   **B.** 5.9 s   **C.** 4.3 s   **D.** 2.7 s

48. A massless, ideal spring projects horizontally from a wall and is connected to a 0.3 kg mass. The mass is oscillating in one dimension, such that it moves 0.4 m from one end of its oscillation to the other. It undergoes 15 complete oscillations in 60 s. How does the frequency change if the spring constant is increased by a factor of 2?

    A. Increases by 200%   **C.** Increases by 41%

    B. Decreases by 59%   **D.** Decreases by 41%

49. A ball swinging at the end of a massless string undergoes simple harmonic motion. At what point(s) is the instantaneous acceleration of the ball the greatest?

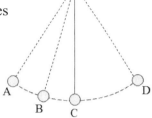

    A. A   **C.** C

    B. B   **D.** A and D

50. A simple pendulum, consisting of a 2 kg weight connected to a 10 m massless rod, is brought to an angle of 90° from the vertical, and then released. What is the speed of the weight at its lowest point? (Use acceleration due to gravity $g = 10$ m/s^2)

    A. 14 m/s   **B.** 10 m/s   **C.** 20 m/s   **D.** 25 m/s

51. A sound source of high frequency emits a wave with a high:

    I. pitch   II. amplitude   III. speed

    A. I only   **B.** II only   **C.** III only   **D.** I, II and III

52. Find the wavelength of a train whistle that is heard by a fixed observer as the train moves toward him with a velocity of 50 m/s. A wind blows at 5 m/s from the observer to the train. The whistle has a natural frequency of 500 Hz. (Use *v* of sound = 340 m/s)

    A. 0.75 m   **B.** 0.43 m   **C.** 0.58 m   **D.** 7.5 m

53. Considering a vibrating mass on a spring, what effect on the system's mechanical energy is caused by doubling of the amplitude only?

    A. Increases by a factor of two   **C.** Increases by a factor of three

    B. Increases by a factor of four   **D.** Produces no change

54. Which of the following is an accurate statement?

    A. Tensile stress is measured in N·m

    B. Stress is a measure of external forces on a body

    C. The ratio stress/strain is called the elastic modulus

    D. Tensile strain is measured in meters

55. An efficient transfer of energy that takes place at a natural frequency is known as:

A. reverberation   C. beats

B. the Doppler effect   D. resonance

56. A simple pendulum and a mass oscillating on an ideal spring both have period T in an elevator at rest. If the elevator now accelerates downward uniformly at 2 m/s², what is true about the periods of these two systems?

A. The period of the pendulum increases, but the period of the spring remains the same

B. The period of the pendulum increases and the period of the spring decreases

C. The period of the pendulum decreases, but the period of the spring remains the same

D. The periods of the pendulum and of the spring both increase

57. All of the following is true of a pendulum that has swung to the top of its arc and has not yet reversed its direction, EXCEPT:

A. The PE of the pendulum is at a maximum

B. The acceleration of the pendulum equals zero

C. The KE of the pendulum equals zero

D. The velocity of the pendulum equals zero

58. The Doppler effect occurs when a source of sound moves:

   I. toward the observer

   II. away from the observer

   III. with the observer

A. I only   B. II only   C. III only   D. I and II only

59. Consider the wave shown in the figure. The amplitude is: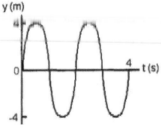

A. 1 m

B. 2 m

C. 4 m

D. 8 m

60. Increasing the mass *m* of a mass-and-spring system causes what kind of change on the resonant frequency *f* of the system?

A. The *f* decreases

B. There is no change in the *f*

C. The *f* decreases only if the ratio *k* / *m* is < 1

D. The *f* increases

61. A simple pendulum that has a bob of mass M has a period T. What is the effect on the period if M is doubled while all other factors remain unchanged?

    A. T/2   **B.** T/√2   **C.** 2T   **D.** T

62. A skipper on a boat notices wave crests passing the anchor chain every 5 s. The skipper estimates that the distance between crests is 15 m. What is the speed of the water waves?

    A. 3 m/s   **B.** 5 m/s   **C.** 12 m/s   **D.** 9 m/s

63. For an object undergoing simple harmonic motion, the:

    A. maximum potential energy is larger than the maximum kinetic energy
    B. acceleration is greatest when the displacement is greatest
    C. displacement is greatest when the speed is greatest
    D. acceleration is greatest when the speed is greatest

64. As the frequency of a wave increases, which of the following must decrease?

    A. The speed of the wave   **C.** The amplitude of the wave
    B. The velocity of the wave   **D.** The period of the wave

65. What is the period for a weight on the end of a spring that bobs up and down one complete cycle every 2 s?

    A. 0.5 s   **B.** 1 s   **C.** 2 s   **D.** 3 s

66. After a rain, one sometimes sees brightly colored oil slicks on the road. These are due to:

    A. selective absorption of different λ by oil   **C.** polarization effects
    B. diffraction effects   **D.** interference effects

67. The natural frequencies for a stretched string of length L and wave speed v are $nv / (2L)$, where n equals:

    A. 0, 1, 3, 5, ...   **B.** 1, 2, 3, 4, ...   **C.** 2, 4, 6, 8, ...   **D.** 0, 1, 2, 3, ...

68. Particles of a material that move back and forth in the same direction the wave is moving are in what type of wave?

    A. Standing   **C.** Transverse
    B. Torsional   **D.** Longitudinal

SOUND

1. A 20 decibel (dB) noise is heard from a cricket 30 m away. How loud would it sound if the cricket were 3 m away?

A. 30 dB   **B.** 40 dB   **C.** 20 × √2 dB   **D.** 80 dB

2. A thunder clap occurs at a distance of 6 km from a stationary person. How soon does the person hear it? (Use speed of sound in air $v = 340$ m/s)

A. 18 s   **B.** 30 s   **C.** 48 s   **D.** 56 s

3. Enrico Caruso, a famous opera singer, is said to have made a crystal chandelier shatter with his voice. This is a demonstration of:

A. ideal frequency   **C.** a standing wave
B. resonance   **D.** sound refraction

4. A taut 2 m string is fixed at both ends and plucked. What is the wavelength corresponding to the third harmonic?

A. 2/3 m   **B.** 1 m   **C.** 4/3 m   **D.** 3 m

5. High-pitched sound has a high:

       I. number of partial tones   II. frequency   III. speed

A. I only   **B.** II only   **C.** III only   **D.** I and II only

6. A light ray in air strikes a medium whose index of refraction is 1.5. If the angle of incidence is 60°, which of the following expressions gives the angle of refraction? (Use $n_{air} = 1$)

A. $\sin^{-1}(0.67 \sin 60°)$ **C.** $\sin^{-1}(1.5 \sin 30°)$
B. $\sin^{-1}(1.5 \cos 60°)$ **D.** $\sin^{-1}(0.67 \sin 30°)$

7. A string, 2 m in length, is fixed at both ends and tightened until the wave speed is 92 m/s. What is the frequency of the standing wave shown?

A. 46 Hz   **B.** 33 Hz   **C.** 240 Hz   **D.** 138 Hz

8. A 0.6 m uniform bar of metal, with a diameter of 2 cm, has a mass of 2.5 kg. A 1.5 MHz longitudinal wave is propagated along the length of the bar. A wave compression traverses the length of the bar in 0.14 ms. What is the wavelength of the longitudinal wave in the metal?

A. 2.9 mm   **B.** 1.8 mm   **C.** 3.2 mm   **D.** 4.6 mm

Questions **9-12** are based on the following:

The velocity of a wave on a wire or string is not dependent (to a close approximation) on frequency or amplitude and is given by $v^2 = T / \rho_L$. T is the tension is the wire. The linear mass density ρ_L (rho) is the mass per unit length of wire. Therefore ρ_L is the product of the mass density and the cross-sectional area (A).

A sine wave is traveling to the right with frequency 250 Hz. Wire A is composed of steel and has a circular cross-section diameter of 0.6 mm and a tension of 2,000 N. Wire B is under the same tension and is made of the same material as wire A, but has a circular cross-section diameter of 0.3 mm. Wire C has the same tension as wire A and is made of a composite material. (Use density of steel wire $\rho = 7$ g/cm^3 and density of the composite material $\rho = 3$ g/cm^3)

9. By how much does the tension need to be increased to increase the wave velocity on a wire by 30%?

    A. 37%   **B.** 60%   **C.** 69%   **D.** 81%

10. What is the linear mass density of wire B compared to wire A?

    A. $\sqrt{2}$ times   **B.** 2 times   **C.** 1/8   **D.** 1/4

11. What must the diameter of wire C be to have the same wave velocity as wire A?

    A. 0.41 mm   **B.** 0.92 mm   **C.** 0.83 mm   **D.** 3.2 mm

12. How does the cross-sectional area change if the diameter increases by a factor of 4?

    A. Increases by a factor of 16   **C.** Increases by a factor of 2
    B. Increases by a factor of 4   **D.** Decreases by a factor of 4

13. A bird, emitting sounds with a frequency of 60 kHz, is moving at a speed of 10 m/s toward a stationary observer. What is the frequency of the sound waves detected by the observer? (Use speed of sound in air $v = 340$ m/s)

    A. 55 kHz   **B.** 62 kHz   **C.** 68 kHz   **D.** 76 kHz

14. What is observed for a frequency heard by a stationary person when a sound source is approaching?

    A. Equal to zero   **C.** Higher than the source
    B. The same as the source   **D.** Lower than the source

15. Which of the following is a false statement?

A. The transverse waves on a vibrating string are different from sound waves
B. Sound travels much slower than light
C. Sound waves are longitudinal pressure waves
D. Sound can travel through a vacuum

16. Which of the following is a real-life example of the Doppler effect?

A. Changing pitch of the siren as an ambulance passes by the observer
B. Radio signal transmission
C. Sound becomes quieter as the observer moves away from the source
D. Human hearing is most acute at 2,500 Hz

17. Two sound waves have the same frequency and amplitudes of 0.4 Pa and 0.6 Pa, respectively. When they arrive at point X, what is the range of possible amplitudes for sound at point X?

A. 0 – 0.4 Pa   **B.** 0.4 – 0.6 Pa   **C.** 0.2 – 1.0 Pa   **D.** 0.4 – 0.8 Pa

18. The intensity of the waves from a point source at a distance d from the source is I. What is the intensity at a distance $2d$ from the source?

A. I/2   **B.** I/4   **C.** 4I   **D.** 2I

19. Sound would be expected to travel most slowly in a medium that exhibited:

A. low resistance to compression and high density
B. high resistance to compression and low density
C. low resistance to compression and low density
D. high resistance to compression and high density

20. Which is true for a resonating pipe that is open at both ends?

A. Displacement node at one end and a displacement antinode at the other end
B. Displacement antinodes at each end
C. Displacement nodes at each end
D. Displacement node at one end and a one-fourth antinode at the other end

21. In a pipe of length L that is open at both ends, the lowest tone to resonate is 200 Hz. Which of the following frequencies does not resonate in this pipe?

A. 400 Hz   **B.** 600 Hz   **C.** 500 Hz   **D.** 800 Hz

22. In general, sound is conducted fastest through:

A. vacuum   **B.** gases   **C.** liquids   **D.** solids

23. If an electric charge is shaken up and down:

A. electron excitation occurs   C. sound is emitted

B. a magnetic field is created   D. light is emitted

24. What is the wavelength of a sound wave of frequency 620 Hz in steel, given that the speed of sound in steel is 5,000 m/s?

A. 1.8 m   B. 6.2 m   C. 8.1 m   D. 2.6 m

25. If the sound from a constant sound source is radiating equally in all directions, as the distance doubles, by what amount is the intensity of the sound reduced?

A. ¼   B. 1/16   C. $1/\sqrt{2}$ D. ½

26. Why does the intensity of waves from a sound source decrease with the square of the distance from the source?

A. The medium through which the waves travel absorbs the energy of the waves

B. The waves speed up as they travel away from the source

C. The waves lose energy as they travel

D. The waves spread out as they travel

Questions **27-30** are based on the following:

Steven is preparing a mailing tube that is 1.5 m long and 4 cm in diameter. The tube is open at one end and sealed at the other. Before he inserted his documents, the mailing tube fell to the floor and produced a note. (Use the speed of sound in air $v = 340$ m/s)

27. What is the wavelength of the fundamental?

A. 0.04 m   B. 6 m   C. 0.75 m   D. 1.5 m

28. If the tube was filled with helium, in which sound travels at 960 m/s, what would be the frequency of the fundamental?

A. 160 Hz   B. 320 Hz   C. 80 Hz   D. 640 Hz

29. What is the wavelength of the fifth harmonic?

A. 3.2 m   B. 1.2 m   C. 2.4 m   D. 1.5 m

30. What is the frequency of the note that Steven heard?

A. 57 Hz   B. 85 Hz   C. 30 Hz   D. 120 Hz

31. A 4 g string, 0.34 m long, is under tension. The string vibrates in the third harmonic. What is the wavelength of the standing wave in the string? (Use the speed of sound in air = 344 m/s)

    A. 0.56 m   **B.** 0.33 m   **C.** 0.23 m   **D.** 0.61 m

32. Two pure tones are sounded together and a particular beat frequency is heard. What happens to the beat frequency if the frequency of one of the tones is increased?

    A. Increases   **C.** Remains the same

    B. Decreases   **D.** Either increase or decrease

33. Consider a closed pipe of length L. What are the wavelengths of the three lowest tones produced by this pipe?

    A. $4L, 4/3L, 4/5L$ **B.** $2L, L, 2/3L$ **C.** $2L, L, \frac{1}{2}L$ **D.** $4L, 2L, L$

34. Mary hears the barely perceptible buzz of a mosquito one meter away from her ear in a quiet room. How much energy does a mosquito produce in 200 s? (Note: an almost inaudible sound has a threshold value of 9.8×10^{-12} W/m^2)

    A. 6.1×10^{-8} J   **B.** 1.3×10^{-8} J   **C.** 6.4×10^{-10} J   **D.** 2.5×10^{-8} J

35. How long does it take for a light wave to travel 1 km through water with a refractive index of 1.33? (Use the speed of light $c = 3 \times 10^8$ m/s)

    A. 4.4×10^{-6} s   **B.** 4.4×10^{-9} s   **C.** 2.8×10^{-9} s   **D.** 2.8×10^{-12} s

36. In designing a music hall, an acoustical engineer deals mainly with:

    A. wave interference   **B.** resonance   **C.** forced vibrations   **D.** modulation

37. Which curve in the figure represents the variation of wave speed (v) as a function of tension (T) for transverse waves on a stretched string?

    A. A
    B. B
    C. C
    D. D

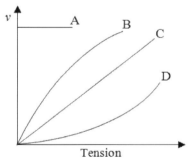

38. A string, 4 meters in length, is fixed at both ends and tightened until the wave speed is 20 m/s. What is the frequency of the standing wave shown?

    A. 13 Hz   **B.** 8.1 Hz   **C.** 5.4 Hz   **D.** 15.4 Hz

39. Compared to the velocity of a 600 Hz sound, the velocity of a 300 Hz sound through air is:

A. one-half as great   **B.** the same   **C.** twice as great   **D.** four times as great

40. A 0.5 m long string, vibrating in the $n = 6$ harmonic, excites an open pipe into second overtone resonance. What is the length of the open pipe? (Use the speed of sound in air $v = 345$ m/s)

A. 0.25 m   **B.** 0.1 m   **C.** 0.17 m   **D.** 0.6 m

41. A string of length L is under tension, and the speed of a wave in the string is v. What is the speed of a wave in the string if the length increases to $2L$ with no change in tension or mass?

A. $v\sqrt{2}$ **B.** $2v$ **C.** $v/2$ **D.** $v/\sqrt{2}$

42. If a guitar string has a fundamental frequency of 500 Hz, which one of the following frequencies can set the string into resonant vibration?

A. 450 Hz   **B.** 760 Hz   **C.** 1,500 Hz   **D.** 2,250 Hz

43. When a light wave is passing from a medium with lower refractive index to a medium with higher refractive index, some of the incident light is refracted, while some is reflected. What is the angle of refraction?

    A. Greater than the angle of incidence and less than the angle of reflection
    B. Less than the angle of incidence and greater than the angle of reflection
    C. Greater than the angles of incidence and reflection
    D. Less than the angles of incidence and reflection

44. The speed of a sound wave in air depends on:

    I. the air temperature   II. its wavelength   III. its frequency

A. I only   **B.** II only   **C.** III only   **D.** I and II only

45. Which of the following statements is false?

    A. The speed of a wave and the speed of the vibrating particles that constitute the wave are different entities
    B. Waves transport energy and matter from one region to another
    C. In a transverse wave, the particle motion is perpendicular to the velocity vector of the wave
    D. Not all waves are mechanical in nature

46. A 2.5 g string, 0.75 m long, is under tension. The string produces a 700 Hz tone when it vibrates in the third harmonic. What is the wavelength of the tone in air? (Use the speed of sound in air $v = 344$ m/s)

A. 0.65 m   **B.** 0.57 m   **C.** 0.33 m   **D.** 0.5 m

47. Suppose that a source of sound is emitting waves uniformly in all directions. If an observer moves to a point twice as far away from the source, what is the frequency of the sound?

   A. $\sqrt{2}$ as large   **B.** Twice as large   **C.** Unchanged   **D.** Half as large

48. A 2.5 kg rope is stretched between supports 8 m apart. If one end of the rope is tweaked, how long will it take for the resulting disturbance to reach the other end? Assume that the tension in the rope is 40 N.

   A. 0.71 s   **B.** 0.62 s   **C.** 0.58 s   **D.** 0.47 s

49. An office machine is making a rattling sound with an intensity of 10^{-5} W/m^2 when perceived by an office worker that is sitting 3 m away. What is the sound level in decibels for the sound of the machine? (Use threshold of hearing $I_0 = 10^{-12}$ W/m^2)

   A. 10 dB   **B.** 35 dB   **C.** 70 dB   **D.** 95 dB

50. A taut 1 m string is plucked. Point B is midway between both ends and a finger is placed on point B such that a waveform exists with a node at B. What is the lowest frequency that can be heard? (Use the speed of waves on the string $v = 3.8 \times 10^4$ m/s)

   A. 4.8×10^5 Hz   **B.** 3.8×10^4 Hz   **C.** 9.7×10^3 Hz   **D.** 7.4×10^3 Hz

51. For a light wave travelling in a vacuum, which of the following properties is true?

   A. Increased f results in increased amplitude
   B. Increased f results in decreased speed
   C. Increased f results in increased wavelength
   D. Increased f results in decreased wavelength

52. Which wave is a different classification than the others (i.e. does not belong to the same grouping)?

   A. Shock waves   **B.** Radio waves   **C.** Ultrasonic waves   **D.** Infrasonic waves

53. Two speakers are placed 2 m apart and both produce a sound wave (in phase) with wavelength 0.8 m. A microphone is placed between the speakers to determine the intensity of the sound at various points. What point is precisely halfway between the two speakers? (Use the speed of sound $v = 340$ m/s)

   A. Both an antinode and a node   **C.** A node
   B. Neither an antinode nor a node   **D.** An antinode

54. The siren of an ambulance blares at 1,200 Hz when the ambulance is stationary. What frequency does a stationary observer hear after this ambulance passes her while traveling at 30 m/s? (Use the speed of sound $v = 342$ m/s)

   A. 1,240 Hz   **B.** 1,128 Hz   **C.** 1,103 Hz   **D.** 1,427 Hz

55. Compared to the wavelength of a 600 Hz sound, the wavelength of a 300 Hz sound in air is:

   A. one-half as long   **B.** the same   **C.** one-fourth as long   **D.** twice as long

56. An organ pipe that is open at both ends is tuned to a given frequency. A second pipe with both ends open resonates with twice this frequency. What is the ratio of the length of the first pipe to the second pipe?

   A. 0.5   **B.** 1   **C.** 2   **D.** 2.5

57. The frequency of the third harmonic of the C_4 string of a piano is 783.7 Hz. The fundamental frequency of the G_5 string is 782.4 Hz. When the key for C_4 is held down so that the string can vibrate, and the G_5 key is stricken loudly, the third harmonic of the C_4 string is excited. Then, when striking the G_5 key again more softly, the volume of the two strings are matched. What phenomenon is demonstrated when the G_5 string is used to excite the vibration of the C_4 string?

   A. Resonance   **B.** Dispersion   **C.** Beats   **D.** Interference

58. Crests of an ocean wave pass a pier every 10 s. If the waves are moving at 4.5 m/s, what is the wavelength of the ocean waves?

   A. 38 m   **B.** 16 m   **C.** 45 m   **D.** 25 m

59. Which statement explains why sound travels faster in water than in air?

   A. Sound shifts to increased frequency
   B. Sound shifts to decreased density
   C. Density of water increases more quickly than its resistance to compression
   D. Density of water increases more slowly than its resistance to compression

60. When visible light is incident upon clear glass, atoms in the glass:

   > I. convert the light energy into internal energy
   > II. resonate
   > III. vibrate

   A. I only   **B.** II only   **C.** III only   **D.** I and II only

61. A sewing machine is making a rattling sound with an intensity is 10^{-6} W/m^2 where a worker is sitting 3 m away. If he moves to a point 9 m away, what would be the intensity?

   A. 9.9×10^{-6} W/m^2 **B.** 3.3×10^{-6} W/m^2 **C.** 3.3×10^{-5} W/m^2 **D.** 1.1×10^{-7} W/m^2

62. A 0.5 m rope under a tension of 50 N is set into oscillation. The mass density of the rope is 140 g/cm. What is the frequency of the fundamental harmonic node (n = 1)?

   A. 1.9 Hz   **B.** 3.8 Hz   **C.** 2.7 Hz   **D.** 1.1 Hz

63. If a person inhales a few breaths from a helium gas balloon, the person would probably experience an amusing change in her voice. What causes her voice to have this high-pitched effect?

    A. Her voice box is resonating at the 2nd harmonic, rather than at the fundamental frequency

    B. Low frequencies are absorbed in helium gas, leaving the high frequency components, which result in the high-pitched sound

    C. The helium causes her vocal cords to tighten and vibrate at a higher frequency

    D. Sound travels faster in helium than in air, causing the velocity to increase

64. A standing wave of the third overtone is induced in a stopped 1.4 m long pipe. A stopped pipe is open at one end and closed at the other. What is the frequency of the sound produced by the pipe? (Use speed of sound $v = 340$ m/s)

    A. 205 Hz   **B.** 260 Hz   **C.** 350 Hz   **D.** 425 Hz

65. Upon measuring the light waves emitted by stars, it was discovered that the measured frequency of the light was lower than the actual frequency. One explanation for this phenomenon is that the:

    A. stars are accelerating   **C.** stars are moving toward the Earth

    B. speed of the stars is decreasing   **D.** stars are moving away from the Earth

66. Two tuning forks have frequencies of 460 Hz and 524 Hz. What is the beat frequency if both are sounding simultaneously and resonating?

    A. 52 Hz   **B.** 64 Hz   **C.** 396 Hz   **D.** 524 Hz

67. Which of the of the following is true of the properties of a light wave as it moves from a medium of lower refractive index to a medium of higher refractive index?

    A. Speed decreases   **C.** Frequency decreases

    B. Speed increases   **D.** Frequency increases

68. Resonance can be looked at as forced vibration with the:

    A. matching of constructive and destructive interference

    B. matching of wave amplitudes

    C. maximum amount of energy input

    D. least amount of energy input

69. The explanation for refraction must involve a change in:

    I. frequency   II. speed   III. wavelength

    A. I only   **B.** II only   **C.** III only   **D.** I and II only

70. Which of the following increases when a sound becomes louder?

    A. Amplitude   **B.** Period   **C.** Frequency   **D.** Wavelength

71. Sound intensity is defined as the:

    A. sound power per unit volume   **C.** sound energy passing through a unit of area
    B. sound power per unit time   **D.** sound energy passing an area per unit time

72. A violin with string length 36 cm and string density 3.8 g/cm resonates with the first overtone of an organ pipe with one end closed. The pipe length is 3 m. What is the tension in the string so that the sound wave resonates at its fundamental frequency? (Use the speed of sound $v = 340$ m/s)

    A. 1,390 N   **B.** 1,946 N   **C.** 1,414 N   **D.** 987 N

73. A speaker is producing a total of 10 W of sound, and Rahul hears the music at 20 dB. His roommate turns up the power to 100 W. What level of sound does Rahul now hear?

    A. 15 dB   **B.** 30 dB   **C.** 40 dB   **D.** 100 dB

74. Seven seconds after a flash of lightning, thunder shakes a house. Approximately how far was the lightning strike from the house? (Use the speed of sound $v = 340$ m/s)

    A. Requires more information   **C.** About one kilometer away
    B. About five kilometers away   **E.** About two kilometers away

75. If two traveling waves with amplitudes of 3 cm and 8 cm interfere, which of the following best describes the possible amplitudes of the resultant wave?

    A. Between 3 and 11 cm   **C.** Between 3 and 5 cm
    B. Between 3 and 8 cm   **D.** Between 8 and 11 cm

76. What is the source of all electromagnetic waves?

    A. electric fields   **C.** heat
    B. vibrating charges   **D.** magnetic fields

77. When a radio is tuned to a certain station, the frequency of the internal electrical circuit is matched to the frequency of that radio station. In tuning the radio, what is being affected?

    A. Beats   **C.** Forced vibrations
    B. Reverberation   **D.** Resonance

DC CIRCUITS

1. What is the new resistance of a wire if the length of a certain wire is doubled and its radius is also doubled?

    A. It is $\sqrt{2}$ times as large   **C.** It stays the same

    B. It is ½ as large   **D.** It is 2 times as large

2. A 6 Ω resistor is connected across the terminals of a 12 V battery. If 0.6 A of current flows, what is the internal resistance of the battery?

    A. 2 Ω   **B.** 26 Ω   **C.** 20 Ω   **D.** 14 Ω

3. Three 8 V batteries are connected in series in order to power light bulbs A and B. The resistance of light bulb A is 60 Ω and the resistance of light bulb B is 30 Ω. How does the current through light bulb A compare with the current through light bulb B?

    A. The current through light bulb A is less

    B. The current through light bulb A is greater

    C. The current through light bulb A is the same

    D. The current through light bulb A is exactly doubled that through light bulb B

4. The current flowing through a circuit of constant resistance is doubled. What is the effect on the power dissipated by that circuit?

    A. Decreases to one-half its original value   **C.** Quadruples its original value

    B. Decreases to one-fourth its original value   **D.** Doubles its original value

5. What current flows when a 400 Ω resistor is connected across a 220 V circuit?

    A. 0.55 A   **B.** 1.8 A   **C.** 5.5 A   **D.** 0.18 A

6. Which statement is accurate for when different resistors are connected in parallel across an ideal battery?

    A. Power dissipated in each is the same

    B. Their equivalent resistance is greater than the resistance of any one of the individual resistors

    C. Current flowing in each is the same

    D. Potential difference across each is the same

7. For an electric motor with a resistance of 35 Ω that draws 10 A of current, what is the voltage drop?

    A. 3.5 V   **B.** 25 V   **C.** 350 V   **D.** 3,500 V

8. The resistor *R* has a variable resistance. Which statement is true when *R* is decreased?

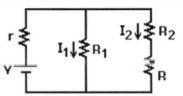

    A. I_1 decreases, I_2 increases
    B. I_1 increases, I_2 remains the same
    C. I_1 remains the same, I_2 increases
    D. I_1 remains the same, I_2 decreases

9. What physical quantity does the slope of the graph represent?

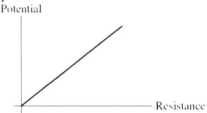

    A. 1 / Current
    B. Voltage
    C. Current
    D. Resistivity

10. Kirchhoff's junction rule is a statement of:

    A. Law of conservation of energy   **C.** Law of conservation of momentum
    B. Law of conservation of angular momentum   **D.** Law of conservation of charge

11. When unequal resistors are connected in series across an ideal battery, the:

    A. current flowing in each is the same
    B. equivalent resistance of the circuit is less than that of the greatest resistor
    C. power dissipated in each turn is the same
    D. potential difference across each is the same

12. Electric current flows only from a point of:

    A. equal potential   **C.** low pressure to a point of higher pressure
    B. high pressure to a point of lower pressure   **D.** high potential to a point of lower potential

13. What is the name of a device that transforms electrical energy into mechanical energy?

    A. Magnet   **B.** Transformer   **C.** Turbine   **D.** Motor

14. Four 6 V batteries (in a linear sequence of A → B → C → D) are connected in series in order to power lights A and B. The resistance of light A is 50 Ω and the resistance of light B is 25 Ω. What is the potential difference at a point between battery C and battery D?

    A. 4 volts   **B.** 12 volts   **C.** 18 volts   **D.** 26 volts

15. What is the quantity that is calculated in units of A·s?

    A. Passivity   **B.** Capacitance   **C.** Potential   **D.** Charge

16. Electric current can only flow:

A. in a region of negligible resistance   **C.** in a perfect conductor

B. though a potential difference   **D.** in the absence of resistance

17. A wire of resistivity ρ is replaced in a circuit by a wire of the same material but four times as long. If the total resistance remains the same, the diameter of the new wire must be:

A. one-fourth the original diameter   **C.** the same as the original diameter

B. two times the original diameter   **D.** one-half the original diameter

18. The addition of resistors in series to a resistor in an existing circuit, while voltage remains constant, would result in [   ] in the original resistor.

A. an increase in current   **C.** an increase in resistance

B. a decrease in resistance   **D.** a decrease in current

19. In an experiment, a battery is connected to a variable resistor R, where resistance can be adjusted by turning a knob. The potential difference across the resistor and the current through it are recorded for different settings of the resistor knob. The battery is an ideal potential source in series with an internal resistor. The emf of the potential source is 9 V and the internal resistance is 0.1 Ω. What is the current if the variable resistor is set at 0.5 Ω?

A. 15 A   **B.** 0.9 A   **C.** 4.5 A   **D.** 45 A

20. What is the quantity that is calculated with units of $kg \cdot m^2 / s \cdot C^2$?

A. Resistance   **B.** Capacitance   **C.** Potential   **D.** Resistivity

21. At a constant voltage, an increase in the resistance of a circuit results in:

A. no change in I or V   **C.** an increase in power

B. an increase in I **D.** a decrease in I

22. Which change to a circuit will always result in an increase in the current?

A. Increased voltage and decreased resistance

B. Decreased voltage and increased resistance

C. Increased voltage and increased resistance

D. Only a decrease in resistance, the voltage has no effect on current

23. When three resistors are added in series to a resistor in a circuit, the original resistor's voltage [   ] and its current [   ].

A. decreases ... increases   **C.** decrease ... decreases

B. increases ... increases   **D.** decreases ... remains the same

24. If two identical storage batteries are connected in series ("+" to "−") and placed in a circuit, the combination provides:

   A. twice the voltage, and the same current flows through each
   B. the same voltage, and the same current flows through each
   C. zero volts, and different currents flow through each
   D. the same voltage, and different currents flow through each

25. The resistivity of gold is 2.22×10^{-8} Ω·m at a temperature of 22 °C. A gold wire, 2 mm in diameter and 18 cm long, carries a current of 500 mA. What is the power dissipated in the wire?

   A. 0.17 mW   **B.** 0.54 mW   **C.** 0.77 mW   **D.** 0.32 mW

26. Consider two copper wires of equal cross-sectional area. One wire has 3 times the length of the other. How do the resistivities of these two wires compare?

   A. The longer wire has 9 times the resistivity of the shorter wire
   B. The longer wire has 27 times the resistivity of the shorter wire
   C. The longer wire has 1/3 the resistivity of the shorter wire
   D. Both wires have the same resistivity

27. A 3 Ω resistor is connected in parallel with a 6 Ω resistor, both resistors are connected in series with a 4 Ω resistor, and all three resistors are connected to a battery as shown. If 3 Ω resistor burnt out and exhibits infinite resistance, which of the following is true?

   A. The power dissipated in the circuit increases
   B. The current provided by the battery remains the same
   C. The current in the 6 Ω resistor increases
   D. The current in the 6 Ω resistor decreases

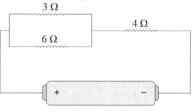

28. The resistivity of gold is 2.44×10^{-8} Ω·m at a temperature of 20 °C. A gold wire, 0.6 mm in diameter and 48 cm long, carries a current of 340 mA. What is the number of electrons per second passing a given cross section of the wire? (Use charge of an electron = -1.6×10^{-19} C)

   A. 2.1×10^{18} electrons   **C.** 1.2×10^{22} electrons
   B. 2.8×10^{14} electrons   **D.** 2.4×10^{17} electrons

29. For the graph shown, what physical quantity does the slope of the graph represent?

   A. 1 / Voltage   **C.** Power
   B. Resistance   **D.** Charge

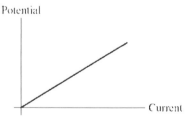

30. What is the voltage across a 15 Ω resistor that has 5 A current passing through it?

   A. 3 V   **B.** 5 V   **C.** 15 V   **D.** 75 V

ELECTROSTATICS

1. How many excess electrons are present for an object that has a charge of -1 Coulomb? (Use Coulomb's constant $k = 9 \times 10^9$ N·m^2/C^2 and charge of an electron $e = -1.6 \times 10^{-19}$ C)

    A. 3.1×10^{19} electrons   **C.** 6.3×10^{18} electrons

    B. 6.3×10^{19} electrons   **D.** 1.6×10^{19} electrons

2. Two charges $Q_1 = 2.4 \times 10^{-10}$ C and $Q_2 = 9.2 \times 10^{-10}$ C are near each other, and charge Q_1 exerts a force F_1 on Q_2. How does F_1 change if the distance between Q_1 and Q_2 is increased by a factor of 4?

    A. Decreases by a factor of 4   **C.** Decreases by a factor of 16

    B. Increases by a factor of 16   **D.** Increases by a factor of 4

3. A 54,000 kg asteroid carrying a negative charge of 15 µC is 180 m from another 51,000 kg asteroid carrying a negative charge of 11 µC. What is the net force the asteroids exert upon each other? (Use gravitational constant $G = 6.673 \times 10^{-11}$ N·m^2/kg^2 and Coulomb's constant $k = 9 \times 10^9$ N·m^2/C^2)

    A. 400,000 N   **B.** 5,700 N   **C.** -8.2×10^{-5} N   **D.** -4×10^{-5} N

4. Two small beads are 30 cm apart with no other charges or fields present. Bead A has 20 µC of charge and bead B has 5 µC. Which of the following statements is true about the electric forces on these beads?

    A. The force on A is 120 times the force on B

    B. The force on A is exactly equal to the force on B

    C. The force on B is 4 times the force on A

    D. The force on A is 20 times the force on B

5. A point charge $Q = -10$ µC. What is the number of excess electrons on charge Q? (Use charge of an electron $e = -1.6 \times 10^{-19}$ C)

    A. 4.5×10^{13} electrons   **C.** 9×10^{13} electrons

    B. 1.6×10^{13} electrons   **D.** 6.3×10^{13} electrons

6. An electron and a proton are separated by a distance of 3 m. What happens to the magnitude of the force on the proton if the electron is moved 1.5 m closer to the proton?

    A. It increases to twice its original value

    B. It decreases to one-fourth its original value

    C. It increases to four times its original value

    D. It decreases to one-half its original value

7. How will the magnitude of the electrostatic force between two objects be affected, if the distance between them and both of their charges are doubled?

A. It will increase by a factor of 4   C. It will decrease by a factor of 2

B. It will increase by a factor of 2   D. It will be unchanged

8. Two oppositely charged particles are slowly separated from each other. What happens to the force as the particles are slowly moved apart?

A. attractive and decreasing   C. attractive and increasing

B. repulsive and decreasing   D. repulsive and increasing

9. Two charges $Q_1 = 3 \times 10^{-8}$ C and $Q_2 = 9 \times 10^{-8}$ C are near each other, and charge Q_1 exerts a force F_1 on Q_2. What is F_2, the force that charge Q_2 exerts on charge Q_1?

A. $F_1 / 3$ B. F_1 C. $3F_1$ D. $2F_1$

10. Two electrons are passing 30 mm apart. What is the electric repulsive force that they exert on each other? (Use Coulomb's constant $k = 9 \times 10^9$ N·m^2/C^2 and charge of an electron $= -1.6 \times 10^{-19}$ C)

A. 1.3×10^{-25} N   C. 1.3×10^{27} N

B. 3.4×10^{-27} N   D. 2.56×10^{-25} N

11. Suppose a van de Graaff generator builds a negative static charge, and a grounded conductor is placed near enough to it so that a 8 μC of negative charge arcs to the conductor. What is the number of electrons that are transferred? (Use charge of an electron $e = -1.6 \times 10^{-19}$ C)

A. 1.8×10^{14} electrons   C. 5×10^{13} electrons

B. 48 electrons   D. 74 electrons

12. Which statement must be true if two objects are electrically attracted to each other?

A. One of the objects could be electrically neutral

B. One object must be negatively charged and the other must be positively charged

C. At least one of the objects must be positively charged

D. At least one of the objects must be negatively charged

13. Two charges ($Q_1 = 2.3 \times 10^{-8}$ C and $Q_2 = 2.5 \times 10^{-9}$ C) are a distance 0.1 m apart. How much energy is required to bring them to a distance 0.01 m apart? (Use Coulomb's constant $k = 9 \times 10^9$ N·m^2/C^2)

A. 2.2×10^{-4} J   B. 8.9×10^{-5} J   C. 1.7×10^{-5} J   D. 4.7×10^{-5} J

14. In the figure below, the charge in the middle is fixed and $Q = -7.5$ nC. For what fixed, positive charge q_1 will non-stationary, negative charge q_2 be in static equilibrium?

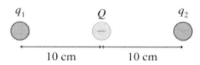

A. 53 nC   **B.** 7.5 nC   **C.** 15 nC   **D.** 30 nC

15. Two charges separated by 1 m exert a 1 N force on each other. If the magnitude of each charge is doubled, the force on each charge is:

A. 1 N   **B.** 2 N   **C.** 4 N   **D.** 6 N

16. In a water solution of NaCl, the NaCl dissociates into ions surrounded by water molecules. Consider a water molecule near a Na^+ ion. What tends to be the orientation of the water molecule?

A. The hydrogen atoms are nearer the Na^+ ion because of their positive charge
B. The hydrogen atoms are nearer the Na^+ ion because of their negative charge
C. The oxygen atom is nearer the Na^+ ion because of the oxygen's positive charge
D. The oxygen atom is nearer the Na^+ ion because of the oxygen's negative charge

17. A metal sphere is insulated electrically and is given a charge. If 30 electrons are added to the sphere in giving a charge, how many Coulombs are added to the sphere? (Use Coulomb's constant $k = 9 \times 10^9$ N·m^2/C^2 and charge of an electron $e = -1.6 \times 10^{-19}$ C)

A. –2.4 C   **B.** –30 C   **C.** -4.8×10^{-18} C   **D.** -4.8×10^{-16} C

18. A positive test charge q is released near a positive fixed charge Q. As q moves away from Q, it experiences:

A. increasing acceleration   C. constant velocity
B. decreasing acceleration   D. decreasing velocity

19. A Coulomb is a unit of electrical:

A. capacity   **B.** resistance   **C.** charge   **D.** potential difference

20. To say that electric charge is conserved means that no case has ever been found where the:

A. net charge has been created or destroyed
B. total charge on an object has increased
C. net negative charge on an object is unbalanced by a positive charge on another object
D. total charge on an object has changed by a significant amount

21. Two charges $Q_1 = 1.7 \times 10^{-10}$ C and $Q_2 = 6.8 \times 10^{-10}$ C are near each other. How would F change if the charges were both doubled, but the distance between them remained the same?

A. F increases by a factor of 2   **C.** F decreases by a factor of $\sqrt{2}$

D. F increases by a factor of 4   **D.** F decreases by a factor of 4

22. Two like charges of the same magnitude are 10 mm apart. If the force of repulsion they exert upon each other is 4 N, what is the magnitude of each charge? (Use Coulomb's constant $k = 9 \times 10^9$ N·m^2/C^2)

A. 6×10^{-5} C   **C.** 2×10^{-7} C

B. 6×10^5 C   **D.** 1.5×10^{-7} C

23. Two identical small charged spheres are a certain distance apart, and each initially experiences an electrostatic force of magnitude F due to the other. With time, charge gradually diminishes on both spheres. What is the magnitude of the electrostatic force when each of the spheres has lost half its initial charge?

A. $1/16\ F$ **B.** $1/8\ F$ **C.** $1/4\ F$ **D.** $2\ F$

24. A charge $Q = 3.1 \times 10^{-5}$ C is fixed in space while another charge $q = -10^{-6}$ C is 6 m away. Charge q is slowly moved 4 m in a straight line directly toward the charge Q. How much work is required to move charge q? (Use Coulomb's constant $k = 9 \times 10^9$ N·m^2/C^2)

A. −0.09 J   **B.** −0.03 J   **C.** 0.16 J   **D.** 0.08 J

25. A point charge $Q = -600$ nC. What is the number of excess electrons in charge Q? (Use the charge of an electron $e = -1.6 \times 10^{-19}$ C)

A. 5.6×10^{12} electrons   **C.** 2.8×10^{11} electrons

B. 2.1×10^{10} electrons   **D.** 3.8×10^{12} electrons

26. If an object is characterized as electrically polarized:

A. its internal electric field is zero   **C.** it is electrically charged

B. it is a strong insulator   **D.** its charges have been rearranged

27. Two equally-charged spheres of mass 1 g are placed 2 cm apart. When released, they begin to accelerate at 440 m/s^2. What is the magnitude of the charge on each sphere? (Use Coulomb's constant $k = 9 \times 10^9$ N·m^2/C^2)

A. 80 nC   **B.** 65 nC   **C.** 115 nC   **D.** 140 nC

28. Two equal and opposite charges a certain distance apart are called an electric 'dipole'. A positive test charge $+q$ is placed as shown, equidistant from the two charges.

Which diagram below gives the direction of the net force on the test charge?

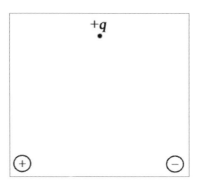

A. $\leftarrow$ C. $\uparrow$

<u>B.</u> $\rightarrow$ D. $\downarrow$

29. Find the magnitude of the electrostatic force between a +3 C point charge and a −12 C point charge if they are separated by 50 cm of empty space. (Use Coulomb's constant $k = 9 \times 10^9$ N·m²/C²)

A. 9.2×10^{12} N   B. 1.3×10^{12} N   C. 7.7×10^{12} N   D. 4.8×10^{12} N

30. Two charges separated by 1 m exert a 1 N force on each other. What is the force on each charge if the charges are pushed to a 0.25 m separation?

A. 1 N   B. 2 N   C. 4 N   D. 16 N

31. In the figure, $Q = 5.1$ nC. What is the magnitude of the electrical force on the charge Q? (Use Coulomb's constant $k = 9 \times 10^9$ N·m²/C²)

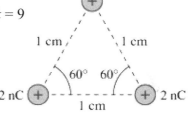

A. 4.2×10^{-3} N   C. 1.6×10^{-3} N

B. 0.4×10^{-3} N   D. 3.2×10^{-3} N

32. Two charges separated by 1 m exert a 1 N force on each other. What is the force on each charge when they are pulled to a separation distance of 3 m?

A. 3 N   B. 0 N   C. 9 N   D. 0.11 N

33. A 4 μC point charge and an 8 μC point charge are initially infinitely far apart. How much work is required to bring the 4 μC point charge to ($x = 2$ mm, $y = 0$ mm), and the 8 μC point charge to ($x = -2$ mm, $y = 0$ mm)? (Use Coulomb's constant $k = 9 \times 10^9$ N·m²/C²)

A. 32.6 J   B. 9.8 J   C. 47 J   D. 72 J

34. A dipole with two ±6 μC charges is positioned so that the negative charge is at the origin and the positive charge is 1 mm to the right. How much work does it take to bring a 10 μC charge from infinity to the position $x = 3$ mm, $y = 0$ mm? (Use Coulomb's constant $k = 9 \times 10^9$ N·m²/C²)

A. 200 J   B. 75 J   C. 450 J   D. 90 J

35. An electron is released from rest at a distance of 5 cm from a proton. How fast will the electron be moving when it is 2 cm from the proton? (Use Coulomb's constant $k = 9 \times 10^9$ N·m^2/C^2, mass of an electron $= 9.1 \times 10^{-31}$ kg, charge of an electron $= -1.6 \times 10^{-19}$ C and charge of a proton $= 1.6 \times 10^{-19}$ C)

    A. 92 m/s   **C.** 147 m/s

    B. 123 m/s   **D.** 1.3×10^3 m/s

36. What is the current in a wire if a total of 2.3×10^{13} electrons pass a given point in a wire in 15 s? (Use charge of an electron $= -1.6 \times 10^{-19}$ C)

    A. 0.25 μA   **B.** 3.2 μA   **C.** 7.1 μA   **D.** 1.3 μA

37. A kilowatt-hour is equivalent to:

    A. 3.6×10^6 J/s   **C.** 3.6×10^3 W

    B. 3.6×10^6 J   **D.** 3.6×10^3 J

DIAGNOSTIC TESTS ANSWER KEYS & EXPLANATIONS

Diagnostic test #1 – Answer Key

1	A	Kinematics & dynamics	26	D	Work & energy
2	D	Force, motion, gravitation	27	B	Waves & periodic motion
3	B	Equilibrium & momentum	28	D	Sound
4	B	Work & energy	29	C	Kinematics & dynamics
5	D	Waves & periodic motion	30	D	Force, motion, gravitation
6	B	Sound	31	C	Equilibrium & momentum
7	A	DC circuits	32	C	Work & energy
8	B	Electrostatics	33	D	Waves & periodic motion
9	B	Kinematics & dynamics	34	B	Sound
10	A	Force, motion, gravitation	35	D	DC circuits
11	B	Equilibrium & momentum	36	C	Electrostatics
12	D	Work & energy	37	C	Kinematics & dynamics
13	A	Waves & periodic motion	38	B	Force, motion, gravitation
14	A	Sound	39	B	Equilibrium & momentum
15	C	Kinematics & dynamics	40	C	Work & energy
16	D	Force, motion, gravitation	41	D	Waves & periodic motion
17	C	Equilibrium & momentum	42	C	Sound
18	A	Work & energy	43	D	Kinematics & dynamics
19	C	Waves & periodic motion	44	C	Force, motion, gravitation
20	D	Sound	45	B	Equilibrium & momentum
21	D	DC circuits	46	C	Work & energy
22	C	Electrostatics	47	C	Waves & periodic motion
23	D	Kinematics & dynamics	48	B	Sound
24	D	Force, motion, gravitation	49	C	DC circuits
25	D	Equilibrium & momentum	50	D	Electrostatics

Diagnostic test #2 – Answer Key

1	D	Kinematics & dynamics	26	A	Work & energy
2	A	Force, motion, gravitation	27	A	Waves & periodic motion
3	C	Equilibrium & momentum	28	C	Sound
4	D	Work & energy	29	B	Kinematics & dynamics
5	B	Waves & periodic motion	30	C	Force, motion, gravitation
6	D	Sound	31	B	Equilibrium & momentum
7	C	DC circuits	32	A	Work & energy
8	D	Electrostatics	33	B	Waves & periodic motion
9	C	Kinematics & dynamics	34	D	Sound
10	C	Force, motion, gravitation	35	A	DC circuits
11	C	Equilibrium & momentum	36	D	Waves & periodic motion
12	C	Work & energy	37	D	Kinematics & dynamics
13	B	Waves & periodic motion	38	B	Force, motion, gravitation
14	C	Sound	39	D	Equilibrium & momentum
15	A	Kinematics & dynamics	40	B	Work & energy
16	B	Force, motion, gravitation	41	A	Waves & periodic motion
17	C	Equilibrium & momentum	42	D	Sound
18	A	Work & energy	43	C	Kinematics & dynamics
19	D	Waves & periodic motion	44	C	Force, motion, gravitation
20	D	Sound	45	B	Equilibrium & momentum
21	C	DC circuits	46	A	Work & energy
22	B	Electrostatics	47	A	Waves & periodic motion
23	A	Kinematics & dynamics	48	D	Sound
24	D	Force, motion, gravitation	49	C	DC circuits
25	C	Equilibrium & momentum	50	C	Kinematics & dynamics

Diagnostic test #3 – Answer Key

1	C	Kinematics & dynamics	26	A	Work & energy
2	A	Force, motion, gravitation	27	D	Waves & periodic motion
3	C	Equilibrium & momentum	28	C	Sound
4	A	Work & energy	29	B	Kinematics & dynamics
5	B	Waves & periodic motion	30	A	Force, motion, gravitation
6	C	Sound	31	D	Equilibrium & momentum
7	B	DC circuits	32	A	Work & energy
8	A	Electrostatics	33	C	Waves & periodic motion
9	B	Kinematics & dynamics	34	D	Sound
10	C	Force, motion, gravitation	35	A	DC circuits
11	A	Equilibrium & momentum	36	A	Electrostatics
12	D	Work & energy	37	D	Kinematics & dynamics
13	A	Waves & periodic motion	38	A	Force, motion, gravitation
14	B	Sound	39	C	Equilibrium & momentum
15	B	Kinematics & dynamics	40	C	Work & energy
16	D	Force, motion, gravitation	41	A	Waves & periodic motion
17	B	Equilibrium & momentum	42	B	Sound
18	B	Work & energy	43	D	Kinematics & dynamics
19	B	Waves & periodic motion	44	D	Force, motion, gravitation
20	B	Sound	45	B	Equilibrium & momentum
21	B	DC circuits	46	B	Work & energy
22	D	Electrostatics	47	D	Waves & periodic motion
23	A	Kinematics & dynamics	48	B	Sound
24	C	Force, motion, gravitation	49	A	Force, motion, gravitation
25	C	Equilibrium & momentum	50	D	Electrostatics

DIAGNOSTIC TEST #1 – EXPLANATIONS

1. A is correct. An object's resistance to change in its state of motion is characterized by its inertia.

Inertia is not a physical property but is directly related to an object's mass. Thus, mass determines resistance to change in motion.

2. D is correct. The three forces are in equilibrium, so the net force $F_{net} = 0$

$$F_{net} = F_1 + F_2 + F_3$$

$$0 = F_1 + F_2 + F_3$$

Since the forces F_1 and F_2 are mirror images of each other along the x-axis, their net force in the y direction is zero. Therefore, F_3 is also zero in the y direction.

The net force along the x direction must add to zero, so set the sum of the x components to zero.

The angles for F_1 and F_2 are equal and measured with respect to the x-axis, so θ_1 and θ_2 are both 20°.

Since F_3 has no y component, $\theta_3 = 0°$. Note that force components to the left are set negative in this answer and components to the right are set positive.

$$0 = F_{1x} + F_{2x} + F_{3x}$$

$$0 = F_1 \cos \theta_1 + F_2 \cos \theta_2 + F_3 \cos \theta_3$$

$$0 = (-4.6 \text{ N} \cos 20°) + (-4.6 \text{ N} \cos 20°) + (F_3 \cos 0°)$$

Since $\cos 0° = 1$:

$$0 = (-4.3 \text{ N}) + (-4.3 \text{ N}) + F_3$$

$$-F_3 = -8.6 \text{ N}$$

$$F_3 = 8.6 \text{ N, to the right}$$

3. B is correct. To balance the torques due to the weight, the fulcrum must be placed 4 times farther from the son than from the man, because the father weighs 4 times more.

Since the total length of the seesaw is 10 m, the fulcrum must be placed 8 m from the son and 2 m from the father who is on the heavier end.

$$x + 4x = 10 \text{ m}$$

$$5x = 10 \text{ m}$$

$$x = 2 \text{ m}$$

Another method to solve the problem:

200 N		800 N
10 − x	Δ	x

$$(200 \text{ N}) \cdot (10 - x) = (800 \text{ N})x$$
$$x = 2 \text{ m}$$

4. B is correct.

$W = Fd$

$W = (20 \text{ N}) \cdot (3.5 \text{ m})$

$W = 70 \text{ J}$

5. D is correct.

Constructive interference occurs when two or more waves of equal frequency and phase produce a single amplitude wave that is the sum of amplitudes of the individual waves.

If there is any phase difference the interference will not be the sum total of the amplitude of each individual wave.

If the phase difference is 180° there will be total destructive interference.

6. B is correct.

The expression for the Doppler shift is:

$f = f_s[(c + v_o) / (c + v_s)]$

where f is the frequency heard by the observer, f_s is the frequency of the source, c is the speed of sound, v_o is the velocity of the observer, v_s is the velocity of the source

The velocity of the source v_s is positive when the source is moving away from the observer and negative when it is moving toward the observer

Since the train is traveling away, once it passes the velocity of the source (i.e. train) is positive.

Kevin is standing still, so the velocity of the observer is zero.

$f = f_s[(c + v_o) / (c + v_s)]$

$f = (420 \text{ Hz}) \cdot [(350 \text{ m/s} + 0 \text{ m/s}) / (350 \text{ m/s} + 50 \text{ m/s})]$

$f = (420 \text{ Hz}) \cdot [(350 \text{ m/s}) / (400 \text{ m/s})]$

$f = (147{,}000 \text{ Hz} \cdot \text{m/s}) / (400 \text{ m/s})$

$f = 368 \text{ Hz}$

7. A is correct.

Find Capacitive Reactance:

$X_c = 1 / 2\pi C f$

$X_c = 1 / (2\pi) \cdot (26 \times 10^{-6} \text{ F}) \cdot (60 \text{ Hz})$

$X_c = 102 \; \Omega$

Find peak current:

$I = V_{rms} / X_c$

$I = 120 \text{ V} / 102 \text{ } \Omega$

$I = 1.2 \text{ A}$

8. B is correct.

By Newton's Third Law, F_1 and F_2 form an *action–reaction* pair.

The ratio of their magnitudes equals 1.

9. B is correct.

$d = \frac{1}{2}gt^2$

$t^2 = 2d / g$

$t^2 = 2(42 \text{ m}) / 10 \text{ m/s}^2$

$t^2 = 8.4 \text{ s}^2$

$t \approx 2.9 \text{ s}$

10. A is correct.

$a = mg \sin \theta$

An object's acceleration down a frictionless ramp (with an incline angle) is constant.

11. B is correct.

A longer barrel gives the propellant a longer time to impart a force upon a bullet and thus a higher velocity. This is characterized by impulse.

$J = F\Delta t$

12. D is correct.

The energy before release and at the top of each bounce equals gravitational PE:

$PE = mgh$

Gravitational potential energy is proportional to height, and mass and g stay constant.

Multiply by 0.8 (80%) to determine the height after a bounce if 20% of the energy is lost.

$h_{\text{initial}} = 250 \text{ cm}$

250 cm × (0.8 × 0.8 × 0.8), equals h after 3 bounces

$h_3 = (250 \text{ cm}) \cdot (0.8)^3$

$h_3 = 128 \text{ cm}$

13. A is correct.

$T = 1 / f$

$T = 1 / (10 \text{ Hz})$

$T = 0.1 \text{ s}$

14. A is correct.

$f = v / \lambda$

$f = (1{,}600 \text{ m/s}) / (2.5 \text{ m})$

$f = 640 \text{ Hz}$

15. C is correct.

16. D is correct.

$F = ma$

$W = mg$

$m = W / g$

$F = (W / g)a$

$a = F / m$

The $F_{\text{friction}} = 8.8 \text{ N}$, and the mass is known from the box's weight.

$8.8 \text{ N} = (40 \text{ N} / 10 \text{ m/s}^2)a$

$a = (8.8 \text{ N}) / (4 \text{ N/m/s}^2)$

$a = 2.2 \text{ m/s}^2$

Since the box moves at constant velocity when force F is applied, F = force due to kinetic friction.

Once the force F is removed, the net force that causes its deceleration is the frictional force.

17. C is correct.

Total momentum of the system is always conserved. Before the ball was thrown the momentum was zero because all mass on the canoe was stationary.

After the ball is thrown and caught on the canoe the momentum must still be equal to zero so the canoe must remain stationary.

$p = mv$

18. A is correct.

$KE_{\text{final}} = 0$ since $v_f = 0$

The length of the skid marks are irrelevant.

$\Delta \text{Energy} = KE_{\text{final}} - KE_{\text{initial}}$

$\Delta E = \frac{1}{2}mv_f^2 - \frac{1}{2}mv_i^2$

$$\Delta E = 0 \text{ J} - \tfrac{1}{2}(1{,}000 \text{ kg}){\cdot}(30 \text{ m/s})^2$$

$$\Delta E = -4.5 \times 10^5 \text{ J}$$

19. C is correct.

The *lowest* harmonic (i.e. fundamental) frequency (f_1) corresponds to the *longest* harmonic (i.e. fundamental) wavelength (λ_1).

$$f_1 = v / \lambda_1$$

$$f_1 = (8 \text{ m/s}) / 4 \text{ m}$$

$$f_1 = 2 \text{ Hz}$$

20. D is correct.

Sound cannot travel through a vacuum because there is no medium to propagate the wave.

In air, sound waves travel through gas, in the ocean they travel through liquid, and in the Earth they travel through solids. These are all mediums in which sound waves can propagate.

However, vacuums are devoid of matter; there is no medium, and the wave cannot pass.

21. D is correct.

$$P = IV$$

$$P = (2 \text{ A}){\cdot}(120 \text{ V})$$

$$P = 240 \text{ W}$$

An ampere (A) is a rate of electric charge flowing in a circuit in coulombs per second (C/s), where 1 A = 1 C/s. The volt (V) measures the difference in electric potential between two points, where 1 V is defined as the electric potential difference when 1 ampere consumes 1 watt (W) of power.

Power is a measure of energy per unit time:

$$1 \text{ W} = 1 \text{ A}{\cdot}\text{V}$$

$$1 \text{ W} = 1 \text{ J} / \text{s}$$

$$1 \text{ W} = 1 \text{ N}{\cdot}\text{m/s}$$

$$1 \text{ W} = 1 \text{ kg}{\cdot}\text{m}^2/\text{s}^3$$

22. C is correct.

If the voltage drop across the 3 Ω resistor is 2 V, the current through the 3 Ω resistor is:

$$I = V / R$$

$$I = 2 \text{ V} / 3 \text{ } \Omega$$

$$I = 2/3 \text{ amp}$$

Since the 1.5 Ω resistor is connected in parallel with the 3 Ω resistor, voltage drop = 2 V (parallel resistors always share the same voltage drop).

The current through the 1.5 Ω resistor is:

$$I = 2 \text{ V} / 1.5 \text{ Ω}$$

$$I = 4/3 \text{ amps}$$

Then, sum the currents:

$$I_{total} = 2/3 \text{ amp} + 4/3 \text{ amps}$$

$$I_{total} = 2 \text{ amps}$$

23. D is correct.

Velocity is in the direction of the current:

$$v_c = at$$

$$v_c = (0.75 \text{ m/s}^2) \cdot (33.5 \text{ s})$$

$$v_c = 25 \text{ m/s}$$

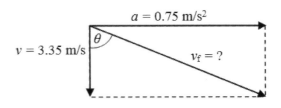

Final velocity:

$$v_f^2 = v^2 + v_c^2$$

$$v_f^2 = (3.35 \text{ m/s})^2 + (25 \text{ m/s})^2$$

$$v_f^2 = 636.2 \text{ m}^2/\text{s}^2$$

$$v_f = 25 \text{ m/s}$$

The angle of motion with respect to the initial velocity:

$$\theta = \tan^{-1} (v_c / v)$$

$$\theta = \tan^{-1} [(25 \text{ m/s}) / (3.35 \text{ m/s})]$$

$$\theta = \tan^{-1} 7.5$$

$$\theta = 82.4°$$

24. D is correct.

According to Newton's First Law: an object at rest tends to stay at rest and an object in motion tends to stay in motion unless acted upon by an outside force.

Lisa fell backwards because the truck accelerated to increase its velocity and Lisa's body tended to stay in its original motion.

25. D is correct.

Divide the problem into three parts: initial acceleration, constant velocity, final deceleration stage.

1) Initial acceleration: determine a, then solve for the displacement during the acceleration. The initial velocity is zero.

Convert the displacement in radians to revolutions.

$\alpha = (\omega_f - \omega_i) / t$

$\alpha = (58 \text{ radians/s}^2 - 0) / 10 \text{ s}$

$\alpha = 5.8 \text{ radians/s}^2$

$\theta = \frac{1}{2}\alpha t^2$

$\theta = \frac{1}{2}(5.8 \text{ radians/s}^2) \cdot (10 \text{ s})^2$

$\theta = 290 \text{ radians}$

$Rev = \theta / 2\pi$

$Rev = 290 \text{ radians} / 2\pi$

$Rev = 46 \text{ revolutions}$

2) Constant velocity: solve θ using constant angular velocity.

Convert radians to revolutions.

$\theta = \omega t$

$\theta = (58 \text{ radians/s}) \cdot (30 \text{ s})$

$\theta = 1,740 \text{ radians}$

$Rev = \theta / 2\pi$

$Rev = 1,740 \text{ radians} / 2\pi$

$Rev = 277 \text{ revolutions}$

3) Final deceleration: determine t for the period of deceleration using the final velocity as zero.

Solve for the displacement during this constant deceleration and convert to revolutions.

$\alpha = (\omega_f - \omega_i) / t$

$t = (\omega_f - \omega_i) / \alpha$

$t = (0 - 58 \text{ radians/s}) / (-1.4 \text{ radians/s}^2)$

$t = 41 \text{ s}$

$\theta = \omega_i t + \frac{1}{2}\alpha t^2$

$\theta = [(58 \text{ radians/s}) \cdot (41 \text{ s})] + [\frac{1}{2}(-1.4 \text{ radians/s}^2) \cdot (41 \text{ s})^2]$

$\theta = 1,201 \text{ radians}$

$Rev = 1,201 \text{ radians} / 2\pi$

$Rev = 191 \text{ revolutions}$

Add the revolutions:

$Rev_{total} = 46 \text{ rev} + 277 \text{ rev} + 191 \text{ rev}$

$Rev_{total} = 514 \approx 510 \text{ revolutions}$

26. D is correct.

$$W = Fd \cos \theta$$

$$W = (20 \text{ N}) \cdot (2 \text{ m})$$

$$W = 40 \text{ J}$$

27. B is correct.

The position of an object in simple harmonic motion (SHM) is represented as a function of time using sine or cosine:

$$x = A \sin (\omega t - \theta)$$

where x = position, A = amplitude (i.e. max displacement of object from equilibrium position), ω = angular velocity in radians/sec (or degrees/sec), t = time elapsed, θ = phase

Here, $\theta = 0$ since the graph matches the phase of the standard sine graph, so there is no need for a phase correction. $A = 1$ is used for simplicity.

$$x = \sin (\omega t)$$

The object's velocity in SHM is represented by the derivative of the position function:

$$v = \omega \cos (\omega t)$$

The object's acceleration in SHM is represented by the derivative of the velocity function:

$$a = -\omega^2 \sin (\omega t)$$

Therefore, the acceleration of objects in SHM is represented as the opposite value of position, multiplied by the square of angular velocity.

ω is constant, so the graphs keep the same wavelengths.

28. D is correct.

Sound is a travelling acoustic pressure wave that is propagated through vibrations of particles such as air or water.

In a vacuum no particles exist so the wave cannot propagate and no sound is heard.

Thus sound can refract in air or water but not in a vacuum.

29. C is correct.

$$y = v_i t + \tfrac{1}{2}at^2$$

$$50 \text{ m} = 0 + \tfrac{1}{2}(10 \text{ m/s}^2)t^2$$

$$50 \text{ m} = \tfrac{1}{2}(10 \text{ m/s}^2)t^2$$

$$t^2 = 50 \text{ m} / 5 \text{ m/s}^2$$

$$t^2 = 10 \text{ s}^2$$

$$t = 3.2 \text{ s}$$

Solve for speed:

$$v_f = v_i + at$$

$$v_f = 0 + (10 \text{ m/s}^2) \cdot (3.2 \text{ s})$$

$$v_f = 32 \text{ m/s}$$

30. D is correct.

Newton's Second Law for each block:

$$ma = F_{net} \text{ acting on the object.}$$

The tension and acceleration on each block are equal in magnitude, but act in different directions.

The only nonzero net forces will be in the horizontal direction for the 15 kg block and in the vertical direction for the 60 kg block.

For the 15 kg block:

$$ma = \text{tension acting to the right}$$

$$(15 \text{ kg})a = F_T$$

For the 60 kg block:

$$ma = (\text{weight acting downward}) - (\text{tension acting upward})$$

$$(60 \text{ kg})a = (60 \text{ kg}) \cdot (10 \text{ m/s}^2) - F_T$$

Substitute F_T from the first equation into the second:

$$(60 \text{ kg})a = (60 \text{ kg}) \cdot (10 \text{ m/s}^2) - (15 \text{ kg})a$$

$$(60 \text{ kg})a + (15 \text{ kg})a = (60 \text{ kg}) \cdot (10 \text{ m/s}^2)$$

$$(75 \text{ kg})a = (60 \text{ kg}) \cdot (10 \text{ m/s}^2)$$

$$a = [(60 \text{ kg}) \cdot (10 \text{ m/s}^2)] / (75 \text{ kg})$$

$$a = 8 \text{ m/s}^2$$

31. C is correct.

Momentum is the product of mass and velocity.

$$p_0 = mv_0$$

If velocity doubles:

$$p = m(2v_0)$$

$$p = 2mv_0$$

$$p = 2p_0$$

Therefore momentum doubles.

32. C is correct.

The kinetic energy of a falling object is directly proportional to height from which it falls. This is because mass and gravity are constants so only the height varies the kinetic energy of a dropped object.

$KE = PE$

$\frac{1}{2}mv^2 = mgh$

33. D is correct.

$\lambda = vt$

$\lambda = (4.6 \text{ m/s})\cdot(10 \text{ s})$

$\lambda = 46 \text{ m}$

34. B is correct.

If the two sound sources are in phase then there is no destructive interference.

The point can be related to the wavelength of the sound wave.

$0.5 \text{ m} = x\lambda$

$0.5 \text{ m} = x(1 \text{ m})$

$x = \frac{1}{2}$

One half of a wavelength is a node.

35. D is correct.

Ohm's law:

$V = IR$

$R = V / I$

36. C is correct.

An object becomes electrostatically charged when a charge imbalance exists.

Charge can only be transferred by electrons because protons are not mobile, thus electron transfer creates electrostatic charge.

37. C is correct.

Distance is direction independent

Displacement is direction dependent

Distance = (16 m North + 12 m South) = 28 m

Displacement = (16 m – 12 m) = 4 m

38. B is correct.

The angle the board makes before the pot slides is dependent upon the static friction coefficient as static friction influences the force of friction before the pot slides. Kinetic friction only occurs after movement of the pot.

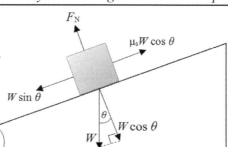

39. B is correct.

Momentum is conserved

$$m_1v_1 + m_2v_2 = m_3v_3$$

momentum before = momentum after

$$p_i = p_f$$

$$p_{total} = m_1v_1 + m_2v_2$$

$$p_{total} = (1 \text{ kg}) \cdot (1 \text{ m/s}) + (6 \text{ kg}) \cdot (0 \text{ m/s})$$

$$p_{total} = 1 \text{ kg·m/s}$$

40. C is correct.

Ignoring air resistance, energy is conserved. The loss in PE = the gain in KE.

$$KE = \tfrac{1}{2}mv^2$$

$$KE = \tfrac{1}{2}(20 \text{ kg}) \cdot (30 \text{ m/s})^2$$

$$KE = 9,000 \text{ J}$$

This equals the amount of PE that is lost (i.e. converted into KE).

41. D is correct.

The wave has to travel for 4 amplitudes of distance in 1 cycle.

Simple harmonic motion can be represented by a wave of one cycle:

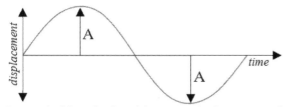

In one half cycle the object travels from zero displacement to A back to zero giving a total displacement of zero but a total distance of 2A. Thus in one complete cycle the object travels 4A.

42. C is correct.

Label the tuning forks I, II, III, and IV.

Beats: I & II, I & III, I & IV, II & III, II & IV and III & IV

From six pairs, there is the possibility of six different beat frequencies.

This is a combination problem since order does not matter.

The formula for combinations is:

$$C(n, k) = n! / (n - k)!k!$$

where n is the given sample size and k is the number of tuning forks per pair.

When solving combination problems, the best way to choose n and k is to ask: "how do I find all the ways to pick n and k?"

$$C(4,2) = 4! / (4 - 2)!2!$$

$$C(4,2) = 4! / 2!2!$$

$$C(4,2) = 6$$

43. D is correct.

The inertia of an object is its resistance to change in motion and is dependent on its mass which has units of kilograms.

44. C is correct.

velocity = acceleration × time

$$a = \Delta v / \Delta t$$

If $\Delta v = 0$, then $a = 0$

45. B is correct.

Check if KE is conserved:

$KE_{before} = KE_{after}$ if collision is elastic

Before:

$$(\tfrac{1}{2})\cdot(4 \text{ kg})\cdot(1.8 \text{ m/s})^2 + (\tfrac{1}{2})\cdot(6 \text{ kg})\cdot(0.2 \text{ m/s})^2 = KE_{before}$$

$$KE_{before} = 6.6 \text{ J}$$

After:

$$(\tfrac{1}{2})\cdot(4 \text{ kg})\cdot(0.6 \text{ m/s})^2 + (\tfrac{1}{2})\cdot(6 \text{ kg})\cdot(1.4 \text{ m/s})^2 = KE_{after}$$

$$KE_{after} = 6.6 \text{ J}$$

Therefore:

$$KE_{before} = KE_{after}$$

The collision was completely elastic because kinetic energy was conserved.

46. C is correct.

The work done by the force can be related to kinetic energy.

4 kg mass:

$$KE = W$$

$$\tfrac{1}{2}(6 \text{ kg}) \cdot (2 \text{ m/s})^2 = F d_1$$

$$d_1 = 12 \, / \, F$$

2 kg mass:

$$KE = W$$

$$\tfrac{1}{2}(3 \text{ kg}) \cdot (4 \text{ m/s})^2 = F d_2$$

$$d_2 = 24 \, / \, F$$

$$d_2 = 2(12 \, / \, F)$$

Therefore:

$$2d_1 = d_2$$

47. C is correct.

$$\text{velocity} = \text{frequency} \times \text{wavelength}$$

$$v = f\lambda$$

$$\lambda = v \, / \, f$$

$$f = 1 \, / \, T$$

$$\lambda = v \times T$$

$$\lambda = 360 \text{ m/s} \times 4.2 \text{ s}$$

$$\lambda \approx 1.5 \text{ m}$$

48. B is correct.

$$PE = \tfrac{1}{2}kx^2$$

$$PE = \tfrac{1}{2}k(2x)^2$$

$$PE = 4(\tfrac{1}{2}kx^2)$$

49. C is correct.

$$V = IR$$

$$I = V \, / \, R$$

$$I = (120 \text{ V}) \, / \, 12 \, \Omega$$

$$I = 10 \text{ A}$$

50. D is correct.

From Coulomb's Law, the electrostatic force is *inversely proportional* to the square of the distance between the charges.

$$F = kq_1q_2 / r^2$$

If the distance increases by a factor of 2, then the force decreases by a factor of $2^2 = 4$.

DIAGNOSTIC TEST #2 – EXPLANATIONS

1. D is correct. There is no acceleration in the horizontal direction, so velocity is constant.

$v_{0x} = v_x$

$d = v_x \times t$

$d = (30 \text{ m/s}) \cdot (75 \text{ s})$

$d = 2{,}250 \text{ m}$

2. A is correct.

$F_{\text{friction}} = \mu_k N$

3. C is correct. Moment of inertia I is defined as the ratio of the angular momentum L of a system to its angular velocity ω around a principal axis.

Moment of inertia:

$I = L / \omega$

Angular acceleration around a fixed axis:

$\tau = \alpha I$

Mass moment of inertia of a thin disk:

$I = \frac{1}{2}mr^2$

$\tau = \alpha(\frac{1}{2}mr^2)$

$m = (2\tau) / \alpha r^2$

$m = [(2) \cdot (14 \text{ N·m})] / [(5.3 \text{ rad/s}^2) \cdot (0.6 \text{ m})^2]$

$m = 14.7 \text{ kg}$

4. D is correct. Energy can exist as work, PE, KE, heat, waves, etc.

The statement ability to do work describes PE

The other statements describe work which is a form of energy.

5. B is correct. The displacement of the tines of a tuning fork from their resting positions is a measure of the amplitude of the resulting sound wave.

6. D is correct.

$I \text{ (dB)} = 10 \log_{10}(I / I_o)$

7. C is correct.

voltage = current × resistance

$V = IR$

$V = (10 \text{ A}) \cdot (5 \text{ } \Omega)$

$V = 55 \text{ V}$

8. D is correct. Acceleration is always positive and away from charge Q.

Therefore, velocity increases (no opposing force of friction).

The energy of the system starts as electrical PE.

$PE_{elec} = (kQq) / r$

where r is the initial distance between the point charges.

Electrical PE is the energy required to bring a system together from the charges starting at infinity.

After charge Q has moved very far away, the energy of the system is only $KE = \frac{1}{2}mv^2$

v has a limit because KE cannot exceed kQq / r

9. C is correct. The slope of the line is the derivative of the position vs. time graph.

The derivative of a position graph gives velocity. Thus, at a single point along the line, the instantaneous velocity is given.

10. C is correct. Centripetal acceleration

$F_c = (m) \cdot (v^2 / r)$

$F_c = (1,200 \text{ kg}) \cdot [(3.5 \text{ m/s})^2 / 4 \text{ m}]$

$F_c = (1,200 \text{ kg}) \cdot [(12.25 \text{ m}^2/\text{s}^2) / 4 \text{ m}]$

$F_c = (1,200 \text{ kg}) \cdot (3 \text{ m/s}^2)$

$F_c = 3,600 \text{ N}$

11. C is correct.

$F = ma$

$m = F / a$

$m_1 = (69 \text{ N}) / (9.8 \text{ m/s}^2)$

$m_1 = 7.04 \text{ kg}$

$m_2 = (94 \text{ N}) / (9.8 \text{ m/s}^2)$

$m_2 = 9.59$ kg

$m_1 r_1 = m_2 r_2$

$m_1 / m_2 = r_2 / r_1$

$m_1 / m_2 = (7.04$ kg$) / (9.59$ kg$)$

$m_1 / m_2 = 0.734$

$r_2 / r_1 = 0.734$

$r_2 + r_1 = 10$ m

Two equations, two unknowns:

Eq$_1$: $r_2 + r_1 = 10$ m

Eq$_2$: $r_2 - (0.734) \cdot (r_1) = 0$

Multiply Eq$_2$ by -1 and add to Eq$_1$:

$(1.734)r_1 = 10$ m

$r_1 = 5.8$ m

12. C is correct.

$v = v_0 + at$

29 m/s $= 0 + (10$ m/s$^2)t$

$v = at$

$t = v / a$

$t = (29$ m/s$) / (10$ m/s$^2)$

$t = 2.9$ s

$y = \frac{1}{2}at^2$

$y = \frac{1}{2}(10$ m/s$^2) \cdot (2.9$ s$)^2 + 1$ m

$y = \frac{1}{2}(10$ m/s$^2) \cdot (8.41$ s$^2) + 1$ m

$y = 42$ m $+ 1$ m

$y = 43$ m

13. B is correct.

Resonant frequency of a spring mass system:

$\omega = \sqrt{(k / m)}$

Increasing the spring constant k results in a higher resonant frequency.

14. C is correct.

Sound velocity in an ideal gas:

$$v_{sound} = \sqrt{(yRT / M)}$$

where y – adiabatic constant, R – gas constant, T – temperature and M = molecular mass of gas.

Increasing the temperature increases the velocity of sound in air.

15. A is correct.

$$v_y = 3.13 \sin 30°$$

$$v_y = 1.6 \text{ m/s}$$

$$v_f = v_o + at$$

$$0 = (1.6 \text{ m/s}) + (-9.8 \text{ m/s}^2)t$$

$$(9.8 \text{ m/s}^2)t = (1.6 \text{ m/s})$$

$$t = (1.6 \text{ m/s}) / (9.8 \text{ m/s}^2)$$

$$t = 0.16 \text{ s}$$

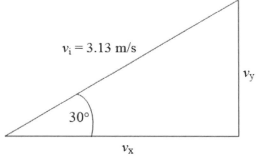

$v_i = 3.13$ m/s

v_y

$30°$

v_x

16. B is correct. Newton's Third Law: for every action there is an equal and opposite reaction force.

17. C is correct. Balance the counterclockwise (CCW) torque with the sum of the two clockwise (CW) torques.

The CCW torque due to the weight of the man is:

$$\tau = r_1F_1$$

$$F = mg$$

where g – acceleration due to gravity

$$\tau = r_1(m_1g)$$

$$\tau = 5.5 \text{ m} \times 105 \text{ kg} \times g$$

$$\tau = 578 \, g$$

The total CW torque due to the weight of the two children is:

$$\tau = r_2F_2 + r_3F_3$$

$$\tau = r_2mg + r_3mg$$

$$\tau = (r_2 \times m_2 \times g) + (r_3 \times m_3 \times g)$$

$$\tau = (r_2 \times 20 \times g) + (10 \times 20 \times g)$$

$$\tau = (20r_2 \times g) + (200 \times g)$$

$$\tau = g(20r_2 + 200)$$

Set the two expressions equal to each other,

$578 \, g = g(20r_2 + 200)$, cancel g from both sides of the expression

$578 = 20r_2 + 200$

$378 = 20r_2$

$r_2 = 378 \, / \, 20$

$r_2 = 19$ m

18. A is correct. The potential energy of a system can be zero because potential energy is defined against an arbitrary reference point. In a gravitational potential problem, if the reference point is ground level and the object is below ground level, it will have a negative potential energy relative to the reference point.

19. D is correct.

$\lambda = 2$ m and $T = 1$ s

$f = 1 \, / \, T$

$f = 1 \, / \, 1$ s

$f = 1$ Hz

$v = f\lambda$

$v = (1 \text{ Hz}) \cdot (2 \text{ m})$

$v = 2$ m/s

20. D is correct. Frequency, length, and velocity are related by:

$f = v \, / \, 2L$

$v = f \times 2L$

$v = (440 \text{ Hz}) \cdot (2 \times 0.14 \text{ m})$

$v = 123.2$ m/s ≈ 123 m/s

$L = v \, / \, 2f$

$L = (123 \text{ m/s}) \, / \, (2) \cdot (520 \text{ Hz})$

$L = 0.118$ m

$\Delta L = 0.14$ m $- 0.118$ m

$\Delta L = 0.022$ m $= 2.2$ cm

21. C is correct.

First, find the total resistance of each set of resistors in parallel.

Resistors in parallel:

$$1 / R_{total} = 1 / R_1 + 1 / R_2 \ldots + 1 / R_n$$

$$1 / R_{total} = 1 / 600 \ \Omega + 1 / 600 \ \Omega$$

$$R_{total} = 300 \ \Omega$$

The two sets of parallel resistors are in series:

Resistors in series:

$$R_{total} = R_1 + R_2 \ldots + R_n$$

$$R_{total} = 300 \ \Omega + 300 \ \Omega$$

$$R_{total} = 600 \ \Omega$$

22. B is correct. Force exerted on a particle of charge q:

$$F = qE$$

Work is being done on the proton because it is speeding up. The acceleration of the proton is to the right so the force is also to the right. Therefore, the electric field must be to the right.

23. A is correct. For constant acceleration, the velocity increases with time. If velocity increases with time, the position vs. time line of the graph is curved over each time interval.

24. D is correct. In a circular path, the object's direction of motion is always changing.

Therefore, the velocity is not constant.

The acceleration (i.e. centripetal force) points toward the center of the circular path.

25. C is correct. Use conservation of momentum for momenta in the x coordinate to solve for the x component of the second ball's final velocity.

Use m as the mass for the first ball and $1.4m$ as mass of the second ball.

$$p_{before} = p_{after}$$

$$m(4 \text{ m/s}) \cos 60° = 1.4mv_x$$

$$v_x = (4 \text{ m/s}) \cdot (\cos 60°) / 1.4$$

$$v_x = (4 \text{ m/s}) \cdot (0.5) / 1.4$$

$$v_x = 1.4 \text{ m/s}$$

26. A is correct.

Work equation:

$$W = Fd$$

$$W = (70 \text{ N}) \cdot (45 \text{ m})$$
$$W = 3{,}150 \text{ J}$$

Power equation:

$$P = W / t$$
$$P = (3{,}150 \text{ J}) / (60 \times 30 \text{ s})$$
$$P = (3{,}150 \text{ J}) / (180 \text{ s})$$
$$P = 18 \text{ W}$$

27. A is correct. Simple harmonic motion equation:

position: $y = A \sin \omega t$

acceleration: $a = -\omega^2 A \sin \omega t$

$a = -\omega^2 y$

From the position and acceleration equations of motion, acceleration is directly proportional to position.

28. C is correct.

Since a beat of frequency 3 Hz is produced, the violin string must be vibrating at either:

$$(340 \text{ Hz} - 4 \text{ Hz}) = 336 \text{ Hz}$$

or

$$(340 \text{ Hz} + 4 \text{ Hz}) = 344 \text{ Hz}$$

Since the string is too taut, the perceived *f* is too high.

Therefore, the string vibrates at 344 Hz.

Period is the reciprocal of frequency.

$$T = 1 / f$$
$$T = 1 / 344 \text{ sec}$$

29. B is correct. First determine how long it takes the ball to drop 50 m:

$$PE = KE$$

$mgh = \frac{1}{2}mv_{yf}^2$, cancel *m* from both sides of the expression

$$gh = \frac{1}{2}v_{yf}^2$$
$$v_{yf}^2 = 2gh$$
$$v_{yf}^2 = (2) \cdot (10 \text{ m/s}^2) \cdot (50 \text{ m})$$
$$v_{yf}^2 = 1{,}000 \text{ m}^2/\text{s}^2$$
$$v_{yf} \approx 32 \text{ m/s}$$

$$t = (v_{yf} - v_{yi}) / a$$

$$t = (32 \text{ m/s} - 0) / (10 \text{ m/s}^2)$$

$$t = 3.2 \text{ s}$$

Calculate the distance traveled horizontally in 3.2 s:

$$d_x = v_x \times t$$

$$d_x = (5 \text{ m/s}){\cdot}(3.2 \text{ s})$$

$$d_x = 16 \text{ m}$$

30. C is correct.

$$F_{\text{tot}} = F_{\text{gravity}} + F_{\text{friction}}$$

$$ma_{\text{tot}} = mg \sin\theta + \mu_k mg \cos\theta, \text{ cancel } m \text{ from both sides}$$

$$a_{\text{tot}} = g(\sin\theta + \mu_k \cos\theta)$$

$$a_{\text{tot}} = -9.8 \text{ m/s}^2(\sin 30^\circ + 0.3 \cos 30^\circ)$$

$$a_{\text{tot}} = -7.44 \text{ m/s}^2$$

Find time taken to reach 0 m/s:

$$v_f = v_0 + at$$

$$0 \text{ m/s} = 14 \text{ m/s} + (-7.44 \text{ m/s}^2)t$$

$$t = 1.88 \text{ s}$$

$$x = x_0 + v_0 t + \tfrac{1}{2}at^2$$

$$x = 0 \text{ m} + (14 \text{ m/s}){\cdot}(1.88 \text{ s}) + \tfrac{1}{2}(-7.44 \text{ m/s}^2){\cdot}(1.88 \text{ s})^2$$

$$x = 13.2 \text{ m}$$

Find vertical component of x:

$$y = x \sin\theta$$

$$y = (13.2 \text{ m}) \sin 30^\circ$$

$$y = 6.6 \text{ m}$$

31. B is correct. The forces on the block (with bullet) are gravity and the tension of the string. The tension is perpendicular to the direction of travel, so the tension does no work. This problem is solved using conservation of energy, assuming a full transfer of KE into gravitational PE.

KE (block with bullet at bottom) = PE (block with bullet at top)

$$\tfrac{1}{2}mv^2 = mgh, \text{ cancel } m \text{ from both sides of the expression}$$

$$\tfrac{1}{2}v^2 = gh$$

$$\tfrac{1}{2}(2 \text{ m/s})^2 = (9.8 \text{ m/s}^2)h$$

$½(4 \text{ m}^2/\text{s}^2) = (9.8 \text{ m/s}^2)h$

$(2 \text{ m}^2/\text{s}^2) = (9.8 \text{ m/s}^2)h$

$h = (2 \text{ m}^2/\text{s}^2) / (9.8 \text{ m/s}^2)$

$h = 0.20 \text{ m} = 20 \text{ cm}$

32. A is correct. Before it is released, the hammer has zero velocity and a gravitational PE of *mgh*. This PE is converted completely into KE when it reaches the ground.

PE (top) = KE (bottom)

$mgh_0 = ½m(v_0^2)$, cancel *m* from both sides of the expression

$v_0 = \sqrt{(2gh_0)}$

If h_0 increases by a factor of 2, substitute $2h_0$ for h_0

$v = \sqrt{[2g(2h_0)]}$

$v = \sqrt{2} \times \sqrt{2gh_0}$

$v = \sqrt{2} \times (v_0)$

The new velocity is $\sqrt{2}$ times faster.

33. B is correct.

Period of a pendulum:

$T = 2\pi\sqrt{(L / s)}$

The period does not depend on mass, so changes to *M* do not affect the period.

34. D is correct. Perceived color of light depends on frequency and wavelength which are related to each other through the speed of light:

$c = f\lambda$

35. A is correct.

Current through 8 Ω resistor:

$V = IR$

$V = 8 \text{ Ω} \times 0.8 \text{ A}$

$V = 6.4$

$I = 6.4 \text{ V} / 16 \text{ Ω}$

$I = 0.4 \text{ A}$

$I_{total} = 0.4 \text{ A} + 0.8 \text{ A}$

$I_{total} = 1.2 \text{ A}$

Voltage drop across 20 Ω resistor:

$V = IR$

$V = (1.2 \text{ A}) \cdot (20 \text{ Ω})$

$V = 24 \text{ V}$

$V_{total} = 6.4 \text{ V} + 24 \text{ V}$

$V_{total} = 30.4 \text{ V}$

Voltage is the same in parallel, thus 30.4 V goes across the 6 Ω and 2 Ω resistors:

$I = V / R$

$I = (30.4 \text{ V}) / (2 \text{ Ω})$

$I = 15.2 \text{ A}$

36. D is correct.

Solve for spring constant k:

$PE = \frac{1}{2}kx^2$

$k = 2(PE) / x^2$

where x is the amplitude (maximum distance traveled from rest).

$k = 2(10 \text{ J}) / (0.2 \text{ m})^2$

$k = 500 \text{ N/m}$

Solve for the period

$T = 2\pi[\sqrt{(m / k)}]$

$T = 2\pi[\sqrt{(0.4 \text{ kg} / 500 \text{ N/m})}]$

$T = 0.18 \text{ s}$

Convert the period to frequency:

$f = 1 / T$

$f = 1 / (0.18 \text{ s})$

$f = 5.6 \text{ Hz}$

37. D is correct.

$v_f^2 = v_0^2 + 2ad$

where $v_0 = 0$

$v_f^2 = 0 + 2ad$

$v_f^2 = 2ad$

Since a is constant, d is proportional to v_f^2

If v_f increases by a factor of 4, then d increases by a factor of $4^2 = 16$.

38. B is correct.

The period of a satellite is found through Kepler's Third Law:

$$T = 2\pi\sqrt{(r^3 / GM)}$$

where T = period, r = distance from Earth's center, G = gravitational constant and M = mass of Earth

The period does not depend on the mass of the satellite so the period remains the same.

39. D is correct.

Find the perimeter (i.e. circumference) of the carousel: distance traveled in one revolution.

$$\text{Perimeter} = \pi \times d$$

$$\text{Perimeter} = \pi \times 18 \text{ m}$$

$$\text{Perimeter} = 56.5 \text{ m}$$

Convert to rev/min, to rev/s:

$$v = (5 \text{ rev/min}) \cdot (1 \text{ min/60 s})$$

$$v = 0.083 \text{ rev/s}$$

Convert rev/s to m/s:

where 1 rev = 56.5 m

$$v = (0.083 \text{ rev/s}) \cdot (56.5 \text{ m/1 rev})$$

$$v = 4.7 \text{ m/s}$$

40. B is correct. The arrows experience the same stopping force when they impart the hay bales.

The kinetic energy can be related to the work done by the force:

Arrow 1: $\quad KE_1 = W$

$$KE_1 = Fd_1$$

$$d_1 = KE_1 / F$$

Arrow 2: $\quad KE_2 = 2KE_1$

$$2KE_1 = W$$

$$2KE_1 = Fd_2$$

$$d_2 = 2KE_1 / F$$

$$d_2 = 2d_1$$

41. A is correct. In a longitudinal wave, the particle displacement is parallel to the direction of the wave, resulting in a distribution of compressions and rarefactions.

Rarefaction is the decrease in an item's density and it is the opposite of compression. Like compression, which can travel in waves (e.g. sound waves), rarefaction waves also exist in nature. A common example of rarefaction is the area of low relative pressure following a shock wave.

Compression is the increase in an items density.

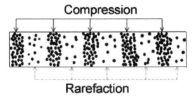

Compression

Rarefaction

42. D is correct.

Decibels use a logarithmic scale.

$$\text{Intensity (dB)} = 10\log_{10} [I / I_0]$$

Where I_0 is the intensity at the threshold of hearing (10^{-12} W/m^2)

$$I = 10\log_{10} [10^{-7} \text{ W/m}^2 / 10^{-12} \text{ W/m}^2]$$

$$I = 10\log_{10} [10^5]$$

$$I = 50 \text{ dB}$$

43. C is correct.

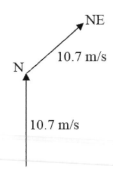

NE

10.7 m/s

N

10.7 m/s

Find the horizontal component of the NE drift:

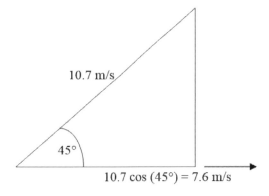

10.7 m/s

45°

10.7 cos (45°) = 7.6 m/s

Find the horizontal component of the NW acceleration:

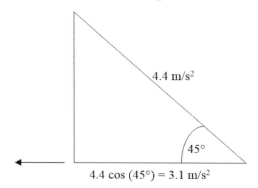

4.4 cos (45°) = 3.1 m/s²

The drift is fully corrected when there is 0 horizontal velocity.

$v_f = v_i + a_x t$

$0 = (7.6 \text{ m/s}) + (3.1 \text{ m/s}^2)(t)$

$t = (7.6 \text{ m/s}) / (3.1 \text{ m/s}^2)$

$t = 2.4 \text{ s}$

44. C is correct. Forces in each axis must be equal.

$F_N = mg \cos \theta$

$F_f = \mu_f F_N$

$F_f = \mu_k mg \cos \theta$

Forces along the incline:

$ma = mg \sin \theta - F_f$

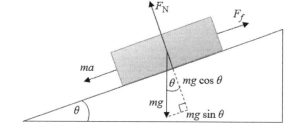

Using the expression for F_N:

$ma = mg \sin \theta - \mu_f mg \cos \theta$, cancel m from both sides of the expression

$a = g \sin \theta - \mu_f g \cos \theta$

$a = [(9.8 \text{ m/s}^2) \sin 40°] - [(0.19)\cdot(9.8 \text{ m/s}^2) \cos 40°]$

$a = (6.3 \text{ m/s}^2) - (1.4 \text{ m/s}^2)$

$a = 4.9 \text{ m/s}^2$

45. B is correct.

Proportionality: find the change in height that doubles the speed of impact

PE = KE

$mgh = mv^2$, cancel m from both sides of the expression

$gh = v^2$

h is proportional to v^2

To double v, h increases by $2^2 = 4$.

46. A is correct.

Power = work / time

Power = (force × distance) / time

Newton's First Law; no force is required to keep the object moving with constant velocity.

The projectile maintains horizontal v since no forces are acting on the horizontal axis.

The vertical forces must also be balanced since it maintains its elevation (only moving horizontally).

Since there is no net force, no work is done, and therefore no power is required.

47. A is correct. The period of a pendulum:

$T = 2\pi\sqrt{(L / g)}$

where L is the length of the pendulum and g is acceleration due to gravity.

Use $g / 6$ for g.

$T = 2\pi\sqrt{(L / (g / 6))}$

$T = 2\pi\sqrt{(6L / g)}$

$T = 2\pi\sqrt{(L / g)} \times \sqrt{6}$

New period $= T\sqrt{6}$

48. D is correct. Electromagnetic waves propagate at the speed of light oscillations of electric and magnetic fields that propagate at the speed of light.

The oscillations of the two fields form a transverse wave perpendicular to each other and perpendicular to the direction of energy and wave propagation.

49. C is correct. Resistance in series experience equal current because there is only one path for the current to travel.

50. C is correct.

$\Delta v = at$

$a = \Delta v / t$

$a = (v_f - v_i) / t$

$(v_f - v_i) = at$

$v_f = at + v_i$

$v_f = (2 \text{ m/s}^2) \cdot (6 \text{ s}) + (5 \text{ m/s})$

$v_f = 17 \text{ m/s}$

DIAGNOSTIC TEST #3 – EXPLANATIONS

1. C is correct.

The slope of a tangent line of a position vs. time graph at a specific time value is the instantaneous velocity. This is equivalent to taking the derivative of the graph at this same time value.

2. A is correct.

An object in motion with constant nonzero velocity experiences no acceleration and thus cannot have any net force upon it.

If v = constant, then:

$a = 0$

$F = ma$

$F = m(0 \text{ m/s}^2)$

$F = 0 \text{ N}$

3. C is correct.

First calculate the stone's speed at impact:

$v^2 = v_0^2 + 2ad$

where $v_0 = 0$ and $a = g$

$v^2 = 2ad$

$v^2 = 2(10 \text{ m/s}^2) \cdot (5 \text{ m})$

$v^2 = 100 \text{ m}^2/\text{s}^2$

$v = 10 \text{ m/s}$

Use the speed of impact to calculate momentum p:

$p = mv$

$p = (3 \text{ kg}) \cdot (10 \text{ m/s})$

$p = 30 \text{ kg} \cdot \text{m/s}$

Another method to solve this problem:

$PE = KE$

$mgh = \frac{1}{2}mv^2$, cancel m from both sides of the expression

$gh = \frac{1}{2}v^2$

$2(gh) = v^2$

$v^2 = 2(10 \text{ m/s}^2 \times 5 \text{ m})$

$v^2 = 100 \text{ m}^2/\text{s}^2$

$v = 10$ m/s

$p = mv$

$p = (3$ kg$)\cdot(10$ m/s$)$

$p = 30$ kg·m/s

4. A is correct.

The spring already has the 0.9 kg mass attached to it so its original equilibrium length is the length needed to counteract the force of gravity.

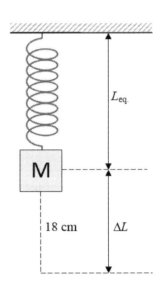

If the spring is stretched further then the net force only includes the component from the spring force:

$F_{spring} = k\Delta x$

$F_{spring} = (3$ N/m$)\cdot(0.18$ m$)$

$F_{spring} = 0.54$ N

5. B is correct.

Convert weight to mass:

$F = ma$

$m = F / a$

$m = 30$ N $/ (9.8$ m/s$^2)$

$m = 3.06$ kg

Frequency of a spring system:

$f = \sqrt{(k / m)}$

$f = \sqrt{(40 \text{ N/m} / 3.06 \text{ kg})}$

$f = 3.6$ rad/s

$f = (3.6$ rad/s$) / (2\pi)$ Hz

$f = 0.57$ Hz

6. C is correct.

$f_{beat} = |f_2 - f_1|$

$f_{beat} = | 786.3 \text{ Hz} - 785.8 \text{ Hz} |$

$f_{beat} = 0.5$ Hz

7. B is correct.

$P = VI$

$V = IR$, substituting into the equation

$P = (IR) \times I$

$P = I^2 \times R$

If P is on y-axis and R is on x-axis,

slope $= P / R$

slope $= I^2$

8. A is correct.

Power = current × voltage

$P = IV$

Power is measured in watts (W), current in amps (A) and voltage in volts (V).

W = A × V

9. B is correct.

The maximum and minimum of position vs. time is always equal to zero velocity.

10. C is correct.

This is due to the nature of objects to resist changes in motion (inertia). An object at rest remains at rest while an object in motion remains in motion (unless acted upon).

The coefficient of static friction (object at rest) is larger than the coefficient of kinetic friction (object in motion).

11. A is correct.

Conservation of momentum:

$m_1 v_1 = m_2 v_2$

$m_1 =$ putty

$m_2 =$ putty + bowling ball

$m_2 = (1 \text{ kg} + 7 \text{ kg})$

$m_2 = 8 \text{ kg}$

$v_2 = (m_1 v_1) / m_2$

$v_2 = (1 \text{ kg}) \cdot (1 \text{ m/s}) / 8 \text{ kg}$

$v_2 = 1/8 \text{ m/s}$

12. D is correct.

Find kinetic energy and set equal to the work done by friction:

$$KE = W_f$$

$$\tfrac{1}{2}mv^2 = F_f \times d$$

$$\tfrac{1}{2}m \,/\, F_f = d \,/\, v^2$$

Because the mass is constant, d / v^2 = constant regardless of velocity.

Solve for the new skid distance:

$$d_1 \,/\, v_1^2 = d_2 \,/\, v_2^2$$

$$d_2 = (d_1){\cdot}(v_2^2) \,/\, (v_1^2)$$

$$d_2 = (30 \text{ m}){\cdot}(150 \text{ km/h})^2 \,/\, (45 \text{ km/h})^2$$

$$d_2 = 333 \text{ m}$$

13. A is correct.

The time it takes to complete on cycle is the period T.

$$T = 1 \,/\, f$$

Period is measured in seconds.

$$\text{Frequency} = s^{-1} \text{ or Hz}$$

14. B is correct.

$$\text{One mosquito} = 1.5 \times 10^{-11} \text{ W}$$

To power a 30 W bulb:

$$(30 \text{ W}) \,/\, (1.5 \times 10^{-11} \text{ W}) = 2 \times 10^{12} \text{ mosquitoes}$$

15. B is correct.

When an object is accelerating its velocity must change in either speed or direction. The speed or direction do not always change but velocity does.

16. D is correct.

$$F_f = \mu_k F_N$$

$$F_f = \mu_k mg \cos \theta$$

Find the length of travel:

$$L = 50 \text{ m} \,/\, \sin 10°$$

$$L = 50 \text{ m} \,/\, 0.174$$

$$L = 288 \text{ m}$$

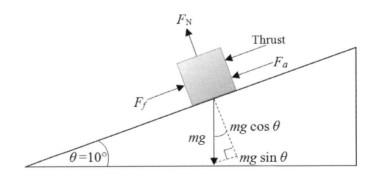

Find acceleration to reach 40 m/s:

$$v_f^2 = v_i^2 + 2ad$$

$$(40 \text{ m/s})^2 = 0 + 2a(288 \text{ m})$$

$$1{,}600 \text{ m}^2/\text{s}^2 = a(576 \text{ m})$$

$$a = (1{,}600 \text{ m}^2/\text{s}^2) / (576 \text{ m})$$

$$a = 2.8 \text{ m/s}^2$$

Find normal (F_N) and gravitational (F_G) forces:

$$F_N = mg \cos \theta$$

$$F_N = (50 \text{ kg}) \cdot (9.8 \text{ m/s}^2) \cos 10°$$

$$F_N = (50 \text{ kg}) \cdot (9.8 \text{ m/s}^2) \cdot (0.985)$$

$$F_N = 483 \text{ N}$$

$$F_G = mg \sin \theta$$

$$F_G = (50 \text{ kg}) \cdot (9.8 \text{ m/s}^2) \sin 10°$$

$$F_G = (50 \text{ kg}) \cdot (9.8 \text{ m/s}^2) \cdot (0.174)$$

$$F_G = 85 \text{ N}$$

$$F_{total} = (260 \text{ N} + 85 \text{ N})$$

$$F_{total} = 345 \text{ N, total force experienced by the skier}$$

The skier experiences acceleration down the slope that was reduced by friction.

The coefficient of kinetic friction can be calculated by:

$$F_{total} - F_{friction} = F_{experienced}$$

$$F_{total} - \mu F_N = F_{experienced}$$

$$345 \text{ N} - \mu_k 483 \text{ N} = (2.8 \text{ m/s}^2 \times 50 \text{ kg})$$

$$345 \text{ N} - \mu_k 483 \text{ N} = 140 \text{ N}$$

$$345 \text{ N} - 140 \text{ N} = \mu_K 483 \text{ N}$$

$$205 \text{ N} = \mu_k 483 \text{ N}$$

$$205 \text{ N} / 483 \text{ N} = \mu_k$$

$$\mu_k = 0.42$$

17. B is correct.

Determine distance in one revolution (the perimeter or circumference):

$$P = \pi d$$

$$P = \pi(18 \text{ m})$$

$$P = 56.55 \text{ m}$$

Convert rev/min to rev/s:

$v = (5.3 \text{ rev/min})\cdot(1 \text{ min/60 s})$

$v = 0.0883 \text{ rev/s}$

Convert rev/s to m/s, where 1 rev = 56.55 m

$v = (0.0883 \text{ rev/s})\cdot(56.55 \text{ m/1 rev})$

$v = 5 \text{ m/s}$

18. B is correct. Upward force due to the spring (Hooke's law):

$F = k\Delta x$

where k is the spring constant and Δx is the distance the spring is stretched

The downward force due to gravity:

$F = mg$

System is in equilibrium so set the expressions equal to each other:

$k\Delta x = mg$

$\Delta x = mg \,/\, k$

$\Delta x = (4 \text{ kg})\cdot(10 \text{ m/s}^2) \,/\, (10 \text{ N/m})$

$\Delta x = 4 \text{ m}$

19. B is correct. The overtone or harmonic can be found by the following:

harmonic	overtone
n^{th} harmonic	$(n^{th} - 1)$ overtone

Thus the third harmonic has the

$(3 - 1) = 2^{nd}$ overtone

20. B is correct.

The two ends count as nodes. From a standing wave with four nodes, there are three antinodes.

Therefore, there are three half-wavelengths.

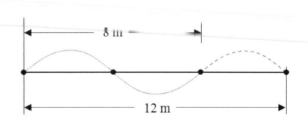

Each dot on the curve represents one of the four nodes.

One complete wave (the solid line) includes three nodes.

1 wave = ¾ entire string

1 wave = ¾(12 m) = 8 m

21. B is correct.

The equivalent resistance of resistors in parallel:

$$R_{eq} = 1 / (1 / R_1 + 1 / R_2 + 1 / R_3 \ldots)$$

The equivalent resistance is always smaller than the smallest resistance:

For example:

$R_1 = 20\ \Omega$, $R_2 = 30\ \Omega$, $R_3 = 30\ \Omega$

$$R_{eq} = 1 / (1 / 20\ \Omega + 1 / 30\ \Omega + 1 / 30\ \Omega \ldots)$$

$$R_{eq} = 8.75\ \Omega$$

$$R_{eq} < R_1$$

22. D is correct.

Coulomb's Law, which describes repulsive force between two particles, is given as:

$$F = k q_1 q_2 / r^2$$

The expression does not include mass, so the repulsive force remains the same when m changes.

Note: gravitational (attractive) forces do rely on the masses of the objects.

23. A is correct.

If acceleration is constant then acceleration is always increasing or decreasing and results in a sloped line (not a straight line).

24. C is correct.

$$F_{net} = ma$$

The only acceleration is centripetal:

$$a_{cent} = v^2 / r$$

$$a_{cent} = (4\ m/s)^2 / 16\ m$$

$$a_{cent} = (16\ m^2/s^2) / 16\ m$$

$$a_{cent} = 1\ m/s^2$$

$$F_{net} = ma$$

$$F_{net} = (40\ kg) \cdot (1\ m/s^2)$$

$$F_{net} = 40\ kg \cdot m/s^2 = 40\ N$$

25. C is correct. If the cylinder's center of mass does not move it must be stationary and the forces must balance:

$$F = mg \sin \theta$$

Force produced by torque is:

$$\tau = I\alpha$$

where I is mass moment of inertia and α is angular acceleration.

I for a solid cylinder is:

$$I = (mr^2) / 2$$

$$\tau = I\alpha$$

$$\tau = Fr$$

$$I\alpha = Fr$$

$$(\tfrac{1}{2}mr^2)\alpha = (mg \sin \theta)r$$

$$\alpha = (2g \sin \theta) / r$$

$$\alpha = (2) \cdot (10 \text{ m/s}^2) \sin 30° / (0.8 \text{ m})$$

$$\alpha = (2) \cdot (10 \text{ m/s}^2) \cdot (0.5) / (0.8 \text{ m})$$

$$\alpha = 12.5 \text{ rad/s}^2$$

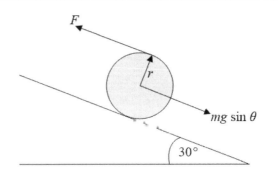

26. A is correct.

Convert PE (before release) into KE (as it is about to strike the ground):

$$mgh = KE$$

KE is proportional to h.

27. D is correct.

A phase change occurs when waves reflect from the surface of a medium with a higher refractive index than the medium they are traveling in. Glass has a higher refractive index than air and therefore, when the light ray moves from glass to air, no change occurs.

28. C is correct.

$$f_{beat} = |f_2 - f_1|$$

$$\pm f_{beat} = f_2 - f_1$$

$$f_2 = \pm f_{beat} + f_1$$

$$f_2 = \pm 5 \text{ Hz} + 822 \text{ Hz}$$

$$f_2 = 817 \text{ Hz}, 827 \text{ Hz}$$

Only 827 Hz is an answer choice.

29. B is correct.

Distance traveled is represented by the area under the velocity vs. time curve.

At the point where each of those curves intersect on this plot, there is more area under the curve of the truck velocity than there is under the curve of the car velocity.

30. A is correct.

Since the velocity is constant, the acceleration is $a = 0$.

$$F_{net} = ma$$

$$F_{net} = 0$$

31. D is correct.

$$\tau = 120 \text{ N·m}$$

$$\tau = I\alpha$$

Mass moment of inertia: mass moment of inertia of disk about z-axis

$$I = \frac{1}{2}mr^2$$

$$\tau = [\frac{1}{2}mr^2]\alpha$$

$$120 \text{ N} = \frac{1}{2}(12 \text{ kg})\cdot(4 \text{ m})^2\, \alpha$$

$$\alpha = (120 \text{ N}) / [\frac{1}{2}(12 \text{ kg})\cdot(4 \text{ m})^2]$$

$$\alpha = 1.25 \text{ rad/s}^2$$

$$\omega = \alpha t$$

$$7.35 \text{ rad/s} = (1.25 \text{ rad/s}^2)t$$

$$t = (7.35 \text{ rad/s}) / (1.25 \text{ rad/s}^2)$$

$$t = 5.9 \text{ s}$$

32. A is correct.

Include the term for work done by air resistance in the conservation of energy equation.

$$KE_i + PE_i + W_{air\ resis} = KE_f + PE_f$$

$$0 + mgh + (-F_{air} \times d) = \frac{1}{2}mv_f^2 + 0$$

$$mgh + (-mad) = \frac{1}{2}mv_f^2$$

$$(1.2 \text{ kg})\cdot(10 \text{ m/s}^2)\cdot(6 \text{ m}) + (-3.4 \text{ kg·m/s}^2)\cdot(6 \text{ m}) = \frac{1}{2}(1.2 \text{ kg})v_f^2$$

$$v_f^2 = 86 \text{ m}^2/\text{s}^2$$

$$v_f = 9.2 \text{ m/s}$$

33. C is correct.

Frequency = # cycles / time

f = 2 cycles / 1 s

$f = 2\ s^{-1}$

$v = \lambda f$

where λ is wavelength

$v = (12\ m) \cdot (2\ s^{-1})$

$v = (12\ m) / (2\ s)$

$v = 6\ m/s$

34. D is correct.

Sound intensity is expressed as power / area:

$I = W/m^2$

$I = J/m^2 t$

This is equivalent to energy through unit area per unit time.

$E = A / t$

35. A is correct.

$P = I^2 R$

$P = (4I)^2 R$

$P = (16)I^2 R$

Power increased by a factor of 16

36. A is correct.

Unit of watt = work / time

Multiply by time, time cancels and work is left.

Alternatively, 1 kilowatt-hour:

1 watt = 1 J/s

1 watt·second = 1 J

$(1\ hr/60\ s) \cdot (60\ min/1\ hr) \cdot (60\ s/1min) = 60^2\ s$

1×10^3 Watt $\times$ (1 hour)·$(60^2\ s/1\ hour) = 36 \times 10^5$ J

Work = force × distance

Joule is a unit of work.

37. D is correct. When an object is thrown into the air, the acceleration vector is always equal to gravity (for objects in free fall). The velocity vector changes direction when the object starts to come down.

38. A is correct. As shown in the diagram, mg (i.e. the force of the mass due to gravity) is broken down into two components.

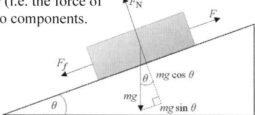

The $mg \sin \theta$ component is parallel to the slope of the road.

39. C is correct.

If the object's velocity is constant, then the net force is zero.

In the y direction:

$$0 = F_N + F_g$$

In the x direction:

$$0 = F_{\text{friction}} + F$$

$$F_N + F_g = F_{\text{friction}} + F$$

$$-F = F_{\text{friction}}$$

Since kinetic friction is exerting a force opposing the object's motion, there must be an equal and opposing force propelling it forward for net force to be zero.

40. C is correct.

$$P = W / t$$

$$W = Fd$$

$$P = (Fd) / t$$

$$F = mg$$

$$P = (mgd \sin \theta) / t$$

$$P = [(54 \text{ kg}) \cdot (9.8 \text{ m/s}^2) \cdot (10 \text{ m}) \sin 30°] / (4 \text{ s})$$

$$P = [(54 \text{ kg}) \cdot (9.8 \text{ m/s}^2) \cdot (10 \text{ m}) \cdot (0.5)] / (4 \text{ s})$$

$$P = 2{,}646 \text{ J} / (4 \text{ s})$$

$$P = 661 \text{ J/s}$$

$$P = 661 \text{ W}$$

Convert watts into horsepower:

$$1 \text{ hp} = 745 \text{ W}$$

$$P = (661 \text{ W}) \cdot (1 \text{ hp} / 745 \text{ W})$$

$$P = 0.89 \text{ hp}$$

41. A is correct.

The amplitude of a wave is a measure of the energy of the wave. Thus if energy is dissipated the amplitude is reduced.

42. B is correct.

To determine the frequency of the fundamental:

$f_n = nf_1$

where f_1 = fundamental

$f_1 = f_3 / 3$

$f_1 = 783 \text{ Hz} / 3$

$f_1 = 261 \text{ Hz}$

43. D is correct.

44. D is correct.

The force of gravity depends only on the *m* and the distance between their centers.

$F_{grav} = GM_1M_2 / d^2$

If one *m* decreases by a factor of 2, then F_{grav} decreases by a factor of 2.

45. B is correct. In projectile motion, the acceleration due to gravity always acts in the vertical component. Thus acceleration due to gravity remains a nonzero constant.

46. B is correct. According to the principle of conservation of mechanical energy: total mechanical energy in a system remains constant as long as the only forces acting are conservative forces.

47. D is correct.

This is a thin film interference problem. When light strikes the surface of the oil some will be transmitted and some light will be reflected off the surface. This process is repeated when the light reaches the oil-water interface.

However, the light reflected from the oil-water interface may combine with the light originally reflected off the oil from before in either constructive or destructive interference.

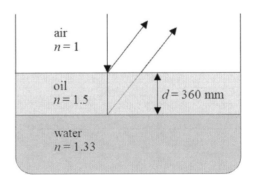

The light which is strongly reflected is formed through constructive interference, the rays that destructively interfere with the originally reflected light cannot be seen.

Use the thin film constructive interference equation:

$$2n_{oil}d = (m + \tfrac{1}{2})\lambda \qquad (m = 0, 1, 2...)$$

where m is the order of the reflected light.

$$\lambda = (2n_{oil}d) / (m + \tfrac{1}{2})$$

Solve for range: 400 nm $\leq \lambda \leq$ 800 nm

Use m = 0

$$\lambda_0 = (2)\cdot(1.5)\cdot(340 \times 10^{-9} \text{ m}) / (0 + \tfrac{1}{2}),$$

$$\lambda_0 = 1{,}020 \times 10^{-9} \text{ m} = 1{,}020 \text{ nm}$$

λ_0 is out of range

Use m = 1

$$\lambda_1 = (2)\cdot(1.5)\cdot(330 \times 10^{-9} \text{ m}) / (1 + \tfrac{1}{2})$$

$$\lambda_1 = 680 \times 10^{-9} \text{ m} = 680 \text{ nm}$$

λ_1 is in range

Use m = 2

$$\lambda_2 = (2)\cdot(1.5)\cdot(330 \times 10^{-9} \text{ m}) / (2 + \tfrac{1}{2})$$

$$\lambda_2 = 408 \times 10^{-9} \text{ m} = 408 \text{ nm}$$

λ_2 is in range

If m is a value greater than 2, it produces wavelength outside the 400 nm to 800 nm range.

Thus the two most strongly reflected wavelengths are:

$$\lambda_1 = 680 \text{ nm}$$

$$\lambda_2 = 408 \text{ nm}$$

48. B is correct.

The harmonic wavelength λ_n occurs when:

$$\lambda_n = (2L) / n$$

where L is the length of the string and n is the harmonic (n = 1, 2, 3…).

The fourth harmonic wavelength occurs at n = 4.

$$\lambda_4 = (2L) / 4$$

$$\lambda_4 = (2 \times 1 \text{ m}) / 4$$

$$\lambda_4 = 0.5 \text{ m}$$

49. A is correct.

$$F_{net} = ma$$

The suitcase is moving in a straight line, at a constant speed, so the suitcase's velocity is constant. Therefore,

$$a = 0$$

$$F_{net} = 0$$

50. D is correct.

Electric field at a distance:

$$E = kQ / d^2$$

Solve for $Q_1 = 18$ μC, where d is half the distance:

$$E_1 = (9 \times 10^9 \text{ N·m}^2\text{·C}^{-2})\cdot(18 \times 10^{-6} \text{ C}) / (0.15 \text{ m})^2$$

$$E_1 = 7.2 \times 10^6 \text{ N/C}$$

Solve for Q_2:

$$E_2 = (9 \times 10^9 \text{ N·m}^2\text{·C}^{-2})\cdot(-6 \times 10^{-6} \text{ C}) / (0.15 \text{ m})^2$$

$$E_2 = -2.4 \times 10^6 \text{ N/C}$$

Note that the negative sign indicates that the electric field goes into the charge, because the charge is negative.

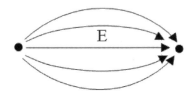

Because the electric fields generated by both charges point in the same direction, sum E_1 and E_2 to find the strength halfway between the charges:

$$E_{total} = E_1 + E_2$$

$$E_{total} = (7.2 \times 10^6 \text{ N/C}) + (2.4 \times 10^6 \text{ N/C})$$

$$E_{total} = 9.6 \times 10^6 \text{ N/C} \text{ towards the negative charge.}$$

TOPICAL
PRACTICE QUESTIONS
ANSWER KEYS &
EXPLANATIONS

Kinematics and Dynamics

1: D	11: C	21: D	31: B	41: C	51: A	61: A	71: C
2: B	12: B	22: A	32: C	42: A	52: A	62: B	72: B
3: B	13: A	23: B	33: D	43: D	53: B	63: D	73: D
4: A	14: C	24: D	34: A	44: B	54: D	64: A	74: A
5: C	15: B	25: B	35: C	45: A	55: A	65: C	75: D
6: B	16: D	26: A	36: D	46: D	56: A	66: B	76: C
7: D	17: A	27: C	37: D	47: B	57: C	67: C	77: D
8: B	18: B	28: D	38: B	48: C	58: C	68: A	
9: A	19: D	29: B	39: C	49: D	59: B	69: D	
10: B	20: C	30: C	40: A	50: C	60: D	70: D	

Force, Motion, Gravitation

1: B	11: A	21: B	31: C	41: A	51: C	61: D	71: C
2: D	12: D	22: A	32: D	42: C	52: B	62: B	72: B
3: A	13: B	23: C	33: D	43: B	53: D	63: D	73: A
4: C	14: C	24: D	34: A	44: C	54: D	64: B	74: B
5: D	15: D	25: D	35: D	45: A	55: B	65: A	75: C
6: D	16: A	26: A	36: A	46: C	56: D	66: C	76: D
7: A	17: D	27: D	37: D	47: D	57: B	67: B	77: D
8: D	18: C	28: D	38: B	48: D	58: D	68: D	78: D
9: A	19: D	29: A	39: B	49: C	59: C	69: A	79: B
10: C	20: B	30: D	40: C	50: A	60: B	70: B	

Equilibrium and Momentum

1: A	13: D	25: D	37: B	49: D	61: C	73: D	85: C
2: D	14: D	26: A	38: C	50: C	62: D	74: B	86: A
3: D	15: D	27: D	39: D	51: D	63: D	75: A	
4: C	16: D	28: C	40: A	52: D	64: C	76: D	
5: D	17: B	29: A	41: B	53: A	65: B	77: A	
6: B	18: D	30: B	42: A	54: D	66: D	78: D	
7: D	19: B	31: C	43: C	55: B	67: A	79: B	
8: A	20: C	32: D	44: B	56: C	68: D	80: D	
9: B	21: D	33: C	45: D	57: D	69: D	81: B	
10: C	22: B	34: B	46: C	58: A	70: D	82: C	
11: D	23: A	35: D	47: B	59: D	71: C	83: D	
12: C	24: D	36: C	48: A	60: B	72: A	84: A	

Work and Energy

1: D	11: D	21: B	31: B	41: A	51: D	61: B	71: D
2: B	12: B	22: D	32: C	42: A	52: C	62: D	72: A
3: A	13: A	23: B	33: D	43: C	53: C	63: A	73: C
4: B	14: C	24: C	34: A	44: B	54: B	64: B	74: C
5: C	15: D	25: D	35: B	45: D	55: C	65: A	75: D
6: A	16: D	26: A	36: B	46: D	56: D	66: D	
7: D	17: A	27: D	37: C	47: A	57: C	67: A	
8: C	18: A	28: C	38: D	48: A	58: C	68: C	
9: A	19: D	29: B	39: A	49: C	59: A	69: D	
10: B	20: A	30: C	40: B	50: B	60: D	70: B	

Waves and Periodic Motion

1: B	11: D	21: B	31: B	41: A	51: A	61: D
2: D	12: A	22: C	32: D	42: C	52: C	62: A
3: B	13: B	23: B	33: A	43: B	53: B	63: B
4: C	14: C	24: A	34: D	44: D	54: C	64: D
5: A	15: A	25: D	35: C	45: A	55: D	65: C
6: D	16: B	26: C	36: D	46: B	56: A	66: D
7: C	17: C	27: D	37: B	47: A	57: B	67: B
8: D	18: B	28: B	38: C	48: C	58: D	68: D
9: A	19: A	29: C	39: D	49: D	59: C	
10: B	20: D	30: A	40: C	50: A	60: A	

Sound

1: B	11: B	21: C	31: C	41: A	51: D	61: D	71: D
2: A	12: A	22: D	32: D	42: C	52: B	62: A	72: C
3: B	13: B	23: B	33: A	43: D	53: D	63: D	73: B
4: C	14: C	24: C	34: D	44: A	54: C	64: D	74: D
5: B	15: D	25: A	35: A	45: B	55: D	65: D	75: A
6: A	16: A	26: D	36: A	46: D	56: C	66: B	76: B
7: D	17: C	27: B	37: B	47: C	57: A	67: A	77: D
8: A	18: B	28: A	38: D	48: A	58: C	68: D	
9: C	19: A	29: B	39: B	49: C	59: D	69: B	
10: D	20: B	30: A	40: C	50: B	60: C	70: A	

DC Circuits

1: B	11: A	21: D
2: D	12: D	22: A
3: C	13: D	23: C
4: C	14: C	24: A
5: A	15: D	25: D
6: D	16: B	26: D
7: C	17: B	27: D
8: A	18: D	28: A
9: C	19: A	29: B
10: D	20: A	30: D

Electrostatics

1: C	11: C	21: B	31: C
2: C	12: A	22: C	32: D
3: D	13: D	23: C	33: D
4: B	14: D	24: A	34: D
5: D	15: C	25: D	35: B
6: C	16: D	26: D	36: A
7: D	17: C	27: D	37: B
8: A	18: B	28: B	
9: B	19: C	29: D	
10: D	20: A	30: D	

KINEMATICS AND DYNAMICS – EXPLANATIONS

1. D is correct.

$$t = (v_f - v_i) \, / \, a$$

$$t = (60 \text{ mi/h} - 0 \text{ mi/h}) \, / \, (13.1 \text{ mi/h·s})$$

$$t = 4.6 \text{ s}$$

Acceleration is in mi/h·s, so miles and hours cancel and the answer is in units of seconds.

2. B is correct. At the top of the parabolic trajectory, the vertical velocity $v_{yf} = 0$

The initial upward velocity is the vertical component of the initial velocity:

$$v_{yi} = v \sin \theta$$

$$v_{yi} = (20 \text{ m/s}) \sin 30°$$

$$v_{yi} = (20 \text{ m/s}) \cdot (0.5)$$

$$v_{yi} = 10 \text{ m/s}$$

$$t = (v_{yf} - v_{yi}) \, / \, a$$

$$t = (0 - 10 \text{ m/s}) \, / \, (-10 \text{ m/s}^2)$$

$$t = (-10 \text{ m/s}) \, / \, (-10 \text{ m/s}^2)$$

$$t = 1 \text{ s}$$

3. B is correct.

$$\Delta d = 31.5 \text{ km} = 31,500 \text{ m}$$

$$1.25 \text{ hr} \times 60 \text{ min/hr} = 75 \text{ min}$$

$$\Delta t = 75 \text{ min} \times 60 \text{ s/min} = 4,500 \text{ s}$$

$$v_{avg} = \Delta d \, / \, \Delta t$$

$$v_{avg} = 31,500 \text{ m} \, / \, 4,500 \text{ s}$$

$$v_{avg} = 7 \text{ m/s}$$

4. A is correct. Instantaneous speed is the scalar magnitude of velocity. It can only be positive or zero (because magnitudes cannot be negative).

5. C is correct.

$$d = (v_i^2 + v_f^2) \, / \, 2a$$

$$d = [(5 \text{ m/s})^2 + (21 \text{ m/s})^2] \, / \, 2(3 \text{ m/s}^2)$$

$$d = (25 \text{ m}^2/\text{s}^2 + 441 \text{ m}^2/\text{s}^2) \, / \, 6 \text{ m/s}^2$$

$$d = (466 \text{ m}^2/\text{s}^2) / 6 \text{ m/s}^2$$
$$d = 69 \text{ m}$$

6. D is correct.

$$a = (v_f - v_i) / t$$
$$a = [0 - (-30 \text{ m/s})] / 0.15 \text{ s}$$
$$a = (30 \text{ m/s}) / 0.15 \text{ s}$$
$$a = 200 \text{ m/s}^2$$

To represent the acceleration in terms of g, divide a by 9.8 m/s^2:

$$\# \text{ of } g = (200 \text{ m/s}^2) / 9.8 \text{ m/s}^2$$
$$\# \text{ of } g = 20 \text{ } g$$

The initial velocity (v_i) is negative due to the acceleration of the car being a positive value. Since the car is decelerating, its acceleration is opposite of its initial velocity.

7. D is correct.

When a bullet is fired it is in projectile motion. The only force in projectile motion (if air resistance is ignored) is the force of gravity.

8. B is correct.

When a car is slowing down, it is decelerating, which is equivalent to acceleration in the opposite direction.

9. A is correct

Uniform acceleration:

$$a = \text{change in velocity / change in time}$$
$$a = \Delta v / \Delta t$$
$$\Delta v = a \Delta t$$
$$\Delta v = (20 \text{ m/s}^2) \cdot (1 \text{ s})$$
$$\Delta v = 20 \text{ m/s}$$

10. B is correct.

Uniform acceleration:

$$a = \text{change in velocity / change in time}$$
$$a = \Delta v / \Delta t$$

$a = (40 \text{ m/s} - 15 \text{ m/s}) / 10 \text{ s}$

$a = (25 \text{ m/s}) / 10 \text{ s}$

$a = 2.5 \text{ m/s}^2$

11. C is correct.

$t = d / v$

$t = (540 \text{ mi}) / (65 \text{ mi/h})$

$t = 8.3 \text{ h}$

The time she can stop is the difference between her total allowed time and the time t that it takes to make the trip:

$t_{\text{stop}} = 9.8 \text{ h} - 8.3 \text{ h}$

$t_{\text{stop}} = 1.5 \text{ h}$

12. B is correct.

Velocity is the change in position with respect to time:

$v = \Delta x / \Delta t$

After one lap, the racecar's final position is the same as its initial position.

Thus $x = 0$, which implies the average velocity of 0 m/s.

13. A is correct.

$d = v_i \Delta t + \frac{1}{2} a \Delta t^2$

$d = (0.2 \text{ m/s}) \cdot (6 \text{ s}) + \frac{1}{2}(-0.05 \text{ m/s}^2) \cdot (5 \text{ s})^2$

$d = 1.2 \text{ m} + \frac{1}{2}(-0.05 \text{ m/s}^2) \cdot (25 \text{ s}^2)$

$d = 1.2 \text{ m} + (-0.625 \text{ m})$

$d = 0.58 \text{ m} \approx 0.6 \text{ m}$

Decelerating is set to negative.

The net displacement is the difference between the final and initial positions after 5 s.

14. C is correct.

$a = $ change in velocity / change in time

$a = \Delta v / \Delta t$

15. B is correct.

Convert the final speed from km/h to m/s:

$$v_f = (210 \text{ km/h}) \times [(1,000 \text{ m}/1 \text{ km})] \times [(1 \text{ h}/3,600 \text{ s})]$$

$$v_f = 58.3 \text{ m/s}$$

Calculate the acceleration necessary to reach this speed:

$$a = (v_i^2 + v_f^2) / 2d$$

$$a = [0 + (58.3 \text{ m/s})^2] / 2(1,800 \text{ m})$$

$$a = (3,399 \text{ m}^2/\text{s}^2) / (3,600 \text{ m})$$

$$a = 0.94 \text{ m/s}^2$$

16. D is correct.

The distance the rocket travels during its acceleration upward is calculated by:

$$d_1 = \tfrac{1}{2}at^2$$

$$d_1 = \tfrac{1}{2}(22 \text{ m/s}^2) \cdot (4 \text{ s})^2$$

$$d_1 = 176 \text{ m}$$

The distance from when the motor shuts off to when the rocket reaches maximum height can be calculated using the conservation of energy:

$$mgd_2 = \tfrac{1}{2}mv^2, \text{ cancel } m \text{ from both sides of the expression}$$

$$gd_2 = \tfrac{1}{2}v^2$$

where $v = at$

$$gd_2 = \tfrac{1}{2}(at)^2$$

$$d_2 = \tfrac{1}{2}(at)^2 / g$$

$$d_2 = \tfrac{1}{2}[(22 \text{ m/s}^2) \cdot (4 \text{ s})]^2 / (10 \text{ m/s}^2)$$

Magnitudes are not vectors but scalars, so no direction is needed

$$d_2 = 387 \text{ m}$$

For the maximum elevation, add the two distances:

$$h = d_1 + d_2$$

$$h = 176 \text{ m} + 387 \text{ m}$$

$$h = 563 \text{ m}$$

17. A is correct.

Speed is a scalar (i.e. one-dimensional physical property), while velocity is a vector (i.e. has both magnitude and direction).

18. B is correct.

Acceleration due to gravity is constant and independent of mass.

19. D is correct.

As an object falls its acceleration is constant due to gravity. However, the magnitude of the velocity increases due to the acceleration of gravity and the displacement increases because the object is going further away from its starting point.

20. C is correct.

The suitcase is not sitting on a surface, so there is no normal force. Jack is pushing upward, but (since the suitcase is moving at constant speed in a straight line) he is not pushing forward.

21. D is correct.

Horizontal velocity (v_x):

$v_x = d_x / t$

$v_x = (44 \text{ m}) / (2.9 \text{ s})$

$v_x = 15.2 \text{ m/s}$

The x component of a vector is calculated by:

$v_x = v \cos \theta$

Rearrange the equation to determine the initial velocity of the ball:

$v = v_x / \cos \theta$

$v = (15.2 \text{ m/s}) / (\cos 45°)$

$v = (15.2 \text{ m/s}) / 0.7$

$v = 21.4 \text{ m/s}$

22. A is correct.

Conservation of energy:

$mgh = \frac{1}{2}mv_f^2$, cancel m from both sides of the expression

$gh = \frac{1}{2}v_f^2$

$(10 \text{ m/s}^2)h = \frac{1}{2}(14 \text{ m/s})^2$

$(10 \text{ m/s}^2)h = \frac{1}{2}(196 \text{ m}^2/\text{s}^2)$

$h = (98 \text{ m}^2/\text{s}^2) / (10 \text{ m/s}^2)$

$h = 9.8 \text{ m} \approx 10 \text{ m}$

23. B is correct.

$$d = v_i t + \tfrac{1}{2}at^2$$

$$d = (20 \text{ m/s}) \cdot (7 \text{ s}) + \tfrac{1}{2}(1.4 \text{ m/s}^2) \cdot (7 \text{ s})^2$$

$$d = (140 \text{ m}) + \tfrac{1}{2}(1.4 \text{ m/s}^2) \cdot (49 \text{ s}^2)$$

$$d = 177 \text{ m}$$

24. D is correct.

Force is not a scalar because it has a magnitude and direction.

25. B is correct.

$$d = \tfrac{1}{2}at^2$$

$$d_A = \tfrac{1}{2}at^2$$

$$d_B = \tfrac{1}{2}a(2t)^2$$

$$d_B = \tfrac{1}{2}a(4t^2)$$

$$d_B = 4 \times \tfrac{1}{2}at^2$$

$$d_B = 4d_A$$

26. A is correct.

$$d = v_{\text{average}} \times \Delta t$$

$$d = \tfrac{1}{2}(v_i + v_f)\Delta t$$

$$d = \tfrac{1}{2}(5 \text{ m/s} + 30 \text{ m/s}) \cdot (10 \text{ s})$$

$$d = 175 \text{ m}$$

27. C is correct.

If there is no acceleration, then velocity is constant.

28. D is correct.

The gravitational force between two objects in space, each having masses of m_1 and m_2, is:

$$F_G = Gm_1m_2 / r^2$$

where G is the gravitational constant and r is the distance between the two objects.

Doubling the distance between the two objects:

$$F_{G2} = Gm_1m_2 / (2r)^2$$

$$F_{G2} = Gm_1m_2 / (4r^2)$$

$$F_{G2} = \tfrac{1}{4}Gm_1m_2 / r^2$$

$$F_{G2} = \tfrac{1}{4}Gm_1m_2 / r^2$$

$$F_{G2} = \tfrac{1}{4}F_G$$

Therefore, when the distance between the objects is doubled, the force (F_G) is one fourth as much.

29. B is correct.

If velocity is non-constant then the average velocity is not equal to the instantaneous velocity. Only when velocity is constant does the instantaneous velocity equal the average velocity.

30. C is correct.

velocity = acceleration × time

$$v = at$$

$$v = (10 \text{ m/s}^2) \cdot (10 \text{ s})$$

$$v = 100 \text{ m/s}$$

31. B is correct.

velocity = distance / time

$$v = d / t$$

d is constant, while t decreases by a factor of 3

32. C is correct. The equation for distance, given a constant acceleration and both the initial and final velocity, is:

$$d = (v_i^2 + v_f^2) / 2a$$

Since the car is coming to rest, $v_f = 0$

$$d = v_i^2 / 2a$$

If the initial velocity is doubled while acceleration and final velocity remain unchanged, the new distance traveled is:

$$d_2 = (2v_i)^2 / 2a$$

$$d_2 = 4(v_i^2 / 2a)$$

$$d_2 = 4d_1$$

Another method to solve this problem:

$$d_1 = (29 \text{ mi/h})^2 / 2a$$

$$d_2 = (59 \text{ mi/h})^2 / 2a$$

$$d_2 / d_1 = [(59 \text{ mi/h})^2 / 2a] / [(29 \text{ mi/h})^2 / 2a]$$

$$d_2 / d_1 = (59 \text{ mi/h})^2 / (29 \text{ mi/h})^2$$

$d_2 / d_1 = (3{,}481) / (841)$

$d_2 / d_1 = 4$

33. D is correct.

$\text{speed}_{average} = \text{total distance} / \text{time}$

$\text{speed} = (400 \text{ m}) / (20 \text{ s})$

$\text{speed} = 20 \text{ m/s}$

If this were velocity, it would be 0.

34. A is correct.

$\Delta v = a\Delta t$

$(v_f - v_i) = a\Delta t$, where $v_f = 0$ m/s (when the car stops)

$a = -0.1$ m/s^2 (negative because deceleration), $\Delta t = 5$ s

$v_i = v_f - a\Delta t$

$v_i = [(0 \text{ m/s}) - (-0.1 \text{ m/s}^2)] \cdot (5 \text{ s})$

$v_i = (0.1 \text{ m/s}^2) \cdot (5 \text{ s})$

$v_i = 0.5$ m/s

35. C is correct. If acceleration is constant then the velocity vs. time graph is linear and the average velocity is the average of the final and initial velocity.

$v_{average} = v_f - v_i / \Delta t$

If acceleration is not constant then the velocity vs. time graph is nonlinear.

$v_{average} \neq v_f - v_i / \Delta t$

36. D is correct. Find velocity of thrown rock:

$v_{f1}{}^2 - v_i{}^2 = 2ad$

$v_{f1}{}^2 = v_i{}^2 + 2ad$

$v_{f1}{}^2 = (10 \text{ m/s})^2 + [2(9.8 \text{ m/s}^2) \cdot (300 \text{ m})]$

$v_{f1}{}^2 = 100 \text{ m}^2/\text{s}^2 + 5{,}880 \text{ m}^2/\text{s}^2$

$v_{f1}{}^2 = 5{,}980 \text{ m}^2/\text{s}^2$

$v_{f1} = 77.33$ m/s

$t_1 = (v_f - v_i) / a$

$t_1 = (77.33 \text{ m/s} - 10 \text{ m/s}) / 9.8 \text{ m/s}^2$

$t_1 = (67.33 \text{ m/s}) / (9.8 \text{ m/s}^2)$

$t_1 = 6.87$ s

Find velocity of dropped rock:

$v_{f2} = \sqrt{2ad}$

$v_{f2} = \sqrt{[(2)\cdot(9.8 \text{ m/s}^2)\cdot(300 \text{ m})]}$

$v_{f2} = 76.7$ m/s

$t_2 = (76.7 \text{ m/s}) / (9.8 \text{ m/s}^2)$

$t_2 = 7.82$ s

$\Delta t = (7.82 \text{ s} - 6.87 \text{ s})$

$\Delta t = 0.95$ s

37. D is correct.

$F = ma$

Force and acceleration are directly proportional so doubling force doubles acceleration.

38. B is correct.

Velocity is defined as having a speed and direction. If either, or both, of these change then the object is experiencing acceleration.

39. C is correct.

The acceleration is negative because it acts to slow the car down against the $+y$ direction.

It is unclear if the acceleration decreases in magnitude from the data provided.

40. A is correct.

Total distance is represented by the area under the velocity-time curve with respect to the x-axis.

This graph can be broken up into sections; calculate the area under the curve.

$d_{total} = d_A + d_B + d_C + d_D$

$d_{total} = [\frac{1}{2}(4 \text{ m/s})\cdot(2 \text{ s})] + [\frac{1}{2}(4 \text{ m/s} + 2 \text{ m/s})\cdot(2 \text{ s})] + [(2 \text{ m/s})\cdot(4 \text{ s})]$
$+ [\frac{1}{2}(2 \text{ m/s})\cdot(2 \text{ s}) + \frac{1}{2}(2 \text{ m/s})\cdot(2 \text{ s})]$

$d_{total} = 4 \text{ m} + 6 \text{ m} + 8 \text{ m} + 2 \text{ m}$

$d_{total} = 20$ m

Since the total distance traveled needs to be calculated, the area under the curve when the velocity is negative is calculated as a positive value.

Distance is a scalar quantity and therefore has no direction.

41. C is correct.

The two bullets different velocities when hitting the water but they both only experience the force due to gravity. Thus the acceleration due to gravity is the same for each bullet.

42. A is correct.

$v_f = v_i + at$

$v_f = 0 + (2.5 \text{ m/s}^2) \cdot (9 \text{ s})$

$v_f = 22.5 \text{ m/s}$

43. D is correct. The equation for impulse is used for contact between two objects over a specified time period:

$F\Delta t = m\Delta v$

$ma\Delta t = m(v_f - v_i)$, cancel m from both sides of the expression

$a\Delta t = (v_f - v_i)$

$a = (v_f - v_i) / \Delta t$

$a = (-2v - v) / (0.45 \text{ s})$

$a = (-3v) / (0.45 \text{ s})$

$a = (-6.7 \text{ s}^{-1})v$

Ratio $a : v = -6.7 \text{ s}^{-1} : 1$

44. B is correct. The time for the round trip is 4 s.

The weight reaches the top of its path in ½ time:

$\frac{1}{2}(4 \text{ s}) = 2 \text{ s}$, where $v = 0$

$a = \Delta v / t$ for the first half of the trip

$a = (v_f - v_i) / t$

$a = (0 - 3.2 \text{ m/s}) / 2 \text{ s}$

$a = -1.6 \text{ m/s}^2$

$|a| = 1.6 \text{ m/s}^2$

Acceleration is a vector and the negative direction only indicates direction.

45. A is correct.

$\Delta v = a\Delta t$

$\Delta v = (0.3 \text{ m/s}^2) \cdot (3 \text{ s})$

$\Delta v = 0.9 \text{ m/s}$

46. D is correct.

47. B is correct.

$$d = d_0 + (v_i^2 + v_f^2) / 2a$$
$$d = 64 \text{ m} + (0 + 60 \text{ m/s})^2 / 2(9.8 \text{ m/s}^2)$$
$$d = 64 \text{ m} + (3{,}600 \text{ m}^2/\text{s}^2) / (19.6 \text{ m/s}^2)$$
$$d = 64 \text{ m} + 184 \text{ m}$$
$$d = 248 \text{ m}$$

48. C is correct.

$$a = (v_f^2 + v_i^2) / 2d$$
$$a = [(60 \text{ m/s})^2 + (0 \text{ m/s})^2] / 2(64 \text{ m})$$
$$a = (3{,}600 \text{ m}^2/\text{s}^2) / 128 \text{ m}$$
$$a = 28 \text{ m/s}^2$$

49. D is correct. Expression for the time interval during constant acceleration upward:

$$d = \tfrac{1}{2}at^2$$

Solving for acceleration:

$$a = (v_f^2 + v_i^2) / 2d$$
$$a = [(60 \text{ m/s})^2 + (0 \text{ m/s})^2] / 2(64 \text{ m})$$
$$a = (3{,}600 \text{ m}^2/\text{s}^2) / (128 \text{ m})$$
$$a = 28.1 \text{ m/s}^2$$

Solving for time:

$$t^2 = 2d / a$$
$$t^2 = 2(64 \text{ m}) / 28.1 \text{ m/s}^2$$
$$t^2 = 4.5 \text{ s}^2$$
$$t = 2.1 \text{ s}$$

50. C is correct.

$$d = (v_i^2 + v_f^2) / 2a, \text{ where } v_i = 0$$
$$d = v_f^2 / 2a$$

For half the final velocity:

$$d_2 = (v_f / 2)^2 / 2a$$

$$d_2 = \frac{1}{4} v_f^2 / 2a$$

$$d_2 \approx \frac{1}{4} d$$

51. A is correct.

$$v_{average} = \Delta d / \Delta t$$

52. A is correct.

Use an equation that relates v, d and t:

$$d = v \times t$$

$$v = d / t$$

If v increases by a factor of 3, then t decreases by a factor of 3.

Another method to solve this problem:

$$d = vt, t = \text{original time and } t_N = \text{new time}$$

$$d = 3vt_N$$

$$vt = d = 3vt_N$$

$$vt = 3vt_N$$

$$t = 3t_N$$

$$t / 3 = t_N$$

Thus, if v increases by a factor of 3, then the original time decreases by a factor of 3.

53. B is correct.

$$v_f = v_i + at$$

$$t = (v_f - v_i) / a$$

Since the ball is thrown straight up, its initial speed upward equals its final speed downward (just before hitting the ground). $v_f = v_i$

$$t = [39 \text{ m/s} - (-39 \text{ m/s})] / 9.8 \text{ m/s}^2$$

$$t = (78 \text{ m/s}) / 9.8 \text{ m/s}^2$$

$$t = 8 \text{ s}$$

54. D is correct.

Since the speed is changing, the velocity is changing, and therefore there *is* an acceleration.

Since the speed is *decreasing*, the acceleration must be *in the reverse direction* (i.e. opposite to the direction of travel).

Since the particle is moving to the right, the acceleration vector points to the left.

If the speed were increasing, the acceleration is in the *same* direction as the direction of travel, and the acceleration vector points to the right.

55. A is correct.

$$W = Fd \cos \theta$$

$$F = ma$$

$$W = ma \times d \times \cos \theta$$

Larry's force is perpendicular to the direction of the package's motion ($\theta = 90°$).

Since $\cos 90° = 0$, $W = 0$

Work done = 0 J

56. A is correct. The slope of a tangent line on a velocity vs. time graph is the acceleration at that time point. Thus is equivalent to taking the derivative of the velocity with respect to time to find the instantaneous acceleration.

57. C is correct.

Since the car is initially traveling North, let North be the positive direction and South be the negative direction:

$$a = (v_f - v_i) / t$$

$$a = (14.1 \text{ m/s} - 17.7 \text{ m/s}) / 12 \text{ s}$$

$$a = (-3.6 \text{ m/s}) / 12 \text{ s}$$

$$a = -0.3 \text{ m/s}^2$$

$$a = 0.3 \text{ m/s}^2 \text{ South}$$

58. C is correct. Speed is represented by the magnitude of the slope of a position vs. time plot.

A steeper slope equates to a higher speed.

59. B is correct. If the object has not reached terminal velocity it continues to accelerate until it does and thus speed is increasing.

60. D is correct.

Let d_1 be the distance the car travels during the initial acceleration, d_2 be the distance during constant speed and d_3 be the distance as the car slows down.

$$d_1 = \frac{1}{2}at^2$$

$$d_1 = \frac{1}{2}(2 \text{ m/s}^2) \cdot (10 \text{ s})^2$$

$d_1 = 100$ m

$d_2 = vt$

$d_2 = (at)t$

$d_2 = at^2$

$d_2 = (2 \text{ m/s}^2) \cdot (10 \text{ s})^2$

$d_2 = 200$ m

$d_3 = (v_i^2 + v_f^2) / 2a$

$d_3 = [(20 \text{ m/s})^2 + (0 \text{ m/s})^2] / 2(2 \text{ m/s}^2)$

$d_3 = (400 \text{ m}^2/\text{s}^2) / (4 \text{ m/s}^2)$

$d_3 = 100$ m

The total distance traveled is the sum of d_1, d_2 and d_3:

$d_{\text{total}} = 100$ m + 200 m + 100 m

$d_{\text{total}} = 400$ m

61. A is correct.

Acceleration has a direction; therefore it is always changing while an object travels in a circular path. Changing direction means that the velocity changes.

$a_c = v^2 / r$

If v stays constant then the centripetal acceleration stays constant. Its direction does not change because a_c always points to the center of a circular path.

62. B is correct.

$d = v_0 t + \frac{1}{2}at^2$, where $v_0 = 0$

$d = \frac{1}{2}at^2$

$t^2 = d / \frac{1}{2}a$

$t = \sqrt{(2d / a)}$

$t = \sqrt{[2 (10 \text{ m}) / 9.8 \text{ m/s}^2]}$

$t = \sqrt{(2.04 \text{ s}^2)}$

$t = 1.4$ s

Another method to solve this problem:

$\Delta y = -10$ m

$a \approx -10 \text{ m/s}^2$

Determine Δt:

$$\Delta y = \tfrac{1}{2}a\Delta t^2$$

$$-10 \text{ m} = \tfrac{1}{2}(-10 \text{ m/s}^2)\Delta t^2$$

$$-10 \text{ m} = (-5 \text{ m/s}^2)\Delta t^2$$

$$\Delta t^2 = -10 \text{ m} / (-5 \text{ m/s}^2)$$

$$\Delta t^2 = 2 \text{ s}^2$$

$$\Delta t = \sqrt{2} \text{ s}^2$$

$$\Delta t = 1.4 \text{ s}$$

63. D is correct.

Before determining the average speed and velocity of the trip, first calculate the total time of the trip:

$$t_{total} = (d_{North} / v_{North}) + (d_{South} / v_{South})$$

$$t_{total} = (95 \text{ km} / 70 \text{ km/h}) + (21.9 \text{ km} / 80 \text{ km/h})$$

$$t_{total} = 1.36 \text{ h} + 0.27 \text{ h}$$

$$t_{total} = 1.63 \text{ h}$$

Calculate the average speed of the trip:

$$speed_{avg} = (d_{North} + d_{South}) / t_{total}$$

$$speed_{avg} = (95 \text{ km} + 21.9 \text{ km}) / 1.63 \text{ h}$$

$$speed_{avg} = (116.9 \text{ km}) / 1.63 \text{ h}$$

$$speed_{avg} = 72 \text{ km/h}$$

Calculate the average velocity of the trip, remembering that velocity is directional so set South as the negative direction:

$$v_{avg} = (d_{North} - d_{South}) / t_{total}$$

$$v_{avg} = (95 \text{ km} - 21.9 \text{ km}) / 1.63 \text{ h}$$

$$v_{avg} = (73.1 \text{ km}) / 1.63 \text{ h}$$

$$v_{avg} = 45 \text{ km/h}$$

The difference between the average speed and average velocity is:

$$speed_{avg} - v_{avg} = 72 \text{ km/h} - 45 \text{ km/h}$$

$$speed_{avg} - v_{avg} = 27 \text{ km/h}$$

64. A is correct.

Uniform acceleration: a = change in velocity / change in time

$$a = \Delta v / \Delta t$$

$$a = 60 \text{ mi/h} / 6 \text{ s}$$
$$a = 10 \text{ mi/h·s}$$
$$a = 10 \text{ mi·h}^{-1}\text{·s}^{-1}$$

65. C is correct.

For uniform acceleration:

$$v_{avg} = \tfrac{1}{2}(v_1 + v_2)$$
$$v_{avg} = \tfrac{1}{2}(5 \text{ m/s} + 30 \text{ m/s})$$
$$v_{avg} = 17.5 \text{ m/s}$$

66. B is correct.

Graph III depicts a non-zero constant velocity process.

Graph I depicts a constant zero velocity process.

Graph II depicts a non-zero constant velocity process.

67. C is correct.

$$a = (v_i^2 + v_f^2) / 2d$$
$$a = [(0 \text{ m/s})^2 + (42 \text{ m/s})^2] / 2(5{,}600 \text{ m})$$
$$a = (1{,}764 \text{ m}^2/\text{s}^2) / 11{,}200 \text{ m}$$
$$a = 0.16 \text{ m/s}^2$$

68. A is correct. At the maximum height, the velocity = 0 and the cannon ball stops moving up and begins to come back.

69. D is correct.

An object's inertia is its resistance to change in motion.

70. D is correct.

$$v = v_0 + at$$

If $a = 2 \text{ m/s}^2$ then the object has a 2 m/s increase in velocity every second.

Example:

$$v_0 = 0 \text{ m/s}, \, a = 2 \text{ m/s}^2, \, t = 1 \text{ s}$$
$$v = 0 \text{ m/s} + (2 \text{ m/s}^2)\cdot(1 \text{ s})$$
$$v = 2 \text{ m/s}$$

71. C is correct.

The acceleration due to gravity is 9.8 m/s^2. If an object is in freefall then every second it increases velocity by 9.8 m/s.

$v = v_0 + at$

$v = v_0 + (9.8 \text{ m/s}^2) \cdot (1 \text{ s})$

$v = v_0 + 9.8 \text{ m/s}$

72. B is correct.

To determine the time at which the marble stops:

$v_2 - v_1 = a\Delta t$

where $v_1 = 0.2$ m/s and $a = -0.05$ m/s^2

$\Delta t = (v_2 - v_1) / a$

$\Delta t = (0 \text{ m/s} - 0.2 \text{ m/s}) / (-0.05 \text{ m/s}^2)$

$\Delta t = (-0.2 \text{ m/s}) / (-0.05 \text{ m/s}^2)$

$\Delta t = 4$ s

73. D is correct.

$v_{avg} = (1/3)v_1 + (2/3)v_2$

73 km/h $= (1/3) \cdot (96.5 \text{ km/h}) + (2/3)v_2$

73 km/h $= (32 \text{ km/h}) + (2/3)v_2$

$(2/3)v_2 = 41$ km/h

$v_2 = (41 \text{ km/h}) \cdot (3/2)$

$v_2 = 62$ km/h

74. A is correct.

The distance to the lightning bolt is calculated by determining the distance traveled by the sound.

Distance = velocity × time

$d = vt$

$d = (340 \text{ m/s}) \cdot (6 \text{ s})$

$d = 2{,}040$ m

75. D is correct.

Calculate the vertical component of the initial velocity:

$$v_{up} = v(\sin \theta)$$

$$v_{up} = (2.74 \text{ m/s}) \sin 60°$$

$$v_{up} = 2.37 \text{ m/s}$$

Then solve for the upward displacement given the initial upward velocity:

$$d = (v_i^2 + v_f^2) / 2a$$

$$d = [(2.37 \text{ m/s})^2 + (0 \text{ m/s})^2] / 2(9.8 \text{ m/s}^2)$$

$$d = 5.62 \text{ m}^2/\text{s}^2 / 19.6 \text{ m/s}^2$$

$$d = 0.29 \text{ m}$$

76. C is correct.

30° North of East is the exact opposite direction of 30° South of West, so set one vector as negative, and the direction of the resultant vector will be in the direction of the larger vector between A and B.

Since the magnitude of A is greater than the magnitude of B and vectors were added "tip to tail," the resultant vector is:

$$AB = A + B$$

$$AB = 6 \text{ m} + (-4 \text{ m})$$

$$AB = 2 \text{ m at } 30° \text{ North of East}$$

77. D is correct.

The solution is measured in feet, so first convert the car velocity into feet per second:

$$v = (49 \text{ mi/h}) \cdot (5280 \text{ ft/mi}) \cdot (1 \text{ h}/3600 \text{ s})$$

$$v = 72 \text{ ft/s}$$

The sober driver's distance:

$$d = vt$$

$$d_{sober} = (72 \text{ ft/s}) \cdot (0.33 \text{ s})$$

$$d_{sober} = 24 \text{ ft}$$

The intoxicated driver's distance:

$$d = vt$$

$$d_{drunk} = (72 \text{ ft/s}) \cdot (1 \text{ s})$$

$$d_{drunk} = 72 \text{ ft}$$

The differences between the distances:

$$\Delta d = 72 \text{ ft} - 24 \text{ ft}$$

$$\Delta d = 48 \text{ ft}$$

FORCE, MOTION, GRAVITATION – EXPLANATIONS

1. B is correct.

The tension of the string keeps the weight traveling in a circular path, otherwise it would move linearly on a tangent path to the circle.

2. D is correct.

Total upward force on the garment bag is equal to the tension in the clothesline.

Therefore, the magnitude of T_{total} equals the garment bag's weight, mg.

$1 \text{ N} = 1 \text{ kg·m/s}^2$

$1 \text{ m/s}^2 = 1 \text{ N / kg}$

$T_{total} = F$

$F = ma$, where a is acceleration due to gravity

$m = T_{total} / a$

$m = (10 \text{ N}) / (10 \text{ N/kg})$ or $m = (10 \text{ kg·m/s}^2) / (10 \text{ kg·m/s}^2/\text{kg})$

$m = 1 \text{ kg}$

3. A is correct.

An object's inertia is its resistance to change in motion.

4. C is correct.

$(F_{net})_y = F_N - F_g$

The car is not moving up or down, so $a_y = 0$:

$(F_{net})_y = 0$

$0 = F_N - F_g$

$F_N = F_g$

$F_N = F_g \cos \theta$

$F_N = mg \cos \theta$

The normal force is a force that is perpendicular to the plane of contact (the slope).

5. D is correct.

$F = ma$

$F = (27 \text{ kg}) \cdot (1.7 \text{ m/s}^2)$

$F = 46 \text{ N}$

---

6. D is correct.

The mass on the table causes a tension force in the string that acts against the force of gravity.

7. A is correct.

Although the net force acting on the object is decreasing with time and the magnitude of the object's acceleration is decreasing there exists a positive acceleration. Therefore, the object's speed continues to increase.

8. D is correct.

Objects moving at constant velocity experience zero net force on them.

9. A is correct.

The sine of an angle is equal to the opposite side over the hypotenuse:

$\sin \theta$ = opposite / hypotenuse

$\sin \theta = h / L$

$h = L \sin \theta$

10. C is correct.

A car accelerating horizontally does not rely on the force of gravity to move it. Since mass does not depend on gravity, a car on Earth and a car on the Moon that experience the same horizontal acceleration also experience the same force.

11. A is correct.

$a = (v_f - v_i) / t$

$a = (3.5 \text{ m/s} - 1.5 \text{ m/s}) / (3 \text{ s})$

$a = (2 \text{ m/s}) / (3 \text{ s})$

$a = 0.67 \text{ m/s}^2$

12. D is correct.

An object with uniform circular motion (i.e. constant angular velocity) only experiences centripetal acceleration directed toward the center of the circle.

13. B is correct.

$F = ma$, so zero force means zero acceleration in any direction.

14. C is correct.

$$F = ma$$
$$a = F / m$$
$$a = 9 \text{ N} / 9 \text{ kg}$$
$$a = 1 \text{ m/s}^2$$

15. D is correct.

The only force acting on a projectile in motion is the force due to gravity. Since that force always acts downward, there is always only a downward acceleration.

16. A is correct.

$$F_{net} = ma$$

If an object moves with constant v, its $a = 0$, so:

$$F_{net} = 0$$

Since gravity pulls down on the can with a force of mg:

$$F_g = mg$$
$$F_g = (10 \text{ kg}) \cdot (10 \text{ m/s}^2)$$
$$F_g = 100 \text{ N}$$

The rope pulls *up* on the can with the same magnitude of force, so the tension is 100 N, for a net force = 0.

17. D is correct.

$$F = ma$$
$$F = (1,000 \text{ kg}) \cdot (2 \text{ m/s}^2)$$
$$F = 2,000 \text{ N}$$

18. C is correct.

$$a_{cent} = v^2 / r$$
$$a_{cent} = (4 \text{ m/s})^2 / (4 \text{ m})$$
$$a_{cent} = (16 \text{ m}^2/\text{s}^2) / (4 \text{ m})$$
$$a_{cent} = 4 \text{ m/s}^2$$

19. D is correct.

Solve for m_1:

$F_{net} = 0$

$m_2g = F_T$

$m_1g \sin \theta + F_f = F_T$

$m_1g \sin \theta + \mu_s m_1g \cos \theta = m_2g$

cancel g from both sides

$m_1(\sin \theta + \mu_s \cos \theta) = m_2$

$m_1 = m_2 / (\sin \theta + \mu_s \cos \theta)$

$m_1 = 2 \text{ kg} / [\sin 20° + (0.55) \cos 20°]$

$m_1 = 2 \text{ kg} / 0.86$

$m_1 = 2.3 \text{ kg}$

Kinetic friction is only used when the mass is in motion.

20. B is correct.

Force only depends on mass and acceleration. Therefore, since the masses are identical and the acceleration is gravity for both masses, they have a net force of zero, and therefore remain stationary.

21. B is correct.

Newton's Third Law states that for every action there is an equal and opposite reaction.

22. A is correct.

Newton's Third Law states that for every action there is an equal and opposite reaction.

23. C is correct.

If w denotes the magnitude of the box's weight, then the component of this force that is parallel to the inclined plane is $w \sin \theta$, where θ is the incline angle.

If θ is less than 90°, then $\sin \theta$ is less than 1.

The component of w parallel to the inclined plane is less than w.

24. D is correct.

The package experiences projectile motion upon leaving the truck, so it experiences no horizontal forces and its initial velocity of 30 m/s remains unchanged.

25. D is correct.

f = revolutions / unit of time

Each revolution represents a length of $2\pi r$.

Velocity is the total distance / time:

$$v = 2\pi r \, / \, t$$

$$v = 2\pi r f$$

If f doubles, then v doubles.

26. A is correct.

$$F = ma$$

$$m = F \, / \, a$$

$$m = 4{,}500 \text{ N} \, / \, 5 \text{ m/s}^2$$

$$m = 900 \text{ kg}$$

27. D is correct.

Newton's Second Law states that every object will remain at rest or in uniform motion unless acted upon by an outside force.

In this case, Steve and the bus are in uniform constant motion until the bus stops due to sudden deceleration (the ground exerts no frictional force on Steve). There is no force acting upon Steve. However, his inertia carries him forward because he is still in uniform motion while the bus comes to a stop.

28. D is correct.

The ball is in a state of rest, so $F_{net} = 0$

$$F_{down} = F_{up}$$

$$F_{external} + F_{w} = F_{buoyant}$$

$$F_{external} = F_{buoyant} - F_{w}$$

$$F_{external} = 8.4 \text{ N} - 4.4 \text{ N}$$

$$F_{external} = 4 \text{ N, in the same direction as the weight}$$

29. A is correct.

The luggage and the train move at the same speed, so when the luggage moves forward with respect to the train, it means the train has slowed down while the luggage is continuing to move at the train's original speed.

---

30. D is correct.

The mass does not change by changing the object's location.

Since the object is outside of Earth's atmosphere, the object's weight is represented by the equation:

$$F_g = GmM_{Earth} / R^2$$

If the altitude is $2R_{Earth}$, then the distance from the center of the Earth is $3R_{Earth}$.

The gravitational acceleration decreases by a factor of $3^2 = 9$ ($g = GmM / R^2$).

Weight decreases by a factor of 9.

New weight = 360 N / 9 = 40 N

31. C is correct.

The rock experiences the same horizontal velocity as the truck, so as a projectile falls, it travels forward at the same velocity as the truck.

32. D is correct.

The acceleration of Jason due to thrust is:

$$F_{net} = ma_1$$

$$ma_1 = F_{ski} - \mu_k mg$$

$$a_1 = (F_{ski} - \mu_k mg) / m$$

$$a_1 = [200 \text{ N} - (0.1) \cdot (75 \text{ kg}) \cdot (9.8 \text{ m/s}^2)] / 75 \text{ kg}$$

$$a_1 = (126.5 \text{ N}) / 75 \text{ kg}$$

$$a_1 = 1.69 \text{ m/s}^2$$

The distance traveled during the acceleration stage is:

$$d_1 = \tfrac{1}{2}a_1 t^2$$

$$d_1 = \tfrac{1}{2}(1.69 \text{ m/s}^2) \cdot (67 \text{ s})^2$$

$$d_1 = 3,793 \text{ m}$$

The distance traveled after the skis run out of fuel is:

$$d_2 = (v_f^2 - v_i^2) / 2a_2$$

a_2 is Jason's acceleration after the fuel runs out:

$$F_{net} = ma_2$$

$ma_2 = -\mu_k mg$, cancel m from both sides of the expression

$$a_2 = -\mu_k g$$

$$a_2 = -(0.1) \cdot (9.8 \text{ m/s}^2)$$

$$a_2 = -0.98 \text{ m/s}^2$$

The acceleration is negative since the frictional force opposes the direction of motion.

v_i is the velocity at the moment when the fuel runs out:

$v_i = a_1 t$

$v_i = (1.69 \text{ m/s}^2) \cdot (67 \text{ s})$

$v_i = 113.2 \text{ m/s}$

Substitute a_2 and v_i into the equation for d_2:

$d_2 = [(0 \text{ m/s})^2 - (113.2 \text{ m/s})^2] / 2(-0.98 \text{ m/s}^2)$

$d_2 = (-12{,}814.2 \text{ m}^2/\text{s}^2) / -1.96 \text{ m/s}^2$

$d_2 = 6{,}538 \text{ m}$

The total distance Jason traveled is:

$d_{total} = d_1 + d_2$

$d_{total} = 3{,}793 \text{ m} + 6{,}538 \text{ m}$

$d_{total} = 10{,}331 \text{ m}$

33. D is correct.

Using energy to solve the problem:

$KE = PE + W_f$

$\frac{1}{2}mv^2 = mgd \sin \theta + \mu_k mgd \cos \theta$, cancel m from the expression

$\frac{1}{2}v^2 = gd \sin \theta + \mu_k gd \cos \theta$

$\frac{1}{2}v^2 = d(g \sin \theta + \mu_k g \cos \theta)$

$d = v^2 / [2g(\sin \theta + \mu_k \cos \theta)]$

$d = (63 \text{ m/s})^2 / [(2) \cdot (9.8 \text{ m/s}^2) \cdot (\sin 30° + 0.3 \times \cos 30°)]$

$d = 267 \text{ m}$

$h = d \sin \theta$

$h = (267 \text{ m}) \sin 30°$

$h = 130 \text{ m}$

Another method using balancing the forces (an alternative method but several more steps):

$F_{net} = F_g + F_{fk}$

$F_g = mg \sin \theta$

$F_g = (0.2 \text{ kg}) \cdot (-9.8 \text{ m/s}^2) \sin 30°$

$F_g = (0.2 \text{ kg}) \cdot (-9.8 \text{ m/s}^2) \cdot (1/2)$

$F_g = -1 \text{ N}$

$F_{fk} = \mu_k F_N$

$$F_{fk} = \mu_k mg \cos \theta$$

$$F_{fk} = (0.3) \cdot (0.2 \text{ kg}) \cdot (-9.8 \text{ m/s}^2) \cos 30°$$

$$F_{fk} = (0.3) \cdot (0.2 \text{ kg}) \cdot (-9.8 \text{ m/s}^2) \cdot (0.866)$$

$$F_{fk} = -0.5 \text{ N}$$

$$F_{net} = -1 \text{ N} + (-0.5 \text{ N})$$

$$F_{net} = -1.5 \text{ N}$$

$$a = F_{net} / m$$

$$a = -1.5 \text{ N} / 0.2 \text{ kg}$$

$$a = -7.5 \text{ m/s}^2$$

The distance it travels until it reaches a velocity of 0 at its maximum height:

$$d = (v_f^2 - v_i^2) / 2a$$

$$d = [(0 \text{ m/s})^2 - (63 \text{ m/s})^2] / 2(-7.5 \text{ m/s}^2)$$

$$d = (-4,000 \text{ m}^2/\text{s}^2) / (-15 \text{ m/s}^2)$$

$$d = 267 \text{ m}$$

The vertical height is:

$$h = d \sin \theta$$

$$h = (267 \text{ m}) \sin 30°$$

$$h = (267 \text{ m}) \cdot (0.5)$$

$$h = 130 \text{ m}$$

34. A is correct.

$$F = ma$$

$$a = F / m$$

$$a_1 = F / 4 \text{ kg}$$

$$a_2 = F / 10 \text{ kg}$$

$$4a_1 = 10a_2$$

$$a_1 = 2.5a_2$$

35. D is correct.

Mass is independent of gravity, however weight is not; as a person moves farther away from any stars or planets, the gravitational pull decreases and, therefore, her weight decreases.

36. A is correct.

Newton's Third Law states that for every action there is an equal and opposite reaction.

37. D is correct.

$m = F / a_{Earth}$

$m = 20\ N / 3\ m/s^2$

$m = 6.67\ kg$

$F_{Moon} = mg_{Moon}$

$F_{Moon} = (6.67\ kg) \cdot (1.62\ m/s^2)$

$F_{Moon} = 11\ N$

38. B is correct.

weight = mass × gravity

$w = (0.4\ kg) \cdot (9.8\ m/s^2)$

$w \approx 4\ N$

39. B is correct. Need an expression which connects time and mass.

Given information for F, v_1, and d:

$a = F / m$

$d = v_1 t + \frac{1}{2}at^2$

Combine the expressions and set $v_i = 0$ m/s because initial velocity is zero:

$d = \frac{1}{2}at^2$

$a = F / m$

$d = \frac{1}{2}(F / m)t^2$

$t^2 = 2dm / F$

$t = \sqrt{(2dm / F)}$

If m increases by a factor of 4, t increases by a factor of $\sqrt{4} = 2$

40. C is correct.

$a = (v_f^2 - v_i^2) / 2d$

$a = [(0\ m/s)^2 - (27\ m/s)^2] / 2(578\ m)$

$a = (-729\ m^2/s^2) / 1,056\ m$

$a = -0.63\ m/s^2$

$F = ma$

$F = (1,100\ kg) \cdot (-0.63\ m/s^2)$

$F = -690\ N$

The car is decelerating, so the acceleration (and therefore the force) is negative.

41. A is correct. Constant speed upward means no net force.

Tension = weight (equals Mg)

42. C is correct.

$$\text{Weight} = mg$$

$$75 \text{ N} = mg$$

$$m = 75 \text{ N} / 9.8 \text{ m/s}^2$$

$$m = 7.65 \text{ kg}$$

$$F_{net} = F_{right} - F_{left}$$

$$F_{net} = 50 \text{ N} - 30 \text{ N}$$

$$F_{net} = 20 \text{ N}$$

$$F_{net} = ma$$

$$a = F_{net} / m$$

$$a = 20 \text{ N} / 7.65 \text{ kg}$$

$$a = 2.6 \text{ m/s}^2$$

43. B is correct. The string was traveling at the same velocity as the plane with respect to the ground outside. When the plane began accelerating backward (decelerating), the string continued to move forward at its original velocity and appeared to go towards the front of the plane.

Since the string is attached to the ceiling at one end, only the bottom of the string moved.

44. C is correct.

If the object slides down the ramp with a constant speed, velocity is constant.

Acceleration and the net force = 0

$$F_{net} = F_{\text{grav down ramp}} - F_{\text{friction}}$$

$$F_{net} = mg \sin \theta - \mu_k mg \cos \theta$$

$$F_{net} = 0$$

$$mg \sin \theta - \mu_k mg \cos \theta = 0$$

$$mg \sin \theta = \mu_k mg \cos \theta$$

$$\mu_k = \sin \theta / \cos \theta$$

45. A is correct.

The net force on an object in free fall is equal to its weight.

46. C is correct.

$a = \Delta v / \Delta t$

$a = (v_f - v_i) / t$

$a = (20 \text{ m/s} - 0 \text{ m/s}) / (10 \text{ s})$

$a = (20 \text{ m/s}) / (10 \text{ s})$

$a = 2 \text{ m/s}^2$

47. D is correct. Since the object does not move, it is in a state of equilibrium, so there are forces acting on it that equal and oppose the force F that Yania applies to the object.

48. D is correct.

Newton's Third Law states that for every action there is an equal and opposite reaction.

49. C is correct.

$F = mg$

$m = F / g$

$m = 685 \text{ N} / 9.8 \text{ m/s}^2$

$m = 69.9 \text{ kg} \approx 70 \text{ kg}$

50. A is correct.

$m_{Bob} = 4m_{Sarah}$

Conservation of momentum:

$m_{Bob}v_{Bob} = m_{Sarah}v_{Sarah}$

$4mv_{Bob} = m(4v_{Sarah})$

51. C is correct. For most surfaces, the coefficient of static friction is greater than the coefficient of kinetic friction. Thus, the force needed to overcome static friction and start the object's motion is greater than the amount of force needed to overcome kinetic friction and keep the object moving at a constant velocity.

52. B is correct.

Weight on Jupiter:

$W = mg$

$W = m(3g)$

$W = (100 \text{ kg}) \cdot (3 \times 10 \text{ m/s}^2)$

$W = 3,000 \text{ N}$

53. D is correct. Neither Joe nor Bill is moving, so the net force is zero:

$$F_{net} = F_{Joe} - F_T$$

$$0 = F_{Joe} - F_T$$

$$F_{Joe} = F_T$$

$$F_T = 200 \text{ N}$$

54. D is correct. Tension in the rope is always equal to F_T.

The net force on block A to the right is:

$$F_{right} = m_A a_A = 2F_T$$

The net force of block B downward is:

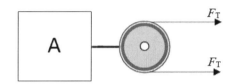

$$F_{down} = m_B a_B = m_B g - F_T$$

Since block A is connected to both the pulley at the end of the table and the wall, it uses twice the amount of rope length to travel the same distance as block B. Therefore, the distance block A moves is half that of block B, the velocity of block A is half the velocity of block B, and the acceleration of block A is half the acceleration of block B:

$$a_A = a_B / 2$$

$$F_{right} = m_A(a_B / 2)$$

$$m_A(a_B / 2) = 2F_T$$

$$m_A a_B = 4F_T$$

$$F_T = \tfrac{1}{4}m_A a_B$$

$$m_B a_B = m_B g - \tfrac{1}{4}m_A a_B$$

$$m_B a_B + \tfrac{1}{4}m_A a_B = m_B g$$

$$a_B[m_B + \tfrac{1}{4}m_A] = m_B g$$

$$a_B = m_B g / [m_B + \tfrac{1}{4}m_A]$$

$$a_B = (5 \text{ kg}) \cdot (9.8 \text{ m/s}^2) / [5 \text{ kg} + \tfrac{1}{4}(4 \text{ kg})]$$

$$a_B = 49 \text{ N} / 6 \text{ kg}$$

$$a_B = 8.2 \text{ m/s}^2$$

$$a_A = a_B / 2$$

$$a_A = (8.2 \text{ m/s}^2) / 2$$

$$a_A = 4.1 \text{ m/s}^2$$

55. B is correct. The force exerted by one surface on another has a perpendicular component (i.e. normal force) and a parallel component (i.e. friction force).

The force of kinetic friction on an object acts opposite to the direction of its velocity.

56. D is correct.

Before slowing down, the elevator rises at a constant velocity, so there is no net force and the scale reads the person's normal weight.

$$F = ma$$

$$600 \text{ N} = m(9.8 \text{ m/s}^2)$$

$$m = 61 \text{ kg}$$

Because the elevator is slowing down the weight will be lower.

$$F_{net} = m(g - a)$$

$$F_{net} = (61 \text{ kg}) \cdot (9.8 \text{ m/s}^2 - 6 \text{ m/s}^2)$$

$$F_{net} = 231 \text{ N}$$

57. B is correct.

Newton's Third Law states that for every action there is an equal and opposite reaction.

58. D is correct.

Since the crate can only move in the horizontal direction, only consider the horizontal component of the applied force when computing the acceleration.

$$F_x = F \cos \theta$$

$$F_x = (140 \text{ N})\cos 30°$$

$$F_x = (140 \text{ N}) \cdot (0.866)$$

$$F_x = 121 \text{ N}$$

$$a = F_x / m$$

$$a = 121 \text{ N} / 40 \text{ kg}$$

$$a = 3 \text{ m/s}^2$$

59. C is correct.

Vectors indicate magnitude and direction, while scalars only indicate magnitude.

60. B is correct.

The gravitational force and the direction of travel are perpendicular:

$$W = Fd \cos \theta$$

$$\cos \theta = 0$$

61. D is correct.

Work = Force × distance

$W_{rope} = Fd_x$

$W_{rope} = Fd \cos \theta$

$d = vt$

$d = (2.5 \text{ m/s}) \cdot (4 \text{ s})$

$W_{rope} = (30 \text{ N}) \cdot (10 \text{ m}) \cos 30°$

$W_{rope} = 260 \text{ J}$

62. B is correct.

Arrow in flight:

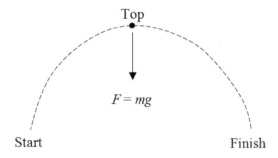

The weight of the arrow is:

$W = mg$

At the top of its flight and throughout its flight, the acceleration of gravity acts on the arrow:

$F = ma$

$F = mg$

$F = W$

63. D is correct.

$F = mg$

$m = F / g$

$m = (740 \text{ N}) / (10 \text{ m/s}^2)$

$m = 74 \text{ kg}$

$g_p = F_p / m$

$g_p = (5{,}180 \text{ N}) / (74 \text{ kg})$

$g_p = 70 \text{ m/s}^2$

64. B is correct.

Newton's Third Law states that for every action there is an equal and opposite reaction.

65. A is correct.

Newton's Second Law ($F = ma$) is rearranged:

$a = F / m$

If F is constant, then a is inversely proportional to m.

A larger mass implies a smaller F / m ratio; the ratio is the acceleration.

66. C is correct.

$F = ma$, so doubling the force doubles the acceleration.

67. B is correct.

Pythagorean Theorem ($a^2 + b^2 = c^2$) to calculate the net force:

$$F_1^2 + F_2^2 = F_{net}^2$$
$$(500 \text{ N})^2 + (1{,}200 \text{ N})^2 = F_{net}^2$$
$$250{,}000 \text{ N}^2 + 1{,}440{,}000 \text{ N}^2 = F_{net}^2$$
$$F_{net}^2 = 1{,}690{,}000 \text{ N}^2$$
$$F_{net} = 1{,}300 \text{ N}$$

Newton's Second Law:

$F = ma$

$a = F_{net} / m$

$a = 1{,}300 \text{ N} / 500 \text{ kg}$

$a = 2.6 \text{ m/s}^2$

68. D is correct.

The acceleration of the 2 kg block is the acceleration of the system because the blocks are linked together. Balance forces and solve for acceleration:

$F_{net} = m_3g - m_2g\mu_k - m_1g$

$(m_3 + m_2 + m_1)a = m_3g - m_2g\mu_k - m_1g$

$a = (m_3 - m_2\mu_k - m_1)g / (m_3 + m_2 + m_1)$

$a = [3 \text{ kg} - (2 \text{ kg})\cdot(0.25) - 1 \text{ kg}]\cdot(9.8 \text{ m/s}^2) / (3 \text{ kg} + 2 \text{ kg} + 1 \text{ kg})$

$a = 2.5 \text{ m/s}^2$

69. A is correct.

Objects moving at constant velocity experience no acceleration and therefore no net force.

70. B is correct.

The cart decelerates, which is acceleration in the opposite direction caused by the force of friction in the opposite direction.

71. C is correct.

Newton's Third Law states that for every action there is an equal and opposite reaction.

72. B is correct.

If the bureau moves in a straight line at a constant speed, its velocity is constant. Therefore, the bureau is experiencing zero acceleration and zero net force.

The force of kinetic friction equals the 30 N force that pulls the bureau.

73. A is correct.

Newton's First Law states that an object at rest tends to stay at rest, and an object in motion tends to maintain that motion, unless acted upon by an unbalanced force. This law depends on a property of an object called inertia, which is inherently linked to the object's mass. More massive objects are more difficult to move and manipulate than less massive objects.

74. B is correct.

$$F_g = Gm_{Earth}m_{moon} / d^2$$

d is the distance between the Earth and the Moon.

If d decreases by a factor of 4, F_g increases by a factor of $4^2 = 16$

75. C is correct.

Find equal and opposite forces:

$$F_{Rx} = -F_1$$

$$F_{Rx} = -(-6.6 \text{ N})$$

$$F_{Rx} = 6.6 \text{ N}$$

$$F_{Ry} = -F_2$$

$$F_{Ry} = -2.2 \text{ N}$$

Pythagorean Theorem ($a^2 + b^2 = c^2$) to calculate the magnitude of the resultant force:

The magnitude of F_R:

$$F_R^2 = F_{Rx}^2 + F_{Ry}^2$$

$$F_R^2 = (6.6 \text{ N})^2 + (-2.2 \text{ N})^2$$

$$F_R^2 = 43.6 \text{ N}^2 + 4.8 \text{ N}^2$$

$$F_R^2 = 48.4 \text{ N}^2$$

$$F_R = 7 \text{ N}$$

The direction of F_R:

$$\theta = \tan^{-1} (-2.2 \text{ N} / 6.6 \text{ N})$$

$$\theta = \tan^{-1} (-1 / 3)$$

$$\theta = 342°$$

The direction of F_R with respect to F_1:

$$\theta = 342° - 180°$$

$$\theta = 162° \text{ counterclockwise of } F_1$$

76. D is correct.

Each scale weighs the fish at 17 kg, so the sum of the two scales is:

$$17 \text{ kg} + 17 \text{ kg} = 34 \text{ kg}$$

77. D is correct.

If θ is the angle with respect to a horizontal line, then:

$$\theta = \frac{1}{2}(40°)$$

$$\theta = 20°$$

In order for a third force to cause equilibrium, the sum of all three forces' components must equal zero. Since F_1 and F_2 mirror each other in the y direction:

$$F_{1y} + F_{2y} = 0$$

Therefore, in order for F_3 to balance the forces in the y direction, its y component must also equal zero:

$$F_{1y} + F_{2y} + F_{3y} = 0$$

$$0 + 0 + F_{3y} = 0$$

$$F_{3y} = 0$$

The x component of F_3:

$$F_{1x} + F_{2x} + F_{3x} = 0$$

$$F_1 \cos \theta + F_2 \cos \theta + F_3 \cos \theta = 0$$

$$F_3 \cos \theta = -(F_1 \cos \theta + F_2 \cos \theta)$$

$F_3 \cos \theta = -[(2.3 \text{ N}) \cos 20° + (2.3 \text{ N}) \cos 20°]$

$F_3 \cos \theta = -(2.15 \text{ N} + 2.15 \text{ N})$

$F_3 \cos \theta = -4.3 \text{ N}$

Since $F_{3y} = 0$,

$F_3 = F_3 \cos \theta$

$F_3 = 4.3 \text{ N}$ to the right

78. D is correct.

At $\theta = 17°$, the force of static friction is equal to the force due to gravity:

$F_f = F_g$

$\mu_s mg \cos \theta = mg \sin \theta$

$\mu_s = \sin \theta / \cos \theta$

$\mu_s = \tan \theta$

$\mu_s = \tan 17°$

$\mu_s = 0.31$

79. B is correct.

The force of the table on the book, the normal force (F_N), is a result of Newton's Third Law of Motion, which states for every action there is an equal and opposite reaction.

A book sitting on the table experiences a force from the table equal to the book's weight:

$W = mg$

$F_N = W$

$F_N = mg$

$F_N = (2 \text{ kg}) \cdot (10 \text{ m/s}^2)$

$F_N = 20 \text{ N}$

EQUILIBRIUM AND MOMENTUM – EXPLANATIONS

1. A is correct. Torque can be written as:

$\tau = I\alpha$

where I = moment of inertia and α = angular acceleration

Thus if no torque acts on the system then the average angular acceleration is zero.

Angular acceleration can be written as:

$\alpha = \Delta\omega \, / \, \Delta t$

where ω = angular speed

Angular momentum can be written as:

$L = I\omega$

If angular acceleration is zero then there is no change in angular velocity so it must be constant. Therefore, angular momentum is constant because the moment of inertia does not change.

2. D is correct. If the velocity is 7 m/s down the mountain, the horizontal component v_x is:

$v_x = v \cos\theta$

1.8 m/s = (7 m/s) $\cos\theta$

$\cos\theta = 0.26$

$\theta \approx 75°$

3. D is correct. The hill exerts a normal force on the sled. However, this force is *perpendicular* to the surface of the hill. There is no parallel force that the hill exerts because it is frictionless.

4. C is correct. Assuming that the water flow is tangent to the wheel, it is perpendicular to the radius vector at the point of contact.

The torque around the center of the wheel is:

$\tau = rF$

$\tau = (10 \text{ m})\cdot(300 \text{ N})$

$\tau = 3,000 \text{ N·m}$

5. D is correct.

1 revolution = 360°, 1 min = 60 s

33 rpm = 33 revs/min

(33 revs/min)·(360°/rev) = 11,880°/min

(11,880°/min)·(1 min/60 s) = 198°/s

Degrees per second is a *rate*:

rate $\times$ time = total degrees

$(198°/s) \cdot (0.32 \text{ s}) \approx 63°$

6. B is correct.

momentum = mass $\times$ velocity

$p = mv$

Since momentum is directly proportional to mass, doubling the mass doubles the momentum.

7. D is correct. The total momentum before the collision is:

$p_{total} = m_I v_I + m_{II} v_{II} + m_{III} v_{III}$

$p_{before} = (1 \text{ kg}) \cdot (0.5 \text{ m/s}) + (1.5 \text{ kg}) \cdot (-0.3 \text{ m/s}) + (3.5 \text{ kg}) \cdot (-0.5 \text{ m/s})$

$p_{before} = (0.5 \text{ kg·m/s}) + (-0.45 \text{ kg·m/s}) + (-1.75 \text{ kg·m/s})$

$p_{before} = -1.7 \text{ kg·m/s}$

8. A is correct. The collision of I and II does not affect the momentum of the system:

$p_{before} = p_{after}$

$p_{I \& II} = (1 \text{ kg}) \cdot (0.5 \text{ m/s}) + (1.5 \text{ kg}) \cdot (-0.3 \text{ m/s})$

$p_{I \& II} = (0.5 \text{ kg·m/s}) - (0.45 \text{ kg·m/s})$

$p_{I \& II} = 0.05 \text{ kg·m/s}$

$p_{III} = (3.5 \text{ kg}) \cdot (-0.5 \text{ m/s})$

$p_{III} = -1.75 \text{ kg·m/s}$

$p_{net} = p_{I \text{ and } II} + p_{III}$

$p_{net} = (0.05 \text{ kg·m/s}) + (-1.75 \text{ kg·m/s})$

$p_{net} = 1.7 \text{ kg·m/s}$

Momentum is conserved at all times.

9. B is correct. Set the initial momentum equal to the final momentum after all the collisions have occurred.

$p_{before} = p_{after}$

$p_{before} = (m_I + m_{II} + m_{III})v_f$

$-1.7 \text{ kg·m/s} = (1 \text{ kg} + 1.5 \text{ kg} + 3.5 \text{ kg})v_f$

$v_f = (-1.7 \text{ kg·m/s}) / (6 \text{ kg})$

$v_f = -0.28 \text{ m/s}$

10. C is correct. Momentum is conserved in this system. The momentum of each car is given by *mv*, and the sum of the momenta before the collision must equal the sum of the momenta after the collision:

$p_{\text{before}} = p_{\text{after}}$

Solve for the velocity of the first car after the collision. Each car is traveling in the same direction before and after the collision, so each velocity value has the same sign.

$m_1 v_{i1} + m_2 v_{i2} = m_1 v_{f1} + m_2 v_{f2}$

(480 kg)·(14.4 m/s) + (570 kg)·(13.3 m/s) = (480 kg)·(v_{f2}) + (570 kg)·(17.9 m/s)

(480 kg)·(v_{f2}) = (480 kg)·(14.4 m/s) + (570 kg)·(13.3 m/s) – (570 kg)·(17.9 m/s)

v_{f2} = [(480 kg)·(14.4 m/s) + (570 kg)·(13.3 m/s) – (570 kg)·(17.9 m/s)] / (480 kg)

v_{f2} = 8.9 m/s ≈ 9 m/s

11. D is correct. Impulse is a force acting over a period of time:

$J = F\Delta t$

An impulse changes a system's momentum, so:

$F\Delta t = \Delta p_{\text{system}}$

The moving block with the lodged bullet comes to a stop when it compresses the spring, losing all momentum.

The initial velocity of the block and bullet separately can be determined by conservation of energy. The two values of interest are the KE of the block and bullet and the PE of the spring.

$(\text{KE} + \text{PE})_{\text{before}} = (\text{KE} + \text{PE})_{\text{after}}$

$\tfrac{1}{2}mv^2 + 0 = 0 + \tfrac{1}{2}kx^2$

x = distance of compression of the spring

k = spring constant

$\tfrac{1}{2}$(4 kg + 0.008 kg)v^2 = $\tfrac{1}{2}$(1,400 N/m)·(0.089 m)^2

v^2 = (1,400 N/m)·(0.089 m)^2 / (4.008 kg)

v^2 = 2.76 m^2/s^2

v = 1.66 m/s

Thus, the block with the lodged bullet hits the spring with an initial velocity of 1.66 m/s.

Since there is no friction, the block is sent in the opposite direction with the same speed of 1.66 m/s when the spring decompresses. Calculate the momentum, with initial momentum toward the spring and final momentum away from the spring.

$\Delta p = p_{\text{final}} - p_{\text{initial}}$

Δp = (4.008 kg)·(–1.66 m/s) – (4.008 kg)·(1.66 m/s)

Δp = (–6.65 kg·m/s) – (6.65 kg·m/s)

Δp ≈ –13 kg·m/s

$\Delta p \approx -13$ N·s

Since $F\Delta t = \Delta p$, the impulse is also -13 kg·m/s $= -13$ N·s

The negative sign signifies the coordinate system chosen in this calculation: toward the spring is the positive direction, and away from the spring is the negative direction.

12. C is correct. Angular momentum is conserved:

$L = I\omega$

where I = moment of inertia and ω = angular velocity

$L = (\frac{1}{2}mr^2)\omega$

If r (radius of arm out from body) decreases, ω increases to conserve angular momentum.

$L_1 = L_2$

$I_1\omega_1 = I_2\omega_2$

$I_1 > I_2$

$\omega_1 < \omega_2$

Thus when the skater brings in her arms the moment of inertia and angular velocity change in proportion to each other.

$KE_R = \frac{1}{2}I\omega^2$

$KE_1 < KE_2$

However, rotational KE increases because I is constant and ω is squared. Thus the resulting KE is greater because it has a greater ω. The increase in KE comes from the work performed by the skater when retracting her arms.

13. D is correct. The centripetal force is the net force required to maintain an object in uniform circular motion.

$F_{centripetal} = mv^2/r$

where r is the radius of the circular path

Since m is constant and r remains unchanged, the centripetal force is proportional to v^2.

$2^2 = 4$

Thus, if v is doubled, then $F_{centripetal}$ is quadrupled.

14. B is correct.

$1 J = kg·m^2/s^2$

$p = mv = kg·m/s$

$J·s/m = (kg·m^2/s^2)·(s/m)$

$J·s/m = kg·m/s$

$kg \cdot m/s = p$

$J \cdot s/m = p$

15. D is correct. Impulse is a change in momentum.

$J = \Delta p$

$J = m\Delta v$

Impulse is also the product of average force and time.

$J = F\Delta t$

$F\Delta t = m\Delta v$

$ma\Delta t = m\Delta v$, cancel m from both sides of the expression

$a\Delta t = \Delta v$

Because acceleration g is constant impulse depends only upon time and velocity.

The speed of the apple affects the impulse as this is included in the Δv term.

Bouncing results in a change in direction. This means a greater change in velocity (the Δv term), so the impulse is greater.

The time of impulse changes the impulse as it is included in the Δt term.

16. D is correct.

$F\Delta t = m\Delta v$

$F = m\Delta v / \Delta t$

Choosing toward the wall as the positive direction, the initial velocity is 25 m/s and the final velocity is –25 m/s:

$F = m(v_f - v_i) / \Delta t$

$F = (0.8 \text{ kg}) \cdot (-25 \text{ m/s} - 25 \text{ m/s}) / (0.05 \text{ s})$

$F = -800 \text{ N}$

Thus, the wall exerts an average force of 800 N on the ball in the negative direction. From Newton's Third Law, the ball exerts a force of 800 N on the wall in the opposite direction.

17. B is correct.

$p = mv$

Sum momentum:

$p_{total} = m_1v_1 + m_2v_2 + m_3v_3$

All objects moving to the left have negative velocity.

$p_{total} = (7 \text{ kg}) \cdot (6 \text{ m/s}) + (12 \text{ kg}) \cdot (3 \text{ m/s}) + (4 \text{ kg}) \cdot (-2 \text{ m/s})$

$p_{total} = (42 \text{ kg·m/s}) + (36 \text{ kg·m/s}) + (-8 \text{ kg·m/s})$

$p_{total} = 70 \text{ kg·m/s}$

18. D is correct.

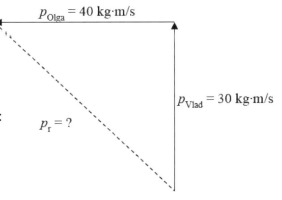

Use conservation of momentum to determine the momentum after the collision. Since they stick together, treat it as a perfectly inelastic collision.

Before the collision, Vladimir's momentum is: $(60 \text{ kg})·(0.5 \text{ m/s}) = 30 \text{ kg·m/s}$ pointing North

Before the collision, Olga's momentum is:

$(40 \text{ kg})·(1 \text{ m/s}) = 40 \text{ kg·m/s}$ pointing West

Write two expressions: one for conservation of momentum on the *y*-axis (North-South) and one for conservation of momentum on the *x*-axis (East-West). They do not interact since they are perpendicular to each other. Since Olga and Vladimir stick together, the final mass is the sum of their masses.

Simply use the Pythagorean Theorem:

$a^2 + b^2 = c^2$

$(30 \text{ kg·m/s})^2 + (40 \text{ kg·m/s})^2 = p^2$

$900 \text{ (kg·m/s)}^2 + 1{,}600 \text{ (kg·m/s)}^2 = p^2$

$2{,}500 \text{(kg·m/s)}^2 = p^2$

$p = 50 \text{ kg·m/s}$

Use this to solve for velocity:

$p = mv$

$50 \text{ kg·m/s} = (100 \text{ kg})v$

$v = 50 \text{ kg·m/s} / 100 \text{ kg}$

$v = 0.5 \text{ m/s}$

Also, this problem can be solved algebraically:

$p_{before} = p_{after}$

$p = mv$

On the *y* coordinate:

$(60 \text{ kg})·(0.5 \text{ m/s}) = (60 \text{ kg} + 40 \text{ kg})v_y$

$v_y = (30 \text{ kg·m/s}) / (100 \text{ kg})$

$v_y = 0.3 \text{ m/s}$

On the *x* coordinate:

$(40 \text{ kg})·(1 \text{ m/s}) = (60 \text{ kg} + 40 \text{ kg})v_x$

$$v_x = (40 \text{ kg·m/s}) / (100 \text{ kg})$$

$$v_x = 0.4 \text{ m/s}$$

Combine these final velocity components using the Pythagorean Theorem since they are perpendicular.

$$v^2 = v_x^2 + v_y^2$$

$$v^2 = (0.4 \text{ m/s})^2 + (0.3 \text{ m/s})^2$$

$$v = 0.5 \text{ m/s}$$

19. B is correct. Use conservation of momentum to determine the momentum after the collision. Since they stick together, treat it as a perfectly inelastic collision.

Before collision, Vladimir's momentum is $(60 \text{ kg})·(0.5 \text{ m/s}) = 30 \text{ kg·m/s}$ pointing North

Before collision, Olga's momentum is $(40 \text{ kg})·(1 \text{ m/s}) = 40 \text{ kg·m/s}$ pointing West

Write two expressions: one for conservation of momentum on the y coordinate (North–South) and one for conservation of momentum on the x coordinate (East-West). They do not interact since they are perpendicular to each other. Since they stick together, the final mass is the sum of their masses.

Simply use the Pythagorean Theorem:

$$a^2 + b^2 = c^2$$

$$(30 \text{ kg·m/s})^2 + (40 \text{ kg·m/s})^2 = p^2$$

$$900(\text{kg·m/s})^2 + 1{,}600(\text{kg·m/s})^2 = p^2$$

$$2{,}500(\text{kg·m/s})^2 = p^2$$

$$p = 50 \text{ kg·m/s}$$

This problem can also be solved algebraically:

$$p_{\text{before}} = p_{\text{after}}$$

$$p = mv$$

On the y coordinate:

$$(60 \text{ kg})·(0.5 \text{ m/s}) = (60 \text{ kg} + 40 \text{ kg})v_y$$

$$v_y = (30 \text{ kg·m/s}) / (100 \text{ kg})$$

$$v_y = 0.3 \text{ m/s}$$

On the x coordinate:

$$(40 \text{ kg})·(1 \text{ m/s}) = (60 \text{ kg} + 40 \text{ kg})v_x$$

$$v_x = (40 \text{ kg·m/s}) / (100 \text{ kg})$$

$$v_x = 0.4 \text{ m/s}$$

Combine these final velocity components using the Pythagorean Theorem since they are perpendicular:

$$v^2 = v_x{}^2 + v_y{}^2$$

$$v^2 = (0.4 \text{ m/s})^2 + (0.3 \text{ m/s})^2$$

$$v = 0.5 \text{ m/s}$$

Use the final weight and final velocity to find the final momentum directly after the collision:

$$p = mv$$

$$p = (60 \text{ kg} + 40 \text{ kg}) \cdot (0.5 \text{ m/s})$$

$$p = 50 \text{ kg·m/s}$$

20. C is correct.

$$p_0 = mv$$

If *m* and *v* are doubled:

$$p = (2m) \cdot (2v)$$

$$p = 4mv$$

$$p = 4p_0$$

The momentum increases by a factor of 4.

21. D is correct. Balance forces on box Q to solve for tension on box P cable:

$$m_Q a = F - T_P$$

$$T_P = F - m_Q a$$

$$0 < T_P < F$$

Thus the tension on the cable connected to box P is less than *F* because it is equal to the difference of *F* and $m_Q a$ but is not equal because the boxes are accelerating.

22. B is correct. At all points on a rotating body the angular velocity is equal. The speed at different points along a rotating body is directly proportional to the radius

$$v = \omega r$$

where *v* = speed, ω = angular velocity and *r* = radius

Thus Melissa and her friend have different speeds due to their different radial locations.

24. D is correct. Angular momentum is always conserved unless a system experiences a net torque greater than zero. This is the rotational equivalent of Newton's First Law of motion.

25. D is correct.

$$F \Delta t = m \Delta v$$

$F = (m\Delta v) / (\Delta t)$

$F = (6.8 \text{ kg}) \cdot (-3.2 \text{ m/s} - 5.4 \text{ m/s}) / (2 \text{ s})$

$F = (-58.48 \text{ kg·m/s}) / (2 \text{ s})$

$F = -29.2 \text{ N}$

$|F| = 29.2 \text{ N}$

26. A is correct.

Before collision, the total momentum of the system = 0 kg·m/s.

Momentum is conserved in the explosion.

The momentum of the moving rifle and bullet are in opposite directions:

Therefore, $p = 0$

The total momentum after the explosion = 0 kg·m/s

27. D is correct.

$p = mv$

Conservation of momentum:

$p_{initial} = p_{final}$

$0 \text{ kg·m/s} = (0.01 \text{ kg}) \cdot (300 \text{ m/s}) + (4 \text{ kg})v_{recoil}$

$0 \text{ kg·m/s} = 3 \text{ kg·m/s} + (4 \text{ kg})v_{recoil}$

$-3 \text{ kg·m/s} = (4 \text{ kg})v_{recoil}$

$(-3 \text{ kg·m/s}) / (4 \text{ kg}) = v_{recoil}$

$v_{recoil} = -0.75 \text{ m/s}$

Velocity is negative since the gun recoils in the opposite direction of the bullet.

28. C is correct.

Since the initial velocity only has a horizontal component, the y component of the initial velocity = 0.

Use 24 m to calculate the time the ball is in the air:

$d_y = \frac{1}{2}at^2$

$t^2 = 2d_y / a$

$t^2 = 2(24 \text{ m}) / (9.8 \text{ m/s}^2)$

$t^2 = 4.9 \text{ s}^2$

$t = 2.2 \text{ s}$

Use the time in the air and the horizontal distance to calculate the horizontal speed of the ball:

$$v_x = d_x / t$$
$$v_x = (18 \text{ m}) / (2.2 \text{ s})$$
$$v_x = 8.2 \text{ m/s}$$

29. A is correct. An object moving in a circle at constant speed is undergoing uniform circular motion. In uniform circular motion the acceleration is due to centripetal acceleration and points inward towards the center of a circle.

30. B is correct.

Impulse:

$$J = F\Delta t$$
$$J = \Delta p$$

where p is momentum

31. C is correct.

Conservation of energy:

$$\text{KE}_i + \text{PE}_i = \text{KE}_f + \text{PE}_f$$
$$\text{KE}_i + \text{PE}_i = \text{KE}_f + 0$$
$$\text{KE}_f = \tfrac{1}{2}mv_i^2 + mgh_i$$
$$\text{KE}_f = \tfrac{1}{2}(4 \text{ kg})\cdot(20 \text{ m/s})^2 + (4 \text{ kg})\cdot(10 \text{ m/s}^2)\cdot(10 \text{ m})$$
$$\text{KE}_f = 800 \text{ J} + 400 \text{ J}$$
$$\text{KE}_f = 1,200 \text{ J}$$

32. D is correct.

The force needed to stop a car can be related to KE and work:

$$\text{KE} = W$$
$$\tfrac{1}{2}mv^2 = Fd$$
$$F = \tfrac{1}{2}mv^2 / d$$

Momentum is included in the KE term.

$$p = mv$$
$$F = \tfrac{1}{2}(mv)v / d$$
$$F = \tfrac{1}{2}(p)v / d$$

If there is less stopping distance the force increases as they are inversely proportional.

If the momentum or mass increase the force increases as they are directly proportional.

33. C is correct.

Impulse:

$$J = F\Delta t$$

Assuming no energy lost in the collision, from Newton's Third Law, the force experienced by these two objects is equal and opposite.

Therefore, the magnitudes of impulse are the same.

34. B is correct. Balance the counterclockwise (CCW) torque with the clockwise (CW) torque. Let the axis of rotation be at the point where the rope attaches to the bar. This placement causes the torque from the rope to be zero since the lever arm is zero.

$$\Sigma\,\tau : \tau_1 - \tau_2 = 0$$

$$\tau_1 = \tau_2$$

The CCW torque due to the weight of the 6 kg mass:

$$\tau = r_1 F_1$$

$$r_1 F_1 = (x)\cdot(6\text{ kg})\cdot(9.8\text{ m/s}^2)$$

The CW torque due to the weight of the 30 kg mass:

$$r_2 F_2 = (5\text{ m} - x)\cdot(30\text{ kg})\cdot(9.8\text{ m/s}^2)$$

Set the two expressions equal to each other

$$(9.8\text{ m/s}^2)\cdot(x)\cdot(6\text{ kg}) = (5\text{ m} - x)\cdot(30\text{ kg})\cdot(9.8\text{ m/s}^2)$$

Cancel g and kg from each side of the equation:

$$6x = 30(5\text{ m} - x)$$

$$6x = 150\text{ m} - 30x$$

$$36x = 150\text{ m}$$

$$x = 4.2\text{ m}$$

35. D is correct.

If the block is at rest then the force of static friction is equal to the force of gravity at angle θ.

$$F_f = mg\sin\theta$$

36. C is correct.

$F_{net} = 0$ is necessary to maintain constant velocity.

If 45 N must be exerted on the block to maintain constant velocity, the force due to kinetic friction against the block equals 45 N.

For a horizontal surface and no other vertical forces acting, the normal force on the block equals its weight.

$$N = mg$$

$$F_{friction} = \mu_k N$$

$$F_{friction} = \mu_k mg$$

$$\mu_k = (F_{friction}) / mg$$

$$\mu_k = (45\text{ N}) / [(30\text{ kg}) \cdot (10\text{ m/s}^2)]$$

$$\mu_k = 0.15$$

37. B is correct.

Newton's Second Law:

$$F = ma$$

The impulse-momentum relationship can be derived by multiplying Δt on both sides:

$$F\Delta t = ma\Delta t$$

$$F\Delta t = m\Delta v$$

$$J = m\Delta v$$

Thus the impulse is equal to the change in momentum.

38. C is correct. Force X acts perpendicular to the short arm of the rectangle, this is the lever arm.

$$\tau = rF$$

$$\tau = (0.5\text{ m}) \cdot (15\text{ N})$$

$$\tau = 7.5\text{ N·m}$$

Since the torque causes the plate to rotate clockwise its sign is negative.

$$\tau = -7.5\text{ N·m}$$

39. D is correct.

$$\tau = rF$$

Force Z acts directly at the pivot so the lever arm equals zero.

$$\tau = (0\text{ m}) \cdot (30\text{ N})$$

$$\tau = 0\text{ N·m}$$

40. A is correct.

$$\tau = rF$$

Force Y acts perpendicular to the long arm of the rectangle, this is the lever arm.

$$\tau = (0.6\text{ m}) \cdot (25\text{ N})$$

$\tau = 15$ N·m

The torque is clockwise, so its sign is negative.

$\tau = -15$ N·m

41. B is correct. The tension in the string provides the centripetal force.

$T = mv^2 / r$

$m = 50$ g $= 0.05$ kg

$T = [(0.05$ kg$)\cdot(20$ m/s$)^2] / (2$ m$)$

$T = [(0.05$ kg$)\cdot(400$ m^2/s$^2)] / (2$ m$)$

$T = (20$ kg·m^2/s$^2) / (2$ m$)$

$T = 10$ N

42. A is correct.

$F = ma$

Newton's Third Law states that each force is paired with an equal and opposite reaction force. Therefore, the small car and the truck each receive the same force.

43. C is correct. Choose the axis of rotation at the point where the bar attaches to the wall. Since the lever arm of the force that the wall exerts is zero, the torque at that point is zero and can be ignored.

The two other torques present arise from the weight of the bar exerting force downward and the cable exerting force upward. The weight of the bar acts at the center of mass, so its lever arm is 1 m. The lever arm for the cable is 2 m, since it acts the full 2 m away from the wall at the end of the bar.

Since torque is calculated with a cross product, only the perpendicular component of force creates torque, so a sin 30° term must be used for the cable.

The sum of torques = 0, since the bar is in rotational equilibrium.

Let the torque of the cable be positive and the torque of the weight be negative.

torque upward (cable) + torque downward (weight) = 0

$(F_T \sin 30°)\cdot(2$ m$) - (10$ kg$)\cdot(10$ m/s$^2)\cdot(1$ m$) = 0$

$F_T = [(10$ kg$)\cdot(10$ m/s$^2)\cdot(1$ m$)] / [(2$ m$)\cdot(\sin 30°)]$

$F_T = [(10$ kg$)\cdot(10$ m/s$^2)\cdot(1$ m$)] / [(2$ m$)\cdot(0.5)]$

$F_T = 100$ N

44. B is correct. Momentum is defined as:

$$p = mv$$

$$m_A = 2m_B$$

$$p_A = 2m_Bv$$

$$p_B = m_Bv$$

$$p_A = 2p_B$$

If both objects reach the ground at the same time they have equal velocities.

However because B is twice the mass it has twice the momentum as object A

45. D is correct. Use conservation of momentum to make equations for momenta along the x-axis and the y-axis. Since the mass ratio is 1 : 4, one car has a mass of m and the other has a mass of $4m$. The entangled cars after the collision have a combined mass of $5m$.

Let the car of mass m be traveling in the positive x direction and the car of mass $4m$ be traveling in the positive y direction. The choice of directions here is arbitrary, but the angle of impact is important.

$$p_{initial} = p_{final} \text{ for both the } x\text{- and } y\text{-axes}$$

$$p = mv$$

For the x-axis:

$$m_iv_i = m_fv_{fx}$$

$$m(12 \text{ m/s}) = 5mv_x, \text{ cancel } m$$

$$12 \text{ m/s} = 5v_x$$

$$v_x = 2.4 \text{ m/s}$$

For the y-axis:

$$m_iv_i = m_fv_{fy}$$

$$4m(12 \text{ m/s}) = 5mv_y, \text{ cancel } m$$

$$4(12 \text{ m/s}) = 5v_y$$

$$v_y = 9.6 \text{ m/s}$$

The question asks for the magnitude of the final velocity, so combine the x and y components of the final velocity using the Pythagorean Theorem.

$$v^2 = (2.4 \text{ m/s})^2 + (9.6 \text{ m/s})^2$$

$$v^2 = 5.76 \text{ m}^2/\text{s}^2 + 92.16 \text{ m}^2/\text{s}^2$$

$$v = 9.9 \text{ m/s}$$

46. C is correct. Use conservation of momentum on the horizontal plane. The horizontal component of the anchor's momentum equals the momentum of the fisherman moving the opposite way.

Use m for the fisherman's mass and $2m$ for the anchor's mass.

$$p = mv$$

$$p_{boat} = p_{anchor}$$

$$m_b v_b = m_a v_a$$

$$m_b(2.9 \text{ m/s}) = 2m_a v \cos 5°, \text{ cancel } m$$

$$v = (2.9 \text{ m/s}) / (2 \cos 5°)$$

$$v = (2.9 \text{ m/s}) / (2)·(0.996)$$

$$v = 1.5 \text{ m/s}$$

47. B is correct.

$$\text{weight} = \text{mass} \times \text{gravity}$$

$$W = mg$$

$$m = W / g$$

$$m = (98 \text{ N}) / (9.8 \text{ m/s}^2)$$

$$m = 10 \text{ kg}$$

Newton's Second Law:

$$F = ma$$

$$F = (10 \text{ kg})·(10 \text{ m/s}^2)$$

$$F = 100 \text{ N}$$

48. A is correct.

KE is constant and conserved because speed is constant.

PE increases because the cart is at a greater height at point B.

The cart as a system is not isolated since the winch does work on it and so its energy is not conserved.

Conservation of energy:

PE increase of the cart = work done by the winch

49. D is correct.

The vertical component of the initial velocity:

$$v_{iy} = (140 \text{ m/s}) \sin 35°$$

$$v_{iy} = (140 \text{ m/s})\cdot(0.57)$$

$$v_{iy} = 79.8 \text{ m/s}$$

The initial velocity upward, time elapsed, and acceleration due to gravity is known.

Determine the final velocity after 4 s.

$$v_y = v_{iy} + at$$

$$v_y = 79.8 \text{ m/s} + (-9.8 \text{ m/s}^2)\cdot(4 \text{ s})$$

$$v_y = 41 \text{ m/s}$$

50. C is correct.

$$\text{impulse} = \text{force} \times \text{time}$$

$$J = F\Delta t$$

51. D is correct.

Conservation of momentum: the momentum of the fired bullet is equal and opposite to that of the rifle.

$$p = mv$$

$$p_{before} = p_{after}$$

$$0 = p_{rifle} + p_{bullet}$$

$$-p_{rifle} = p_{bullet}$$

$$-(2 \text{ kg})v = (0.01 \text{ kg})\cdot(220 \text{ m/s})$$

$$v = (0.01 \text{ kg})\cdot(220 \text{ m/s}) / (-2 \text{ kg})$$

$$v = -1.1 \text{ m/s}$$

Thus, the velocity of the rifle is 1.1 m/s in the opposite direction as the bullet.

52. D is correct.

Airbags reduce force by increasing the time of contact between the passenger and surface.

In a collision, an impulse is experienced by a passenger:

$$J = F\Delta t$$

$$F = J / \Delta t$$

The impulse is a constant but the force experienced by the passenger is inversely related to time of contact. Airbags increase the time of impact and thus reduce the forces experienced by the person.

53. A is correct. Since Force I is perpendicular to the beam, the entire force acts to produce torque without any horizontal force component.

$$\tau = rF$$

$$\tau = (0.5 \text{ m}) \cdot (10 \text{ N})$$

$$\tau = 5 \text{ N·m}$$

Because the force causes the beam to rotate clockwise against the positive counterclockwise direction, the torque sign should be negative:

$$\tau = -5 \text{ N·m}$$

54. D is correct. To calculate torque, use the 35° angle.

For torque:

$$\tau = rF \sin \theta$$

$$\tau = (1 \text{ m}) \cdot (5 \text{ N}) \sin 35°$$

$$\tau = 2.9 \text{ N·m}$$

The torque is counterclockwise, so the sign is positive.

55. B is correct. Force III acts purely in tension with the beam and has no component acting vertically against the beam. Torque can only be calculated using a force with some component perpendicular to the length vector. Because Force III has no perpendicular component to the length vector, torque is zero.

$$\tau = rF$$

$$\tau = (1 \text{ m}) \cdot (0 \text{ N})$$

$$\tau = 0 \text{ N·m}$$

56. C is correct.

Impulse can be written as:

$$J = m\Delta v$$

$$J = F\Delta t$$

Impulse is the change in momentum of an object. Because the yellow ball bounced higher, it can be concluded that its upward velocity after the collision must be higher than that of the red ball:

$$\Delta v_{\text{yellow}} > \Delta v_{\text{red}}$$

Thus, because the mass of both balls are the same, the yellow ball must have a greater impulse according to the impulse equation:

$$m\Delta v_{\text{yellow}} > m\Delta v_{\text{red}}$$

57. D is correct.

$J = F\Delta t$

$J = (4.5 \text{ N}) \cdot (1.4 \text{ s})$

$J = (4.5 \text{ kg·m/s}^2) \cdot (1.4 \text{ s})$

$J = 6.3 \text{ kg·m/s}$

58. A is correct. Both trucks experience the same acceleration due to gravity so their acceleration and velocity are equal because these do not depend on mass:

$v_f = v_0 + a\Delta t$

However, their momentum are different and the heavier truck has a larger momentum because of its larger mass.

$p = mv$

$m_H > m_L$

$p_H = m_H v$

$p_L = m_L v$

$p_H > p_L$

59. D is correct. The time elapsed from release until collision is calculated by:

time from release until collision = round trip time / 2

$t = (4 \text{ s}) / 2$

$t = 2 \text{ s}$

The time of contact is negligible to the round trip time, so this calculation ignores it. Since this collision is elastic, the time from release until the collision is the same as the time from the collision until the ball reaches the same height again.

Given this time in the air, find the velocity of the ball immediately before impact:

$v = v_i + at$

$v = 0 + (9.8 \text{ m/s}^2) \cdot (2 \text{ s})$

$v = 19.6 \text{ m/s}$

Find the KE of the ball before impact:

$KE = \frac{1}{2}mv^2$

$KE = \frac{1}{2}(0.078 \text{ kg}) \cdot (19.6 \text{ m/s})^2$

$KE = 15 \text{ J}$

The KE of the ball is stored as elastic energy during the collision and is then converted back to KE to send the ball upward in the opposite direction. This stored elastic energy is equivalent to the KE before the collision.

60. B is correct.

There is no unbalanced external force, so use the equation for conservation of momentum:

$p_{before} = p_{after}$

$m_1 v_i = (m_1 + m_2)v_f$

$(5 \text{ kg}) \cdot (2 \text{ m/s}) = (5 \text{ kg} + 10 \text{ kg})v_f$

$10 \text{ kg·m/s} = (15 \text{ kg})v_f$

$v_f = (10 \text{ kg·m/s}) / (15 \text{ kg})$

$v_f = 0.67 \text{ m/s}$

61. C is correct.

$J = F\Delta t$

$J = m\Delta v$

$F\Delta t = m\Delta v$

$\Delta t = (m\Delta v) / F$

Let towards the batter be the positive direction and away from batter be the negative direction:

$t = m(v_f - v_i) / F$

$t = (0.12 \text{ kg}) \cdot (-34 \text{ m/s} - 23 \text{ m/s}) / (-5,000 \text{ N})$

$t = 0.0014 \text{ s}$

$t = 1.4 \times 10^{-3} \text{ s}$

62. D is correct.

$KE = \tfrac{1}{2}mv^2$

$p = mv$

$m = p / v$

$v = p / m$

$KE = \tfrac{1}{2}(p / v)v^2$

$KE = \tfrac{1}{2}pv$

$KE = \tfrac{1}{2}p(p / m)$

$KE = \tfrac{1}{2}(p^2 / m)$

$KE = p^2 / 2m$

---

63. D is correct.

Conservation of momentum:

$mv_i = mv_f + Mv$

$m(v_i - v_f) = Mv$

$(2.2 \text{ kg}) \, [(9.2 \text{ m/s} - (-2.5 \text{ m/s})] = Mv$

$Mv = 25.75 \text{ kg·m/s}$

Conservation of KE:

$\frac{1}{2}mv_i^2 = \frac{1}{2}mv_f^2 + \frac{1}{2}Mv^2$

$mv_i^2 = mv_f^2 + Mv^2$

$m(v_i^2 - v_f^2) = Mv^2$

$(2.2 \text{ kg})[9.2 \text{ m/s}^2 - (-2.5 \text{ m/s})^2] = Mv^2$

$Mv^2 = 172.5 \text{ kg·m/s}^2$

$v(Mv) = Mv^2$

$v(25.75 \text{ kg·m/s}) = 172.5 \text{ kg·m/s}^2$

$v = (172.5 \text{ kg·m/s}^2) / (25.75 \text{ kg·m/s})$

$v = 6.7 \text{ m/s}$

$M(6.7 \text{ m/s}) = 25.75 \text{ kg·m/s}$

$M = (25.75 \text{ kg·m/s}) / (6.7 \text{ m/s})$

$M = 3.8 \text{ kg}$

64. C is correct.

Momentum is conserved:

$p = mv$

$p_{before} = p_{after}$

Set to the left as the negative direction.

$m_1v_{1i} + m_2v_{2i} = m_1v_{1f} + m_2v_{2f}$

$(1 \text{ kg})·(7 \text{ m/s}) + (3 \text{ kg})·(-2 \text{ m/s}) = (1 \text{ kg})·(-3 \text{ m/s}) + (3 \text{ kg})v$

$7 \text{ kg·m/s} + (-6 \text{ kg·m/s}) = -3 \text{ kg·m/s} + (3 \text{ kg})v_f$

$1 \text{ kg·m/s} = -3 \text{ kg·m/s} + (3 \text{ kg})v_f$

$4 \text{ kg·m/s} = (3 \text{ kg})v_f$

$(4 \text{ kg·m/s}) / (3 \text{ kg}) = v_f$

$v_f = 1.3 \text{ m/s}$, the direction of cart II is to the right because the vector is positive.

65. B is correct.

Newton's Third Law states that every action has an equal and opposite reaction.

66. D is correct. Equation for torque $\tau = r \times F$, where r is the length at which the force is acting.

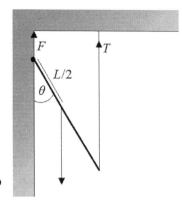

$\tau_{net} = 0$, system is in equilibrium

$0 = -\tau_{mg} + \tau_T$

The torque due to gravity is working in the clockwise direction, therefore it is negative.

Tension is working counter-clockwise, so it is positive.

Let the length of the rod be L; then the torque upward (due to the tension T in the string) $= LT \sin \theta$.

The torque downward is due to the weight of the rod, and the weight vector acts at the rod's center of mass, which is halfway ($L / 2$) down the rod.

$0 = -(L / 2)Mg \sin \theta + (L)T \sin \theta$

$0 = -(L / 2)Mg + (L)T$

$T = Mg / 2$

Mg acts in the middle of the rod, as it is uniform. T acts at the full length.

$0 = -(½)Mg + T$

$T = Mg / 2$

67. A is correct. If no force acts there is no acceleration.

$F_{net} = 0$

$0 = ma$

$m \neq 0$

$a = 0$

Impulse is:

$F\Delta t = m\Delta v$

$J = 0$

Force is zero, so impulse is zero.

The momentum is constant because momentum is the product of mass and velocity:

$p = mv$

$m \neq 0$

$v \neq 0$

Since neither the mass nor velocity are changing, momentum is constant.

68. D is correct. In projectile motion the only force acting on the projectile (if air resistance is ignored) is the force of gravity. Therefore the horizontal component of the velocity does not change and is constant because gravity only acts vertically.

69. D is correct. Use conservation of momentum to find the velocity of the objects after the collision. Note that the objects stick together in a perfectly inelastic collision, and the initial momentum of the stationary 4 kg object is zero.

$$p = mv$$

$$m_1v_1 = (m_1 + m_2)v_2$$

$$(3.3 \text{ kg}) \cdot (6.9 \text{ m/s}) = (3.3 \text{ kg} + 3.6 \text{ kg})v_f$$

$$v_f = 3.3 \text{ m/s}$$

Calculate the initial KE and final KE of the system:

$$KE_{initial} = \tfrac{1}{2}mv^2$$

$$KE_{initial} = \tfrac{1}{2}(3.3 \text{ kg}) \cdot (6.9 \text{ m/s})^2$$

$$KE_{initial} = 78.6 \text{ J}$$

$$KE_{final} = \tfrac{1}{2}mv^2$$

$$KE_{final} = \tfrac{1}{2}(3.3 \text{ kg} + 3.6 \text{ kg}) \cdot (3.3 \text{ m/s})^2$$

$$KE_{final} = 37.6 \text{ J}$$

Use KE to find the percentage of initial kinetic energy lost:

$$\% \, KE_{lost} = (100) \cdot [(78.6 \text{ J} - 37.6 \text{ J}) / (78.6 \text{ J})]$$

$$\% \, KE_{lost} = 52\%$$

70. D is correct. In circular motion, all points on a rotating body experience the same angular displacement. The angular displacement is not equal to zero if the carousel is in motion.

71. C is correct.

$$p = mv, \text{ or}$$

$$p = m_1v_1 = m_2v_2$$

$$v_2 = (m_1v_1) / m_2$$

$$m_2 = m_1 + m_{ore}$$

$$m_2 = 1{,}200 \text{ kg} + 800 \text{ kg}$$

$$m_2 = 2{,}000 \text{ kg}$$

$$v_2 = [(1{,}200 \text{ kg}) \cdot (10 \text{ m/s})] / 2{,}000 \text{ kg}$$

$$v_2 = 6 \text{ m/s}$$

72. A is correct. By Newton's Third Law the car and the truck experience equal and opposite forces during the collision. The time of contact for the car and truck is also equal.

Thus the car and truck have the same impulse:

$J_{car} = J_{truck}$

$J = F\Delta t$

$J = \Delta p$

$\Delta p_{car} = \Delta p_{truck}$

The car and truck experience the same change in momentum.

73. D is correct.

$F_{net\ pully} = 2F_T$

$F_{net\ pully} = 2(750\ N)$

$F_{net\ pully} = 1,500\ N$

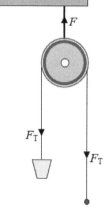

Since the bucket is not accelerating, the tension in the rope is 750 N.

Therefore, the pulley experiences two tension forces (one on each side of the pulley), each 750 N pulling downward.

The pulley, to remain stationary, experiences a total tension force of 1,500 N.

74. B is correct. Momentum is conserved so the momentum of the ball equals the momentum of the cannon.

$m_B v_B = m_C v_C$

However the cannon has more mass than the ball so its recoil velocity is much less than the velocity of the cannon ball to conserve momentum.

$m_B < m_C$

$v_B > v_C$

75. A is correct. Since the momentum is conserved during the collision, the change is $p = 0$.

$p_{initial} = p_{final}$

$m_1 v_1 + m_2 v_2 = (m_1 + m_2) v_3$

76. D is correct.

$J = \Delta p = m\Delta v$

$\Delta v = J\ /\ m$

$\Delta v = (30,000\ N \cdot s)\ /\ (1,120\ kg)$

$$\Delta v = 27 \text{ m/s}$$
$$\Delta v = v_f - v_i$$
$$27 \text{ m/s} = 0 - v_i$$
$$v_i = 27 \text{ m/s}$$

77. A is correct. In uniform circular motion the centripetal force does no work because the force and displacement vectors are at right angles to each other.

$$W = Fd$$

The work equation is only applicable if force and displacement direction are the same.

78. D is correct.

$$J = F\Delta t$$

Impulse remains constant so the time of impact increases and the impact force decreases.

79. B is correct. Consider a dropped baseball on Earth:

$$d_E = -\tfrac{1}{2}gt^2$$

On the Moon:

$$d_M = -\tfrac{1}{2}(g/6)t^2$$
$$d_E / d_M = (-\tfrac{1}{2}gt^2) / (-\tfrac{1}{2}(g/6)t^2)$$
$$d_E / d_M = 1/6, \text{ so the distance is 6 times greater on the Moon}$$

80. D is correct. The total downward force on the meter stick is:

$$20 \text{ N} + 50 \text{ N} + 30 \text{ N} = 100 \text{ N}$$

The total upward force on the meter stick – which is provided by the tension in the supporting rope – must also be 100 N to keep the meter stick in static equilibrium.

Let x be the distance from the left end of the meter stick to the suspension point.

From the pivot point, balance the torques.

The counterclockwise (CCW) torque due to the 50 N weight at the left end is $50\,x$.

The total clockwise (CW) torque due to the weight of the meter stick and the 30 N weight at the right end is:

$$50x = 20(50 \text{ cm} - x) + 30(100 \text{ cm} - x)$$
$$50x = (1,000 \text{ cm} - 20x) + (3,000 \text{ cm} - 30x)$$
$$50x = 4,000 \text{ cm} - 50x$$
$$100x = 4,000 \text{ cm}$$
$$x = 40 \text{ cm}$$

81. B is correct.

$J = F\Delta t$ is constant

increased t = decreased F

82. C is correct.

$m_1v_1 = (m_1 + m_2)v_2$

$v_2 = (m_1v_1) / (m_1 + m_2)$

$v_2 = (1,200 \text{ kg})\cdot(15.6 \text{ m/s}) / (1,200 \text{ kg} + 1,500 \text{ kg})$

$v_2 = (18,720 \text{ kg}\cdot\text{m/s}) / (2,700 \text{ kg})$

$v_2 = 6.9 \text{ m/s}$

83. D is correct.

$F\Delta t = m\Delta v$

$F = (m\Delta v) / \Delta t$

$F = [(0.05 \text{ kg})\cdot(100 \text{ m/s} - 0 \text{ m/s})] / (0.0008 \text{ s})$

$F = (5 \text{ kg}\cdot\text{m/s}) / (0.0008 \text{ s})$

$F = 6,250 \text{ N} = 6.3 \text{ kN}$

84. A is correct.

In circular motion all points along the rotational body have the same angular velocity regardless of their radial distance from the center of rotation.

85. C is correct.

In both elastic and inelastic collisions, momentum is conserved.

However, in an ideal elastic collision, KE is also conserved, but not in an inelastic collision.

To determine if the collision is elastic or inelastic, compare the KE before and after the collision.

Initial KE:

$KE_i = \frac{1}{2}m_1v_1^2$

$KE_i = \frac{1}{2}(2 \text{ kg})\cdot(0.6 \text{ m/s})^2$

$KE_i = 0.36 \text{ J}$

Conservation of momentum:

$m_1v_1 + m_2v_2 = m_1u_1 + m_2u_2$

$$m_1 v_1 = m_2 u_2$$

$$(m_1 / m_2) v_1 = u_2$$

$$u_2 = (2\ \text{kg} / 2.5\ \text{kg}) \cdot (0.6\ \text{m/s})$$

$$u_2 = 0.48\ \text{m/s}$$

Final KE:

$$KE_f = \tfrac{1}{2} m_2 u_2^{\,2}$$

$$KE_f = \tfrac{1}{2}(2.5\ \text{kg}) \cdot (0.48\ \text{m/s})^2$$

$$KE_f = 0.29\ \text{J}$$

KE_i does not equal KE_f and thus KE is not conserved.

The collision is therefore inelastic and only momentum is conserved.

86. A is correct.

A longer barrel gives the expanding gas more time to impart force upon the bullet and thus increase the impulse upon the bullet.

$$J = F\Delta t$$

WORK AND ENERGY – EXPLANATIONS

1. D is correct.

The final velocity in projectile motion is related to the maximum height of the projectile through conservation of energy:

$$KE = PE$$

$$\tfrac{1}{2}mv^2 = mgh$$

When the stone thrown straight up passes its starting point on its way back down, its downward speed is equal to its initial upward velocity (2D motion). The stone thrown straight downward contains the same magnitude of initial velocity as the stone thrown upward, and thus both the stone thrown upward and the stone thrown downward have the same final speed.

A stone thrown horizontally (or for example, a stone thrown at 45°) does not achieve the same height h as a stone thrown straight up, so it has smaller final vertical velocity.

2. B is correct.

Work = force × displacement × cos θ

$W = Fd \cos \theta$, where θ is the angle between the vectors F and d

$W = (5 \text{ N}) \cdot (10 \text{ m}) \cos 45°$

$W = (50 \text{ J}) \cdot (0.7)$

$W = 35 \text{ J}$

3. A is correct.

$$KE = \tfrac{1}{2}mv^2$$

KE is influenced by mass and velocity. However, since velocity is squared, its influence on KE is greater than the influence of mass.

4. B is correct.

Work = force × displacement × cos θ

$W = Fd \cos \theta$

$\cos 90° = 0$

$W = 0$

Since the force of gravity acts perpendicular to the distance traveled by the ball, the force due to gravity does no work in moving the ball.

5. C is correct.

$$KE = \tfrac{1}{2}mv^2$$

$$KE = \tfrac{1}{2}(5 \text{ kg})\cdot(2 \text{ m/s})^2$$

$$KE = 10 \text{ J}$$

6. A is correct.

$$W = Fd \cos\theta$$

$$\cos\theta = 1$$

$$F = W / d$$

$$F = (360 \text{ J}) / (8 \text{ m})$$

$$F = 45 \text{ N}$$

$$F = ma$$

$$m = F / a$$

$$m = (45 \text{ N}) / (10 \text{ m/s}^2)$$

$$m = 4.5 \text{ kg}$$

7. D is correct.

On a displacement (x) vs. force (F) graph, the displacement is the y-axis and the force is the x-axis.

The slope is x / F, (in units of m/N) which is the reciprocal of the spring constant k, which is measured in N/m.

8. C is correct.

Work done by a spring equation:

$$W = \tfrac{1}{2}kx^2$$

$$W = \tfrac{1}{2}(22 \text{ N/m}) (3 \text{ m})^2$$

$$W = 99 \text{ J}$$

9. A is correct.

The force due to gravity always acts downward. When the ball is traveling upward, the gravitational force applied over the traveled distance is negative, and therefore the work done by gravity is negative.

When the ball travels downward, the gravitational force is applied over the traveled distance is positive, and therefore the work done by gravity is positive.

10. B is correct. Work done by gravity is an object's change in gravitational PE.

$$W = -PE$$

$$A_1 = 400 \text{ J}$$

By the work-energy theorem,

$$W = KE$$

$$B_1 = 400 \text{ J}$$

11. D is correct. Work is calculated as the product of force and displacement parallel to the direction of the applied force:

$$W = Fd \cos \theta$$

where some component of d is in the direction of the force.

12. B is correct. Work only depends on force and distance:

$$W = Fd \cos \theta$$

Power = W / t is the amount of work done in a unit of time.

13. A is correct.

The area under the curve on a graph is the product of the values of $y \times x$.

Here, the y value is force and the x value is distance:

$$Fd = W$$

14. C is correct.

This is the conservation of energy. The only force acting on the cat is gravity.

$$KE = PE_g$$

$$KE = mgh$$

$$KE = (3 \text{ kg}) \cdot (10 \text{ m/s}^2) \cdot (4 \text{ m})$$

$$KE = 120 \text{ J}$$

15. D is correct.

Static friction only acts on stationary objects to prevent them from moving.

Since no movement is involved, no distance is covered, and therefore the work done is zero.

$$W = Fd \cos \theta$$

If $d = 0$,

$$W = 0$$

16. D is correct.

$W = Fd$

$d = W / F$

$d = (350 \text{ J}) / (900 \text{ N})$

$d = 0.39 \text{ m}$

17. A is correct.

Conservation of energy between kinetic energy and potential energy:

KE = PE

$KE = \frac{1}{2}mv^2$ and $PE = mgh$

Set the equations equal to each other:

$\frac{1}{2}mv^2 = mgh$, cancel m from both sides

$\frac{1}{2}v^2 = gh$

h is only dependent on the initial v, which is equal between both objects, so the two objects rise to the same height.

18. A is correct.

Work = Power × time

$P_1 = W / t$

$P_2 = (3 \text{ W}) / (1/3 \ t)$

$P_2 = 3(3/1) \cdot (W / t)$

$P_2 = 9(W / t)$

$P_2 = 9(P_1)$

19. D is correct.

Conservation of energy.

KE = PE

$KE = mgh$

$W = mg$

$KE = Wh$

$KE = (450 \text{ N}) \cdot (9 \text{ m})$

$KE = 4{,}050 \text{ J}$

20. A is correct. $F_1 = -kx_1$

Solve for the spring constant k:

$k = F / x_1$

$k = (160 \text{ N}) / (0.23 \text{ m})$

$k = 696 \text{ N/m}$

$F_2 = -kx_2$

$F_2 = (696 \text{ N/m}) \cdot (0.34 \text{ m})$

$F_2 = 237 \text{ N}$

21. B is correct. There is a frictional force since the net force = 0

The mule pulls in the same direction as the direction of travel so $\cos \theta = 1$

$W = Fd \cos \theta$

$d = v\Delta t$

$W = Fv\Delta t$

22. D is correct.

$W = Fd \cos \theta$

$F_T = W / (d \times \cos \theta)$

$F_T = (540 \text{ J}) / (18 \text{ m} \times \cos 32°)$

$F_T = (540 \text{ J}) / (18 \text{ m} \times 0.848)$

$F_T = 35 \text{ N}$

23. B is correct.

$F = -kx$

$ma = -kx$

By adding an extra 100 grams, the mass is doubled:

$2ma = -kx$

Since acceleration and the spring constant are constant, only x changes.

Thus after the addition of 100 g, x doubles:

$PE_1 = \frac{1}{2}kx^2$

$PE_2 = \frac{1}{2}k(2x)^2$

$PE_2 = \frac{1}{2}k(4x^2)$

$PE_2 = 4(\frac{1}{2}kx^2)$

The potential energy increases by a factor of 4.

24. C is correct.

The force due to kinetic friction is related to the normal force on an object.

The normal force is equal and opposite to the object's weight:

$$F_f = \mu_k F_n$$

$$F_f = \mu_k mg$$

Therefore, the frictional force increases for larger masses.

As the force increases, so does the work done on the object, because:

$$W = F \times d$$

25. D is correct.

The hammer does work on the nail as it drives it into the wood. The amount of work done is proportional to the amount of kinetic energy lost by the hammer:

$$\Delta KE = \Delta W$$

26. A is correct.

The only force doing work is the road's friction, so the work done by the road's friction is the total work. This work equals the change in KE.

$$W = \Delta KE$$

$$W = KE_f - KE_i$$

$$W = \tfrac{1}{2}mv_2^2 - \tfrac{1}{2}mv_1^2$$

$$W = 0 - [\tfrac{1}{2}(1{,}500 \text{ kg}) \cdot (25 \text{ m/s})^2]$$

$$W = -4.7 \times 10^{-5} \text{ J}$$

27. D is correct.

Convert 17 km/hr to m/s:

$$v = (17 \text{ km/h}) \cdot (1{,}000 \text{ m/km}) \, (1 \text{ h/60 min}) \cdot (1 \text{ min/60 s})$$

$$v = 4.72 \text{ m/s}$$

$$KE = \tfrac{1}{2}mv^2$$

$$KE_{car} = \tfrac{1}{2}(1{,}000 \text{ kg}) \cdot (4.72 \text{ m/s})^2$$

$$KE_{car} = 11{,}139 \text{ J}$$

Calculate the KE of the 2,000 kg truck with 20 times the KE:

$$KE_{truck} = KE_{car} \times 20$$

$$KE_{truck} = (11{,}139 \text{ J}) \times 20$$

$$KE_{truck} = 222.7 \text{ kJ}$$

Calculate the speed of the 2,000 kg truck:

$$KE = \tfrac{1}{2}mv^2$$

$$v^2 = 2KE \,/\, m$$

$$v^2 = 2(222.7 \text{ kJ}) \,/\, (2,000 \text{ kg})$$

$$v_{\text{truck}} = \sqrt{[2(222.7 \text{ kJ}) \,/\, (2,000 \text{ kg})]}$$

$$v_{\text{truck}} = 14.9 \text{ m/s}$$

Convert back to km/h:

$$v_{\text{truck}} = (14.9 \text{ m/s}){\cdot}(60 \text{ s/min}){\cdot}(60 \text{ min/h}){\cdot}(1 \text{ km}/1,000 \text{ m})$$

$$v_{\text{truck}} = 53.6 \text{ km/h} \approx 54 \text{ km/h}$$

28. C is correct.

Gravity and the normal force are balanced, vertical forces.

Since the car is slowing (i.e. accelerating backwards) there is a net force backwards, due to friction (i.e. braking).

Newton's First Law of Motion states that in the absence of any forces, the car would keep moving forward.

29. B is correct.

Energy is always conserved so the work needed to lift the piano is 0.15 m is equal to the work needed to pull the rope 1 m:

$$W_1 = W_2$$

$$F_1 d_1 = F_2 d_2$$

$$F_1 d_1 \,/\, d_2 = F_2$$

$$F_2 = (6,000 \text{ N}){\cdot}(0.15 \text{ m}) \,/\, 1 \text{ m}$$

$$F_2 = 900 \text{ N}$$

30. C is correct.

The area under the curve on a graph is the product of the values of $y \times x$.

Here, the y value is force and the x value is distance:

$$Fd = W$$

31. B is correct.

The vast majority of the Earth's energy comes from the sun, which produces radiation that penetrates the Earth's atmosphere. Likewise, radiation is emitted from the Earth's atmosphere.

32. C is correct.

$$W = Fd$$

$$W = \Delta KE$$

$$F \times d = \tfrac{1}{2}mv^2$$

If v is doubled.

$$F \times d_2 = \tfrac{1}{2}m(2v)^2$$

$$F \times d_2 = \tfrac{1}{2}m(4v^2)$$

$$F \times d_2 = 4(\tfrac{1}{2}mv^2)$$

For equations to remain equal to each other, d_2 must be 4 times d.

33. D is correct.

$$\text{Work} = \text{Power} \times \text{time}$$

$$P = W \, / \, t$$

$$W = Fd$$

$$P = (Fd) \, / \, t$$

$$P = [(2{,}000 \text{ N}){\cdot}(320 \text{ m})] \, / \, (60 \text{ s})$$

$$P = 10{,}667 \text{ W} = 10.7 \text{ kW}$$

34. A is correct.

Find acceleration:

$$\Delta x = v_0 t + \tfrac{1}{2}at^2$$

$$3 \text{ m} = 0 + (\tfrac{1}{2}){\cdot}(a){\cdot}(3 \text{ s})^2$$

$$a = 0.67 \text{ m/s}^2$$

Find power:

Power = Work / time

$$P = W \, / \, t$$

Work = Force × distance

$$W = Fd$$

$$W = (ma)d$$

Therefore,

$$P = (ma_{\text{total}})d \, / \, t$$

$$P = (25 \text{ kg}){\cdot}(0.67 \text{ m/s}^2 + 9.8 \text{ m/s}^2){\cdot}(3 \text{ m}) \, / \, (3 \text{ s})$$

$$P = 262 \text{ J}$$

35. B is correct.

The bag was never lifted off the ground and moved horizontally at constant velocity.

$F = 0$

$W = Fd$

$W = 0$ J

Because there is no acceleration, the force is zero and thus the work is zero.

36. B is correct.

$F = ma$

$a = F / m$

$a = (9{,}600$ N$) / (1{,}000$ kg$)$

$a = 9.6$ m/s^2

$v_f^2 = v_0^2 + 2a\Delta d$

$(v_f^2 - v_0^2) / 2a = \Delta d$

Note that acceleration is negative due to it acting opposite the velocity.

$\Delta d = [(22$ m/s$)^2 - (30$ m/s$)^2] / 2(-9.6$ m/s$^2)$

$\Delta d = (484$ m^2/s$^2 - 900$ m^2/s$^2) / (-19.2$ m/s$^2)$

$\Delta d = (-416$ m^2/s$^2) / (-19.2$ m/s$^2)$

$\Delta d = 21.7$ m ≈ 22 m

Or using energy conservation to solve the problem:

$W = |\,\Delta KE\,|$

$Fd = |\,\tfrac{1}{2}m(v_f^2 - v_0^2)\,|$

$d = |\,m(v_f^2 - v_0^2) / 2F\,|$

$d = |\,(1{,}000$ kg$)\cdot[(22$ m/s$)^2 - (30$ m/s$)^2] / (2)\cdot(9{,}600$ N$)\,|$

$d = |\,(1{,}000$ kg$)\cdot(484$ m^2/s$^2 - 900$ m^2/s$^2) / 19{,}200$ N$\,|$

$d = 22$ m

37. C is correct.

$W = 100$ J

Work = Power × time

$P = W / t$

$P = 100$ J $/ 50$ s

$P = 2$ W

38. D is correct.

$$v_f^2 = v_0^2 + 2a\Delta x$$

$$v_f^2 = 0 + 2a\Delta x$$

$$v_f = \sqrt{2a\Delta x}$$

$$v_f = \sqrt{[2(10 \text{ m/s}^2) \cdot (58 \text{ m})]}$$

$$v_f = \sqrt{(1{,}160 \text{ m}^2/\text{s}^2)}$$

$$v_f = 34 \text{ m/s}$$

39. A is correct.

$$PE = mgh$$

If height and gravity are constant then potential energy is directly proportional to mass.

As such, if the second stone has four times the mass of the first, then it must have four times the potential energy of the first stone.

$$m_2 = 4m_1$$

$$PE_2 = 4PE_1$$

Therefore, the second stone has four times the potential energy.

40. B is correct.

$$W = Fd$$

$W = mgh$, work done by gravity

$$W = (1.3 \text{ kg}) \cdot (10 \text{ m/s}^2) \cdot (6 \text{ m})$$

$$W = 78 \text{ J}$$

41. A is correct.

$$PE = mgh$$

42. A is correct.

$$F_{spring} = F_{centripetal}$$

$$F_{spring} = kx$$

$$kx = 15 \text{ N}$$

$$x = (15 \text{ N}) / (65 \text{ N/m})$$

$$x = 0.23 \text{ m}$$

$$PE_{spring} = \tfrac{1}{2}kx^2$$

$$PE_{spring} = \tfrac{1}{2}(65 \text{ N/m}) \cdot (0.23 \text{ m})^2$$

$$PE_{spring} = 1.7 \text{ J}$$

43. C is correct.

total time = (3.5 h/day)·(7 days)·(5 weeks)

total time = 122.5 h

cost = (8.16 cents/kW·h)·(122.5 h)·(0.12 kW/1)

cost = 120 cents = $1.20

44. B is correct.

$x = 5.1$ m $\times (\cos 32°)$

$x = 4.33$ m

$h = 5.1$ m $- 4.33$ m

$h = 0.775$ m

$W = Fd$

$W = mg \times h$

$m = W / gh$

$m = (120$ J$) / (9.8$ m/s$^2)·(0.775$ m$)$

$m = 15.8$ kg

45. D is correct.

Potential energy of spring:

$PE = \frac{1}{2}k\Delta x^2$

87 J $= \frac{1}{2}k(2.9$ m$)^2 - (1.4$ m$)^2$

87 J $= \frac{1}{2}k(8.41$ m$^2) - (1.96$ m$^2)$

87 J $= \frac{1}{2}k(6.45$ m$^2)$

$k = 2(111$ J$) / (6.45$ m$^2)$

$k = 34$ N/m

Unit check:

$J = kg·m^2/s^2$

$J/m^2 = (kg·m^2/s^2)·(1/m^2)$

$J/m^2 = (kg/s^2)$

$N/m = (kg·m/s^2)·(1/m)$

$N/m = (kg/s^2)$

46. D is correct.

Potential energy, kinetic energy and work are all measured in joules:

$$J = kg \cdot m^2/s^2$$

$$KE = \tfrac{1}{2}mv^2 = kg(m/s)^2 = J$$

$$PE = mgh = kg(m/s^2) \cdot (m/1) = J$$

$$W = Fd = J$$

47. A is correct.

Potential energy of spring:

$$PE = \tfrac{1}{2}kx^2$$

Kinetic energy of mass:

$$KE = \tfrac{1}{2}mv^2$$

Set equal to each other and rearrange:

$\tfrac{1}{2}kx^2 = \tfrac{1}{2}mv^2$, cancel $\tfrac{1}{2}$ from both sides of the expression

$$kx^2 = mv^2$$

$$x^2 = (mv^2) / k$$

$$x^2 = (m / k)v^2$$

Since m / k is provided:

$$x^2 = (0.038 \ kg \cdot m/N) \cdot (18 \ m/s)^2$$

$$x^2 = 12.3 \ m^2$$

$$x = \sqrt{12.3} \ m$$

$$x = 3.4 \ m$$

48. A is correct.

$$m_t = 2m_c$$

$$v_t = 2v_c$$

KE of the truck:

$$KE_t = \tfrac{1}{2}m_t v_t^2$$

Replace mass and velocity of the truck with the equivalent mass and velocity of the car:

$$KE_t = \tfrac{1}{2}(2m_c) \cdot (2v_c)^2$$

$$KE_t = \tfrac{1}{2}(2m_c) \cdot (4v_c^2)$$

$$KE_t = \tfrac{1}{2}(8m_c v_c^2)$$

The truck has 8 times the kinetic energy of the car.

49. C is correct. When a car stops the KE is equal to the work done by the force of friction from the brakes.

Through friction the KE is transformed into heat.

50. B is correct. When the block comes to rest at the end of the spring, the upward force of the spring balances the downward force of gravity.

$F = kx$

$mg = kx$

$x = mg / k$

$x = (30 \text{ kg}) \cdot (10 \text{ m/s}^2) / 900 \text{ N/m}$

$x = 0.33 \text{ m}$

51. D is correct.

$KE = \frac{1}{2}mv^2$

$KE = \frac{1}{2}(0.33 \text{ kg}) \cdot (40 \text{ m/s})^2$

$KE = 264 \text{ J}$

52. C is correct. Work is the area under a force vs. position graph.

$\text{area} = Fd = W$

The area of the triangle as the object moves from 0 to 4 m:

$A = \frac{1}{2}bh$

$A = \frac{1}{2}(4 \text{ m} \cdot)(10 \text{ N})$

$A = 20 \text{ J}$

$W = 20 \text{ J}$

53. C is correct.

$KE = PE$

$\frac{1}{2}mv^2 = mgh$

$v^2 / 2g = h$

If v is doubled:

$h_B = v_B^2 / 2g$

$v_J = 2v_B$

$(2v_B)^2 / 2g = h_J$

$4(v_B^2 / 2g) = h_J$

$4h_B = h_J$

James's ball travels 4 times higher than Bob's ball.

---

54. B is correct.

Hooke's Law is given as:

$$F = -kx$$

The negative is only by convention to demonstrate that the spring force is a restoring force. Graph B is correct because force is linearly increasing with increasing distance. All other graphs are either constant or exponential.

55. C is correct. A decrease in the KE for the rocket causes either a gain in its gravitational PE, or the transfer of heat, or a combination.

The rocket loses some KE due to air resistance (friction).

Thus, some of the rocket's KE is converted to heat that causes the temperature of the air surrounding the rocket to increase. Therefore, the average KE of the air molecules increases.

56. D is correct.

Kinetic energy is given as:

$$KE_1 = \tfrac{1}{2}mv^2$$
$$KE_2 = \tfrac{1}{2}m(4v)^2$$
$$KE_2 = \tfrac{1}{2}m(16v^2)$$

Increasing the velocity by a factor of 4 increases the KE by a factor of 16.

57. C is correct. Energy is conserved and converted from potential to kinetic.

$$PE = KE$$
$$\tfrac{1}{2}kx^2 = \tfrac{1}{2}mv^2$$
$$kx^2 = mv^2$$
$$x\sqrt{k} = v\sqrt{m}$$

The velocity and the compression distance of the spring are directly proportional. Thus if the spring is compressed by four times the original distance then the velocity is four times the original.

$$x_2 = 4x_1$$
$$v_2 = 4v_1$$

58. C is correct.

Force: $F = ma$ (N)

Work: $W = Fd$ (N·m)

Power: $P = W / t$ (N·m/s)

59. A is correct.

$$W_{net} = \Delta KE$$

$$\Delta KE = KE_f - KE_i$$

$$\Delta KE + KE_i = KE_f$$

60. D is correct.

$$v = (70 \text{ km/h}) \cdot (1,000 \text{ m/km}) \cdot (1 \text{ h/60 min}) \cdot (1 \text{ min/60 s})$$

$$v = 19.4 \text{ m/s}$$

Force acting against the car:

$$F = mg \sin \theta$$

$$F = (1,320 \text{ kg}) \cdot (9.8 \text{ m/s}^2) \sin 5°$$

$$F = (1,320 \text{ kg}) \cdot (9.8 \text{ m/s}^2) \cdot (0.09)$$

$$F = 1,164 \text{ N}$$

$$N = \text{kg} \cdot \text{m/s}^2$$

Rate of energy is power:

$$\text{Watts} = \text{kg} \cdot \text{m}^2/\text{s}^3$$

Multiply velocity by the downward force:

$$P = Fv$$

$$P = (1,164 \text{ N}) \cdot (19.4 \text{ m/s})$$

$$P = 22.6 \text{ kW}$$

61. B is correct. When the pebble falls, KE at impact = PE before.

$$PE = KE$$

$$mgh = KE$$

$$mg(2h) = 2KE$$

$$2PE = 2KE$$

If the mass and gravity are constant, then the height must be doubled.

62. D is correct. Power = Work / time

A: Power = 50 J / 20 min = 2.5 J/min

B: power = 200 J / 30 min = 6.67 J/min

C: power = 10 J / 5 min = 2 J/min

D: power = 100 J / 20 min = 5 J/min

Typically, power is measured in watts or J/s.

63. A is correct.

> kilowatt = unit of power
>
> hour = unit of time
>
> kW·h = power × time
>
> power = work / time
>
> kW·h = (work / time) × time
>
> kW·h = work

64. B is correct. Mechanical advantage:

> d_1 / d_2
>
> where d_1 and d_2 are the effort arm and load arm, respectively.

If d_1 is greater than d_2, energy output is increased.

65. A is correct.

> $v_0 = 10$ m/s
>
> $W = Fd$
>
> $W = (ma)d$
>
> $ad = W / m$
>
> $ad = (4.5 \times 10^5 \text{ J}) / (1{,}150 \text{ kg})$
>
> $ad = (4.5 \times 10^5 \text{ kg·m}^2/\text{s}^2) / (1{,}150 \text{ kg})$
>
> $ad = 391$ m^2/s^2
>
> $ad = ax$
>
> $v_f^2 = v_0^2 + 2a(x - x_0)$
>
> $v_f^2 = v_0^2 + 2a(x - 0)$
>
> $v_f^2 = v_0^2 + 2ax$
>
> $v_f^2 = (10 \text{ m/s})^2 + (2)\cdot(391 \text{ m}^2/\text{s}^2)$
>
> $v_f^2 = 882$ m^2/s^2
>
> $v_f = 29.7$ m/s ≈ 30 m/s

66. D is correct.

> Work = Force × distance
>
> $W = Fd$

The unit kg·m/s cannot be manipulated to achieve this.

67. A is correct.

The Law of Conservation of Energy states that energy cannot be created or destroyed and remains constant. Energy can only transform from one form to another.

68. C is correct.

$$a_{total} = 1.4 \text{ m/s}^2 + 9.8 \text{ m/s}^2$$

$$a_{total} = 11.2 \text{ m/s}^2$$

$$W = Fd$$

$$W = ma \times d$$

$$W = (300 \text{ kg}) \cdot (11.2 \text{ m/s}^2) \cdot (110 \text{ m})$$

$$W = 3.7 \times 10^5 \text{ J}$$

69. D is correct.

$$\text{Work} = \text{Force} \times \text{displacement} \times \cos \theta$$

$$W = Fd \cos \theta$$

If $d = 0$, then work $= 0$

70. B is correct.

Relative to the ground, an object's gravitational PE $= mgh$, where h is the altitude.

PE is proportional to h; doubling h doubles PE.

71. D is correct.

$$W = Fd$$

$$P = W / t$$

$$P = Fd / t$$

$$P = (1 \text{ N}) \cdot (1 \text{ m}) / 1 \text{ s}$$

$$P = 1 \text{ W}$$

72. A is correct.

$$KE = PE$$

$$KE = mgh$$

h is directly proportional to KE.

If h doubles, then the KE doubles.

73. C is correct.

$\Delta KE = \Delta PE$

$\frac{1}{2}mv^2 = \frac{1}{2}k\Delta x^2$

$\Delta x = (0.6 \text{ m}) \cdot (0.23)$

$\Delta x = 0.138 \text{ m}$

$k / m = v^2 / \Delta x^2$

23% is lost as heat

$k / m = (v^2 / \Delta x^2) \cdot (0.77)$

$k / m = [(4.5 \text{ m/s})^2 / (0.138 \text{ m})^2] \cdot (0.77)$

$k / m = 819 \text{ s}^{-1} = 0.8 \text{ kN/kg·m}$

74. C is correct.

$PE = mgh$

$PE = (21 \times 10^3 \text{ kg}) \cdot (9.8 \text{ m/s}^2) \cdot (2.6 \times 10^3 \text{ m})$

$PE = 535 \text{ MJ}$

75. D is correct.

$h_0 = 3.5 \text{ m}$

$PE_0 = mgh$

$PE_1 = mgh(0.69) \rightarrow$ after first bounce

$PE_2 = mgh(0.69)^2 \rightarrow$ after second bounce

$PE_3 = mgh(0.69)^3 \rightarrow$ after third bounce

Because mass and gravity are constant, the final height is:

final height $= h(0.69)^3$

final height $= (4 \text{ m}) \cdot (0.69)^3$

final height $= 1.31 \text{ m}$

final height $= 131 \text{ cm}$

WAVES AND PERIODIC MOTION – EXPLANATIONS

1. B is correct.

Frequency is the measure of the amount of cycles per second a wave experiences, which is independent of the wave's amplitude.

2. D is correct.

Hooke's Law:

$$F = kx$$

It is known that the force on each spring must be equal if they are in static equilibrium, therefore:

$$F_A = F_B$$

Therefore, the expression can be written as:

$$k_A L_A = k_B L_B$$

Solve for the spring constant of spring B:

$$k_B = (k_A L_A) / L_B$$

3. B is correct. Wave motion is the result of oscillating (or vibrating) particles traveling in a perpendicular direction to their oscillations.

4. C is correct.

speed = wavelength × frequency

$$v = \lambda f$$

$$v = (0.25 \text{ m}) \cdot (1{,}680 \text{ Hz})$$

$$v = 420 \text{ m/s}$$

5. A is correct.

$$E_{total} = PE + KE$$

$$E_{stored} = \tfrac{1}{2}k\text{A}^2$$

Stored energy is potential energy. In simple harmonic motion, the equation for gravitational potential energy is similar to the equation for the potential energy of a spring.

$$PE = \tfrac{1}{2}kx^2 \text{ or } \tfrac{1}{2}k\text{A}^2,$$

where k is a constant and A (or x) is the distance from equilibrium

A is the amplitude of a wave in simple harmonic motion (SHM).

---

6. D is correct.

The period of the spring's oscillation is:

$$T = 2\pi\sqrt{(L / g)}$$
$$T = 2\pi\sqrt{(0.03 \text{ m} / 9.8 \text{ m/s}^2)}$$
$$T = 2\pi(0.055 \text{ s})$$
$$T = 0.35 \text{ s}$$

The frequency is the reciprocal of the period.

$$f = 1 / T$$
$$f = 1 / (0.35 \text{ s})$$
$$f = 2.9 \text{ Hz}$$

7. C is correct.

$$T = 1 / f$$

8. D is correct.

The period of a pendulum:

$$T = 2\pi\sqrt{(L / g)}$$

The period only depends on the pendulum's length and gravity.

In an elevator, gravity only changes if the elevator is accelerating in either direction.

9. A is correct. The period is the reciprocal of the frequency:

$$T = 1 / f$$
$$T = 1 / 100 \text{ Hz}$$
$$T = 0.01 \text{ s}$$

10. B is correct.

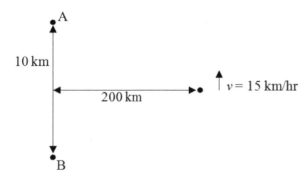

Convert v to m/s:

$v = (15 \text{ km}/1 \text{ h}) \cdot (1 \text{ h}/60 \text{ min}) \cdot (1 \text{ min}/60 \text{ s}) \cdot (10^3 \text{ m}/1 \text{ km})$

$v = 4.2$ m/s

Convert frequency to λ:

$\lambda = c / f$

$\lambda = (3 \times 10^8 \text{ m/s}) / (4.7 \times 10^6 \text{ Hz})$

$\lambda = 63.8$ m

According to Young's Equation:

$\lambda = yd / mL$, where $m = 0, 1, 2, 3, 4...$

Solve for y by rearranging to isolate y:

$y = \lambda L m / d$

y = distance travelled by boat:

$y = vt$

Therefore, the value of m must be within the range of the given times, find highest value of m.

Because m must be an integer and the ship travelled some distance, $m \geq 1$.

$t = mL\lambda / vy$

$t = (1) \cdot (200{,}000 \text{ m}) \cdot (63.8 \text{ m}) / (4.2 \text{ m/s}) \cdot (10{,}000 \text{ m})$

$t = 304$ s

Convert time from seconds to minutes:

$t = (304 \text{ s}) \cdot (1 \text{ min}/60 \text{ s})$

$t = 5.06 \text{ min} \approx 5.1$ min

For all m values greater than 1, the calculated times are beyond the answer choices so 5.1 min is the correct answer.

11. D is correct. The tension in the rope is given by the equation:

$T = (mv^2) / L$

where v is the velocity of the wave and L is the length of the rope.

Substituting:

$v = L / t$

$T = [m(L / t)^2] / L$

$T = mL / t^2$

$t^2 = mL / T$

$t = \sqrt{(mL / T)}$

$t = \sqrt{[(2.31 \text{ kg}) \cdot (10.4 \text{ m}) / 74.4 \text{ N}]}$

$t = \sqrt{(0.323 \text{ s}^2)}$

$t = 0.57$ s

12. A is correct.

$f_A \quad 2 f_B$

frequency = 1 / period

$f = 1 / T$

The period is the reciprocal of the frequency

$T = 1 / f$

$f_A = 2 f_B$

$T_A = \frac{1}{2} f_B$

$T_A = \frac{1}{2} T_B$

$T = 2\pi \sqrt{(L / g)}$

$L_B = g(T_B / 2\pi)^2$

$L_A = g(\frac{1}{2} T_B / 2\pi)^2$

$L_A = \frac{1}{4} g(T_B / 2\pi)^2$

$L_A = \frac{1}{4} L_B$

13. B is correct. $F = -kx$

Since the motion is simple harmonic, the restoring force is proportional to displacement.

Therefore, if the displacement is 5 times greater, then so is the restoring force.

14. C is correct.

Period = (60 s) / (10 oscillations)

$T = 6$ s

The period is the time for one oscillation.

If 10 oscillations take 60 s, then one oscillation takes 6 s.

15. A is correct. Conservation of Energy:

total ME = ΔKE + ΔPE = constant

$\frac{1}{2} mv^2 + \frac{1}{2} kx^2$ = constant

16. B is correct. A displacement from the position of maximum elongation to the position of maximum compression represents *half* a cycle. If it takes 1 s, then the time required for a complete cycle is 2 s.

$f = 1 / T$

$f = 1 / 2$ s

$f = 0.5$ Hz

17. C is correct.

Sound waves are longitudinal waves.

18. B is correct.

speed = wavelength × frequency

speed = wavelength / period

$v = \lambda / T$

$\lambda = vT$

$\lambda = (362$ m/s$)\cdot(0.004$ s$)$

$\lambda = 1.5$ m

19. A is correct.

$a = -A\omega^2 \cos(\omega t)$

where A is the amplitude, or displacement from resting position.

20. D is correct.

The acceleration of a simple harmonic oscillation is:

$a = -A\omega^2 \cos(\omega t)$

Its maximum occurs when $\cos(\omega t)$ is equal to 1

$a_{max} = -\omega^2 x$

If ω is doubled:

$a = -(2\omega)^2 x$

$a = -4\omega^2 x$

The maximum value of acceleration changes by a factor of 4.

21. B is correct.

Resonant frequency of a spring and mass system in any orientation:

$$\omega = \sqrt{(k / m)}$$
$$f = \omega / 2\pi$$
$$T = 1 / f$$
$$T = 2\pi\sqrt{(k / m)}$$

Period of a spring does not depend on gravity

The period remains constant because only mass and the spring constant affect the period.

22. C is correct.

$$v = \lambda f$$
$$\lambda = v / f$$

An increase in v and a decrease in f must increase λ.

23. B is correct. Frequency is the measure of oscillations or vibrations per second.

> frequency = 60 vibrations in 1 s
> frequency = 60 Hz
> speed = 30 m / 1 s
> speed = 30 m/s

24. A is correct.

$$T = (mv^2) / L$$
$$m = TL / v^2$$
$$m = (60 \text{ N}) \cdot (16 \text{ m}) / (40 \text{ m/s})^2$$
$$m = (960 \text{ N·m}) / (1,600 \text{ m}^2/\text{s}^2)$$
$$m = 0.6 \text{ kg}$$

25. D is correct. Amplitude is independent of frequency.

26. C is correct.

$$f = \text{\# cycles} / \text{time}$$
$$f = 60 \text{ drips} / 40 \text{ s}$$
$$f = 1.5 \text{ Hz}$$

27. D is correct.

Transverse waves are characterized by their crests and valleys, which are caused by the particles of the wave traveling "up and down" with respect to the lateral movement of the wave.

The particles in longitudinal waves travel parallel to the direction of the wave.

28. B is correct.

For a particle in simple harmonic motion, at each end of its oscillation when the amplitude is maximum, the particle's velocity is zero since it is stopped and about to "turn around" in its motion. At this point, the particle's acceleration is at a maximum and directed toward the equilibrium position since the particle is at the farthest distance from equilibrium and requires the largest acceleration to get there.

Once the particle reaches the equilibrium position, it stops moving; since the acceleration is always directed toward equilibrium, the acceleration is zero at the equilibrium position. But due to the previous acceleration the particle just experienced, its velocity reaches a maximum as it passes through the equilibrium position, then decreases.

29. C is correct.

The speed of a wave is determined by the characteristics of the medium (and the type of wave). Speed is independent of amplitude.

30. A is correct.

$f = 1$ / period

$f = $ # cycles / second

$f = 1$ cycle / 2 s

$f = \frac{1}{2}$ Hz

31. B is correct.

$f = v / \lambda$

$\lambda = v / f$

$\lambda = (340 \text{ m/s}) / (2,100 \text{ Hz})$

$\lambda = 0.16$ m

32. D is correct.

Period (T) $= 2\pi\sqrt{(L / g)}$

The period is independent of the mass.

33. A is correct.

$$v = \omega x$$

$$\omega = v / x$$

$$\omega = (15 \text{ m/s}) / (2.5 \text{ m})$$

$$\omega = 6.0 \text{ rad/s}$$

34. D is correct.

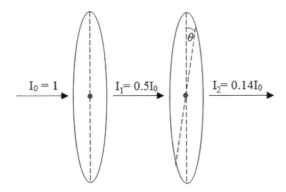

Unpolarized light on a polarizer reduces the intensity by ½.

$$I = (\tfrac{1}{2})I_0$$

After that, the light is further reduced in intensity by the second filter.

Law of Malus:

$$I = I_0 \cos^2 \theta$$

$$(0.14 \, I_0) = (0.5 \, I_0) \cos^2 \theta$$

$$0.28 = \cos^2 \theta$$

$$\cos^{-1} \sqrt{(0.28)} = \theta$$

$$\theta = 58°$$

35. C is correct. At a maximum distance from equilibrium, the energy in the system is potential energy and the speed is zero, therefore kinetic energy is also zero. Since there is no kinetic energy, the mass has no velocity.

At a minimum distance: $KE_{system} \geq 0$ Joules.

36. D is correct.

$$v = \lambda f$$

$$f = v / \lambda$$

$$f = (240 \text{ m/s}) / (0.1 \text{ m})$$

$$f = 2,400 \text{ Hz}$$

37. B is correct.

In a transverse wave the vibrations of particles are perpendicular to the direction of travel of the wave. Transverse waves have crests and troughs that move along the wave.

In a longitudinal wave the vibrations of particles are parallel to the direction of travel of the wave. Longitudinal waves have compressions and rarefactions that move along the wave.

38. C is correct.

$v = \sqrt{(T / \mu)},$

where μ is the linear density of the wire.

$T = v^2 \mu$

$\mu = \rho A$

where A is the cross-sectional area of the wire.

$\mu = (2{,}700 \text{ kg/m}^3)\pi(4.6 \times 10^{-3} \text{ m})^2$

$\mu = 0.045 \text{ kg/m}$

$T = (36 \text{ m/s})^2 \cdot (0.045 \text{ kg/m})$

$T = 58 \text{ N}$

39. D is correct.

Refraction is the change in direction of a wave, caused by the change in the wave's speed. Examples of waves include sound waves and light waves. Refraction is seen most often when a wave passes from one medium to a different medium (e.g. from air to water and vice versa).

40. C is correct.

$f = \#$ cycles / second

$f = 2$ cycles / 1 s

$f = 2 \text{ Hz}$

41. A is correct.

pitch = frequency

A higher pitch means a greater f.

42. C is correct.

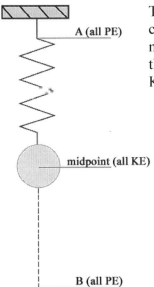

A (all PE)

midpoint (all KE)

B (all PE)

The KE is maximum when the spring is neither stretched nor compressed. If the object is bobbing, KE is maximum at the midpoint between fully stretched and fully compressed because this is where all of the spring's energy is KE rather than a mix of KE and PE.

43. B is correct.

Torque = $rF \sin \theta$

$F = ma$, substitute mg for F

$\tau = rmg \sin \theta$

$\tau = (1 \text{ m}) \cdot (0.5 \text{ kg}) \cdot (10 \text{ m/s}^2) \sin 60°$

$\tau = (5 \text{ kg} \cdot \text{m}^2/\text{s}^2) \times 0.87$

$\tau = 4.4 \text{ N} \cdot \text{m}$

44. D is correct.

The Doppler effect can be observed to occur in all types of waves.

45. A is correct.

$v = \sqrt{(T / \mu)}$ where μ is the linear density of the wire.

$F_T = ma$

$F_T = (2,500 \text{ kg}) \cdot (10 \text{ m/s}^2)$

$F_T = 25,000 \text{ N}$

$v = \sqrt{(25,000 \text{ N} / 0.65 \text{ kg/m})}$

$v = 196 \text{ m/s}$

The weight of the wire can be assumed to be negligible compared to the cement block.

46. B is correct.

$f = \frac{1}{2}\pi[\sqrt{(g / L)}]$, frequency is independent of mass

47. A is correct.

$T = 2\pi\sqrt{(L / g)}]$

$T = 2\pi\sqrt{(3.3 \text{ m} / 10 \text{ m/s}^2)}$

$T = 3.6 \text{ s}$

48. C is correct.

$f = \sqrt{(k / m)}$

If k increases by a factor of 2, then f increases by a factor of $\sqrt{2}$ (or 1.41).

Increasing by a factor of 1.41 or 41%

49. D is correct.

In simple harmonic motion, the acceleration is greatest at the ends of motions (points A and D) where velocity is zero.

Velocity is greatest at the nadir where acceleration is equal to zero (point C).

50. A is correct.

At the lowest point, the KE is at a maximum and the PE is at a minimum.

The loss of gravitational PE equals the gain in KE:

$mgh = \frac{1}{2}mv^2$, cancel m from both sides of the expression

$gh = \frac{1}{2}v^2$

$(10 \text{ m/s}^2) \cdot (10 \text{ m}) = \frac{1}{2}v^2$

$(100 \text{ m}^2/\text{s}^2) = \frac{1}{2}v^2$

$200 \text{ m}^2/\text{s}^2 = v^2$

$v = 14 \text{ m/s}$

51. A is correct. Pitch is equivalent to frequency and amplitude. It is a measurement of wave energy but does not relate to speed which is constant.

52. C is correct.

Because wind is blowing in the reference frame of both the train and the observer, it does not need to be taken into account.

$$f_{observed} = [v_{sound} / (v_{sound} - v_{source})]f_{source}$$

$$f_{observed} = [340 \text{ m/s} / (340 \text{ m/s} - 50 \text{ m/s})] \cdot 500 \text{ Hz}$$

$$f_{observed} = 586 \text{ Hz}$$

$$\lambda = v / f$$

$$\lambda = 340 \text{ m/s} / 586 \text{ Hz}$$

$$\lambda = 0.58 \text{ m}$$

53. B is correct.

$$PE = \tfrac{1}{2}kx^2$$

Doubling the amplitude x increases PE by a factor of 4.

54. C is correct.

The elastic modulus is given by:

$$E = \text{tensional strength} / \text{extensional strain}$$

$$E = \sigma / \varepsilon$$

55. D is correct.

Resonance is the phenomenon where one system transfers its energy to another at that system's resonant frequency (natural frequency). It is forced vibration with the least energy input.

56. A is correct.

Period of a pendulum:

$$T_P = 2\pi\sqrt{(L / g)}$$

Period of a spring:

$$T_S = 2\pi\sqrt{(m / k)}$$

The period of a spring does not depend on gravity and is unaffected.

57. B is correct.

At the top of its arc, the pendulum comes to rest momentarily; the KE and the velocity equal zero.

Since its height above the bottom of its arc is at a maximum at this point, its (angular) displacement from the vertical equilibrium position is at a maximum also.

The pendulum constantly experiences the forces of gravity and tension, and is therefore continuously accelerating.

58. D is correct.

The Doppler effect is the observed change in frequency when a sound source is in motion relative to an observer (away or towards). If the sound source moves with the observer then there is no relative motion between the two and the Doppler effect does not occur.

59. C is correct.

The amplitude of a wave is the magnitude of its oscillation from its equilibrium point.

60. A is correct.

$$f = \sqrt{(k \, / \, m)}$$

An increase in m causes a decrease in f.

61. D is correct.

$$T = 2\pi[\sqrt{(L \, / \, g)}]$$

No effect on the period because T is independent of mass.

62. A is correct.

speed = wavelength × frequency

period = 1 / frequency

$v = \lambda f$

$v = \lambda \, / \, T$

$v = 15 \text{ m} \, / \, 5 \text{ s}$

$v = 3 \text{ m/s}$

63. B is correct.

When displacement is greatest, the force on the object is greatest. When force is maximized, then acceleration is maximum.

64. E is correct.

$\lambda = vf$

$f = v \, / \, \lambda$

$f = 1 \, / \, T$

The period is the reciprocal of the frequency.

If f increases, then T decreases.

65. C is correct.

The definition of period is the time required to complete one cycle.

Period = time / # cycles

T = 2 s / 1 cycle

T = 2 s

66. D is correct.

When it rains the brightly colored oil slicks on the road are due to thin film interference effects. This is when light reflects from the upper and lower boundaries of the oil layer and form a new wave due to interference effects. These new waves are perceived as different colors.

67. B is correct.

A stretched string has all harmonics of the fundamental.

68. D is correct.

In a longitudinal wave, particles of a material are displaced parallel to the direction of the wave.

SOUND – EXPLANATIONS

1. B is correct. Intensity is inversely proportional to distance (In W/m^2, not dB).

$$I_2 / I_1 = (d_1 / d_2)^2$$
$$I_2 / I_1 = (3 \text{ m} / 30 \text{ m})^2$$
$$100 \, I_2 = I_1$$

The intensity is 100 times greater at 3 m away than 30 m away.

Intensity to decibel relationship:

$$I \text{ (dB)} = 10 \log_{10} (I / I_0)$$

The intensity to dB relationship is logarithmic. Thus if I_1 is 100 times the original intensity then it is two times the dB intensity because:

$$\log_{10} (100) = 2$$

Thus the decibel level at 3 m away is:

$$I \text{ (dB)} = (2) \cdot (20 \text{ dB})$$
$$I = 40 \text{ dB}$$

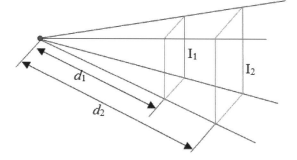

2. A is correct.

$$\text{distance} = \text{velocity} \times \text{time}$$
$$d = vt$$
$$t = d / v$$
$$t = (6,000 \text{ m}) / (340 \text{ m/s})$$
$$t = 18 \text{ s}$$

3. B is correct. Resonance occurs when a wave oscillates at a relative maximum amplitude, which translates into greater energy of the system. When this energy exceeds the stability of the glass, the glass shatters.

4. C is correct. The third harmonic is shown in the figure below:

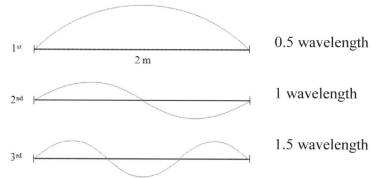

1st   0.5 wavelength
    2 m

2nd   1 wavelength

3rd   1.5 wavelength

There are $(3/2)\lambda$ in the 2 m wave in the third harmonic

$L = (n / 2)\lambda$ (for n harmonic)

$L = (3 / 2)\lambda$ (for 3rd harmonic)

$L(2 / 3) = \lambda$

λ (2 m)·(2 / 3)

$\lambda = 4/3$ m

5. B is correct.

6. A is correct.

Snell's law:

$n_1 \sin \theta_1 = n_2 \sin \theta_2$

Solve for θ_2:

$(n_1 / n_2) \sin \theta_1 = \sin \theta_2$

$\sin \theta_1 = (n_1 / n_2) \sin \theta_2$

$\theta_2 = \sin^{-1}[(n_1 / n_2) \sin \theta_1]$

Substituting the given values:

$\theta_2 = \sin^{-1}[(1 / 1.5) \sin 60°]$

$\theta_2 = \sin^{-1}(0.67 \sin 60°)$

7. D is correct.

For a standing wave, the length and wavelength are related:

$L = (n / 2)\lambda$ (for n harmonic)

From the diagram, the wave is the 6th harmonic:

$L = (6 / 2)\lambda$

$\lambda = (2 \text{ m})·(2 / 6)$

$\lambda = 0.667$ m

$f = v / \lambda$

$f = (92 \text{ m/s}) / (0.667 \text{ m})$

$f = 138$ Hz

8. A is correct.

$v = d / t$

$v = (0.6 \text{ m}) / (0.00014 \text{ s})$

$v = 4{,}286 \text{ m/s}$

$\lambda = v / f$

$\lambda = (4{,}286 \text{ m/s}) / (1.5 \times 10^6 \text{ Hz})$

$\lambda = 0.0029 \text{ m} = 2.9 \text{ mm}$

9. C is correct.

The wave velocity is increased by a factor of 1.3.

$v^2 = T / \rho_L$

$T = v^2 \times \rho_L$

Increasing v by a factor of 1.3:

$T = (1.3v)^2 \rho_L$

$T = 1.69 v^2 \rho_L$

T increases by 69%

10. D is correct.

$\rho_L = \rho A$

$\rho_L = \rho (\pi r^2)$

Thus if the diameter decreases by a factor of 2, then the radius decreases by a factor of 2, and the area decreases by a factor of 4. The linear mass density decreases by a factor of 4.

11. B is correct.

The v and period (T) of wire C are equal to wire A so the ρ_L must be equal as well.

$\rho_{LA} = \rho_{LC}$

$\rho_A A_A = \rho_C A_C$

$A_C = (\rho_A A_A) / \rho_C$

$(\pi / 4) \cdot (d_C)^2 = (7 \text{ g/cm}^3)(\pi / 4) \cdot (0.6 \text{ mm})^2 / (3 \text{ g/cm}^3)$

$(d_C)^2 = (7 \text{ g/cm}^3) \cdot (0.6 \text{ mm})^2 / (3 \text{ g/cm}^3)$

$d_C^2 = 0.84 \text{ mm}^2$

$d_C = \sqrt{(0.84 \text{ mm}^2)} = 0.92 \text{ mm}$

12. A is correct.

$A = \pi r^2$

If d increases by a factor of 4, r increases by a factor of 4.

A increases by a factor of 16.

13. B is correct. Since the bird is moving toward the observer, the $f_{observed}$ must be higher than f_{source}.

Doppler shift for an approaching sound source:

$$f_{observed} = (v_{sound} / v_{sound} - v_{source})f_{source}$$

$$f_{observed} = [340 \text{ m/s} / (340 \text{ m/s} - 10 \text{ m/s})]f_{source}$$

$$f_{observed} = (340 \text{ m/s} / 330 \text{ m/s})\cdot(60 \text{ kHz})$$

$$f_{observed} = (1.03)\cdot(60 \text{ kHz})$$

$$f_{observed} = 62 \text{ kHz}$$

14. C is correct. When an approaching sound source is heard, the observed frequency is higher than the frequency from the source due to the Doppler effect.

15. D is correct. Sound requires a medium of solid, liquid or gas substances to be propagated through. A vacuum is none of these.

16. A is correct.

pitch = frequency

According to the Doppler effect pitch increases as the sound source moves towards the observer because consecutive waves which are closer together have a higher frequency and therefore a higher pitch.

Conversely, as the sound source moves away from the observer, its pitch decreases.

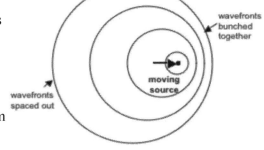

17. C is correct. If waves are out of phase, the combination has its minimum amplitude of $(0.6 - 0.4)$ Pa = 0.2 Pa.

If waves are in phase, the combination has its maximum amplitude of $(0.6 + 0.4)$ Pa = 1.0 Pa.

18. B is correct.

$$I = P / A$$

$$I = P / \pi d^2$$

Intensity at $2d$:

$$I_2 = P / \pi(2d)^2$$

$$I_2 = P / 4\pi d^2$$

$$I_2 = \tfrac{1}{4}P / \pi d^2$$

The new intensity is ¼ the original.

19. A is correct.

speed of sound = √[resistance to compression / density]

$v_{sound} = \sqrt{(E / \rho)}$

Low resistance to compression and high density result in low velocity because this minimizes the term under the radical and thus minimizes velocity.

20. B is correct. Pipes resonate at harmonic frequencies, which are integer multiples of the pipe's fundamental frequency.

At these frequencies, there are antinodes on the wave at each end of the open pipe.

21. C is correct.

For a pipe open at both ends, the resonance frequency:

$f_n = nf_1$

where n = 1, 2, 3, 4…

Therefore only a multiple of 200 Hz can be a resonant frequency.

22. D is correct. Unlike light, sound waves require a medium to travel through and its speed is dependent upon the medium.

Sound is fastest in solids, then liquids and slowest in air.

$v_{solid} > v_{liquid} > v_{air}$

23. B is correct. Magnetic fields are induced by currents or moving charges.

24. C is correct.

$\lambda = v / f$

$\lambda = (5{,}000 \text{ m/s}) / (620 \text{ Hz})$

$\lambda = 8.1 \text{ m}$

25. A is correct. Sound intensity radiating spherically:

$I = P / 4\pi r^2$

If *r* is doubled:

$I = P / 4\pi (2r)^2$

$I = \frac{1}{4}P / 4\pi r^2$

The intensity is reduced by a factor of ¼.

26. D is correct.

As the sound propagates through a medium it spreads out in an approximately spherical pattern. Thus the power is radiated along the surface of the sphere and the intensity can be given by:

$I = P / (4\pi r^2)$ ← for surface area of a sphere

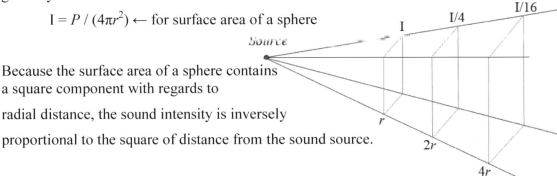

Because the surface area of a sphere contains a square component with regards to radial distance, the sound intensity is inversely proportional to the square of distance from the sound source.

27. B is correct.

The closed end is a node and the open end is an antinode.

$\lambda = (4 / n)L$

where n = 1, 3, 5 …

For the fundamental n = 1:

$\lambda = (4 / 1)\cdot(1.5 \text{ m})$

$\lambda = 6 \text{ m}$

The 1.5 m tube (open at one end) is a quarter of a full wave, so the wavelength is 6 m.

28. A is correct. The 1.5 m is ¼ a full wave, so the wavelength is 6 m, for the fundamental.

$f = v / \lambda$

$f = (960 \text{ m/s}) / 6 \text{ m}$

$f = 160 \text{ Hz}$

29. B is correct. For a closed-ended pipe the wavelength to the harmonic relationship is:

$\lambda = (4 / n)L$

where n = 1, 3, 5…
For the 5th harmonic n = 5

$\lambda = (4 / 5)\cdot(1.5 \text{ m})$

$\lambda_n = 1.2 \text{ m}$

Closed end tube

Harmonic # (n)	# of waves in tube	# of nodes	# of antinodes	Wavelength to length
1	1/4	1	1	$\lambda = 4L$
3	3/4	2	2	$\lambda = 4/3 \, L$
5	5/4	3	3	$\lambda = 4/5 \, L$
7	7/4	4	4	$\lambda = 4/7 \, L$

30. A is correct.

$$f = v / \lambda$$

$$f = (340 \text{ m/s}) / (6 \text{ m})$$

$$f = 57 \text{ Hz}$$

31. C is correct. Wavelength to harmonic number relationship in a standing wave on a string:

$$\lambda = (2L / n)$$

$$\text{where } n = 1, 2, 3, 4, 5 \ldots$$

For the 3rd harmonic:

$$\lambda = (2) \cdot (0.34 \text{ m}) / 3$$

$$\lambda = 0.23 \text{ m}$$

32. D is correct. Beat frequency equation:

$$f_{\text{beat}} = |f_2 - f_1|$$

If one of the tones increases in frequency, then the beat frequency increases or decreases, but this cannot be determined unless the two tones are known.

33. A is correct. For a closed-ended pipe, the wavelength to harmonic relationship is:

$$\lambda = (4 / n)L$$

$$\text{where } n = 1, 3, 5, 7 \ldots$$

The lowest three tones are n = 1, 3, 5

$$\lambda = (4 / 1)L; \lambda = (4 / 3)L; \lambda = (4 / 5)L$$

34. D is correct. The sound was barely perceptible, the intensity at Mary's ear is $I_0 = 9.8 \times 10^{-12}$ W/m^2.

Since the mosquito is 1 m away, imagine a sphere 1 m in radius around the mosquito.

If 9.8×10^{-12} W emanates from each area 1 m^2, then the surface area is $4\pi(1 \text{ m})^2$.

This is the power produced by one mosquito:

$$P = 4\pi r^2 I_0$$

$$P = 4\pi(1 \text{ m})^2 \times (9.8 \times 10^{-12} \text{ W/m}^2)$$

$$P = 1.2 \times 10^{-10} \text{ W}$$

$$\text{energy} = \text{power} \times \text{time}$$

$$E = Pt$$

Energy produced in 200 s:

$$Pt = (1.2 \times 10^{-10} \text{ W}) \cdot (200 \text{ s})$$

$$E = 2.5 \times 10^{-8} \text{ J}$$

35. A is correct.

$$v = c / \text{n}$$

where c is the speed of light in a vacuum

$$v = \Delta x / \Delta t$$

$$\Delta x / \Delta t = c / \text{n}$$

$$\Delta t = \text{n}\Delta x / c$$

$$\Delta t = (1.33) \cdot (10^3 \text{ m}) / (3 \times 10^8 \text{ m/s})$$

$$\Delta t = 4.4 \times 10^{-6} \text{ s}$$

36. A is correct. When waves interfere constructively (i.e. in phase), the sound level is amplified. When they interfere destructively (i.e. out of phase), they cancel and no sound is heard. Acoustic engineers work to ensure that there are no "dead spots" and the sound waves add.

An engineer should minimize destructive interference which can distort sound.

37. B is correct.

Velocity of a wave on a string in tension can be calculated by:

$$v = \sqrt{(TL / m)}$$

Graph B gives a curve of a square root relationship which is how velocity and tension are related.

$$y = x^{\frac{1}{2}}$$

38. D is correct. From the diagram, the wave is a 6th harmonic standing wave.

Find wavelength:

$$\lambda = (2L / \text{n})$$

$$\lambda = (2) \cdot (4 \text{ m}) / (6)$$

$$\lambda = 1.3 \text{ m}$$

Find frequency:

$$f = v / \lambda$$

$$f = (20 \text{ m/s}) / (1.3 \text{ m})$$

$$f = 15.4 \text{ Hz}$$

39. B is correct.

Sound wave velocity is independent of frequency and does not change.

40. C is correct.

For a standing wave on a string the frequency to harmonic relationship is:

$f = (nv) / (2L)$

For the 6th harmonic, n = 6:

$f = (6)\cdot(345 \text{ m/s}) / (2)\cdot(0.5 \text{ m})$

$f = 2{,}070 \text{ Hz}$

The open pipe resonating in the 2nd overtone is resonating at twice its fundamental frequency.

$2{,}070 \text{ Hz} = 2f_{\text{fundamental pipe}}$

$f_{\text{fundamental pipe}} = 1{,}035 \text{ Hz}$

Find the length of the pipe. The frequency to harmonic relationship for a standing wave on a string is the same for a pipe open at both ends.

$f = (nv) / (2L)$

$L = (nv) / (2f)$

$L = (1)\cdot(345 \text{ m/s}) / (2)\cdot(1{,}035 \text{ Hz})$

$L = 0.17 \text{ m}$

41. A is correct.

$v = \sqrt{(T / \mu)}$

$\mu = m / L$

$v = \sqrt{(TL / m)}$

$v_2 = \sqrt{(T(2L) / m)}$

$v_2 = \sqrt{2} \sqrt{(TL / m)}$

$v_2 = v\sqrt{2}$

42. C is correct. For a standing wave, the resonance frequency:

$f_n = nf_1$

where n is the harmonic number, n = 1, 2, 3, 4 …

Therefore, only a multiple of 500 Hz can be a resonant frequency.

43. D is correct. The angle of incidence always equals the angle of reflection.

A light beam entering a medium with a greater refractive index than the incident medium refracts *toward* the normal. Thus, the angle of refraction is less than the angles of incidence and reflection.

Snell's law:

$$n_1 \sin \theta_1 = n_2 \sin \theta_2$$

where $n_1 < n_2$

For Snell's law to be true, then:

$$\theta_1 > \theta_2$$

44. A is correct. Speed of sound in gas:

$$v_{sound} = \sqrt{(yRT / M)}$$

where y = adiabatic constant, R = gas constant, T = temperature and M = molecular mass

The speed of sound in a gas is only dependent upon temperature and not frequency or wavelength.

45. B is correct.

Waves only transport energy and not matter.

46. D is correct.

$$v = \lambda f$$

$$\lambda = v / f$$

$$\lambda = (344 \text{ m/s}) / (700 \text{ s}^{-1})$$

$$\lambda = 0.5 \text{ m}$$

The information about the string is unnecessary, as the only contributor to the wavelength of the sound in air is the frequency and the speed.

47. C is correct.

$$v = \lambda f$$

$$f = v / \lambda$$

Distance from sound source is not part of the equation for frequency.

48. A is correct.

Velocity of a wave in a rope:

$$v = \sqrt{[T / (m / L]}$$

$t = d / v$

$d = L$

$t = d / \sqrt{[T / (m / L)]}$

$t = (8 \text{ m}) / [40 \text{ N} / (2.5 \text{ kg} / 8 \text{ m})]^{\frac{1}{2}}$

$t = 0.71 \text{ s}$

49. C is correct.

Intensity to decibel relationship:

$I \text{ (dB)} = 10 \log_{10} (I_1 / I_0)$

where I_0 = threshold of hearing

$dB = 10 \log_{10}[(10^{-5} \text{ W/m}^2) / (10^{-12} \text{ W/m}^2)]$

$I = 70$ decibels

50. B is correct.

The diagram represents the described scenario.

The wave is in the second harmonic with a wavelength of:

$\lambda = (2 / n)L$

$\lambda = (2 / 2)\cdot(1 \text{ m})$

$\lambda = 1 \text{ m}$

$f = v / \lambda$

$f = (3.8 \times 10^4 \text{ m/s}) / (1 \text{ m})$

$f = 3.8 \times 10^4 \text{ Hz}$

The lowest frequency corresponds to the lowest possible harmonic number.

For this problem, n = 2.

51. D is correct.

The speed of light travelling in a vacuum is c.

$c = \lambda v$

$c = \lambda f$

$f = c / \lambda$

Frequency and wavelength are inversely proportional so an increase in frequency results in a decreased wavelength.

52. B is correct.

Radio waves are electromagnetic waves while all other choices are mechanical waves.

53. D is correct. Find the extreme path difference (EPD) which is the path length from speaker 1 to the microphone minus the path length from speaker 2.

$$\text{EPD} = |L_1 - L_2|$$

$$L = \text{path} / \lambda$$

$$\text{EPD} = |(1 \text{ m} / 0.8 \text{ m}) - (1 \text{ m} / 0.8 \text{ m})|$$

$$\text{EPD} = 0$$

For constructive interference:

$$\text{EPD} = m\lambda$$

where $m = 0, 1, 2, 3 \dots$

For destructive interference:

$$\text{EPD} = \tfrac{1}{2}(2m - 1)\lambda$$

where $m = 1, 2, 3 \dots$

The wave is constructively interfering because EPD = 0 which can only be produced when $m = 0$.

Thus point m must be an antinode.

54. C is correct. Doppler equation for receding source of sound:

$$f_{observed} = [v_{sound} / (v_{sound} + v_{source})]f_{source}$$

$$f_{observed} = [(342 \text{ m/s}) / (342 \text{ m/s} + 30 \text{ m/s})]\cdot(1{,}200 \text{ Hz})$$

$$f_{observed} = 1{,}103 \text{ Hz}$$

The observed frequency is always lower when the source is receding.

55. D is correct.

$$f_1 = 600 \text{ Hz}$$

$$f_2 = 300 \text{ Hz}$$

$$f_2 = \tfrac{1}{2}f_1$$

$$\lambda_1 = v / f_1$$

$$\lambda_2 = v / (\tfrac{1}{2}f_1)$$

$$\lambda_2 = 2 (v / f_1)$$

The wavelength of the 300 Hz frequency is twice as long as the wavelength of the 600 Hz frequency.

56. C is correct.

$f_2 = 2f_1$

$f = v / \lambda$

$v / \lambda_2 = (2)v / \lambda_1$, cancel v from both sides of the expression

$1 / \lambda_2 = 2 / \lambda_1$

$\lambda = (2 / n)L$, for open-ended pipes

$1 / (2 / n)L_2 = 2 / (2 / n)L_1$

$L_1 = 2L_2$

$L_1 / L_2 = 2$

57. A is correct.

Resonance occurs when energy gets transferred from one oscillator to another of similar f by a weak coupling. Dispersion is the spreading of waves due to the dependence of wave speed on frequency.

Interference is the addition of two waves in the same medium, which is what happens when waves from both strings combine, but that is not the excitation of the C_4 string.

58. C is correct.

frequency = 1 / period

$f = 1 / T$

$f = 1 / 10$ s

$f = 0.1$ Hz

Find wavelength:

$\lambda = v / f$

$\lambda = (4.5 \text{ m/s}) / (0.1 \text{ Hz})$

$\lambda = 45$ m

59. D is correct.

$v = \sqrt{K / \rho}$

where K = bulk modulus (i.e. resistance to compression) and ρ = density.

Since ρ for water is greater than for air, the greater v for water implies that water's bulk modulus (K) must be much greater than for air.

60. C is correct.

When visible light strikes glass, it causes the electrons of the atoms in the glass to vibrate at their non-resonant frequency. The vibration is passed from one atom to the next transferring the energy of the light. Finally, the energy is passed to the last atom before the light is re-mitted out of the glass at its original frequency.

If the light energy were converted into internal energy the glass would heat up and not transfer the light.

61. D is correct.

Sound intensity varies as the inverse square of the distance.

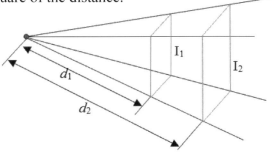

$I_2 / I_1 = (d_1 / d_2)^2$

where $d_1 = 3$ m and $d_2 = 9$ m

$I_2 = (10^{-6}$ W/m$^2) \cdot (3$ m $/ 9$ m$)^2$

$I_2 = 1.1 \times 10^{-7}$ W/m^2

62. A is correct.

Convert linear density to appropriate units:

$\mu = (140$ g/cm$) \cdot (1$ kg$/10^3$ g$) \cdot (100$ cm $/ 1$ m$)$

$\mu = 14$ kg/m

Find velocity:

$v = \sqrt{(T / \mu)}$

$v = \sqrt{(50$ N $/ 14$ kg/m$)}$

$v = 1.9$ m/s

Find frequency:

$f_n = nv / 2L$

$f_1 = (1) \cdot (1.9$ m/s$) / (2)(0.5$ m$)$

$f_1 = 1.9$ Hz

63. D is correct.

Sound travels faster in helium than in air due to its lower density. The different speed of sound alters the timbre of her voice but frequency remains constant.

64. D is correct.

An overtone is any frequency higher than the fundamental.

In a stopped pipe (i.e. open at one end and closed at the other):

Harmonic #	Tone
1	fundamental tone
3	1st overtone
5	2nd overtone
7	3rd overtone

Find wavelength for the third overtone:

$$\lambda_n = (4L \,/\, n)$$

where n = 1, 3, 5, 7…

$$\lambda_n = [(4)\cdot(1.4 \text{ m}) \,/\, (7)]$$

$$\lambda_n = 0.8 \text{ m}$$

Find frequency:

$$f = v \,/\, \lambda$$

$$f = (340 \text{ m/s}) \,/\, (0.8 \text{ m})$$

$$f = 425 \text{ Hz}$$

65. D is correct.

The Doppler effect for light is similar to that for sound. The movement of the sound source away from the observer results in a decrease in the detected frequency.

66. B is correct.

Beat frequency equation:

$$f_{beat} = |f_2 - f_1|$$

$$f_{beat} = |\,524 \text{ Hz} - 460 \text{ Hz}\,|$$

$$f_{beat} = 64 \text{ Hz}$$

67. A is correct. The frequency of a wave does not change when it enters a new medium.

$$v = (1 \,/\, n)c$$

where c = speed of light in a vacuum and n = refractive index.

The speed v decreases when light enters a medium with a higher refractive index.

68. D is correct.

Resonance is the phenomenon where one system transfers its energy to another at that system's resonant frequency (natural frequency). It is forced vibrations with the least energy input.

69. B is correct.

Refraction is the bending of a light wave when it enters a medium where its speed is different.

The index of refraction is based upon:

$n = c / v$

where n = index of refraction, c = speed of light in a vacuum and v = speed of light in the medium.

70. A is correct.

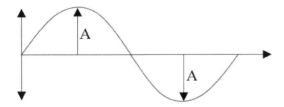

When a sound becomes louder, the energy of the sound wave becomes higher.

Amplitude is directly related to the energy of the sound wave:

more energy = higher amplitude

less energy = lower amplitude

71. D is correct.

Intensity is the power per unit area:

$I = W/m^2$

Loudness is a subjective measurement of the strength of the ear's perception to sound.

72. C is correct.

An overtone is any frequency higher than the fundamental.

In a stopped pipe (i.e. open at one end and closed at the other):

Harmonic #	Tone
1	fundamental tone
3	1st overtone
5	2nd overtone
7	3rd overtone

The first overtone is the 3rd harmonic.

Find wavelength:

$\lambda_n = (4L / n)$, for stopped pipe

where n = 1, 3, 5, 7...

$\lambda_3 = [(4) \cdot (3 \text{ m}) / 3)]$

$\lambda_3 = 4 \text{ m}$

Find frequency:

$f = v / \lambda$

$f = (340 \text{ m/s}) / (4 \text{ m})$

$f = 85 \text{ Hz}$

Find velocity of a standing wave on the violin:

$f = v / 2L$

$v = (2L) \cdot (f)$

$v = (2) \cdot (0.36 \text{ m}) \cdot (85 \text{ Hz})$

$v = 61 \text{ m/s}$

Convert linear density to kg/m:

$\mu = (3.8 \text{ g/cm}) \cdot (1 \text{ kg/} 10^3 \text{ g}) \cdot (100 \text{ cm} / 1 \text{ m})$

$\mu = 0.38 \text{ kg/m}$

Find tension:

$v = \sqrt{(T / \mu)}$

$T = v^2 \mu$

$T = (61 \text{ m/s})^2 \times (0.38 \text{ kg/m})$

$T = 1,414 \text{ N}$

73. B is correct.

I = Power / area

The intensity *I* is proportional to the power, so an increase by a factor of 10 in power leads to an increase by a factor of 10 in intensity.

$I \text{ (dB)} = 10\log_{10} (I / I_0)$

dB is related to the logarithm of intensity.

If the original intensity was 20 dB then:

$20 \text{ dB} = 10\log_{10} (I_1 / I_0)$

$2 = \log_{10} (I_1 / I_0)$

$100 = I_1 / I_0$

The new intensity is a factor of 10 higher than before:

$I_2 = 10 I_1$

$1,000 = I_2 / I_0$

$I \text{ (dB)} = 10\log_{10}(1,000)$

$I \text{ (dB)} = 30 \text{ dB}$

74. D is correct.

velocity = distance / time

$v = d / t$

$d = vt$

$d = (340 \text{ m/s}) \cdot (7 \text{ s})$

$d = 2,380 \text{ m} \approx 2 \text{ km}$

75. A is correct.

Constructive interference: the maximal magnitude of amplitude of the resultant wave is the sum of the individual amplitudes:

3 cm + 8 cm = 11 cm

Destructive interference: the minimal magnitude of amplitude of the resultant wave is the difference between the individual amplitudes:

8 cm − 3 cm = 5 cm

The magnitude of amplitude of the resultant wave is between 5 and 11 cm.

76. B is correct.

All electromagnetic waves arise from accelerating charges. When a charge is vibrating it is accelerating (change in direction of motion is acceleration).

77. D is correct.

When tuning a radio the tuner picks up certain frequencies by resonating at those frequencies. This filters out the other radio signals so only that specific frequency is amplified. By changing the tuner on the radio a particular frequency is chosen that the tuner resonates at and the signal is amplified.

DC CIRCUITS – EXPLANATIONS

1. B is correct. $R = \rho L / A$, where ρ is the resistivity of the wire material.

If the length L is doubled, the resistance R is doubled.

If the radius r is doubled, the area $A = \pi r^2$ is quadrupled and the resistance R is decreased by ¼.

If these two changes are combined:

$R_{new} = \rho(2L) / \pi(2r)^2$

$R_{new} = (2/4) \cdot (\rho L / \pi r^2)$

$R_{new} = (2/4)R = \frac{1}{2}R$

2. D is correct. Internal resistance of battery is in series with resistors in circuit:

$R_{eq} = R_1 + R_{battery}$

where R_{eq} is equivalent resistance and R_1 is resistor connected to battery

$V = IR_{eq}$

$V = I(R_1 + R_{battery})$

$R_{battery} = V / I - R_1$

$R_{battery} = (12 \text{ V} / 0.6 \text{ A}) - 6 \text{ } \Omega$

$R_{battery} = 14 \text{ } \Omega$

3. C is correct. An ohm Ω is defined as the resistance between two points of a conductor when a constant potential difference of 1 V, applied to these points, produces in the conductor a current of 1 A.

A series circuit experiences the same current through all resistors regardless of their resistance.

However, the voltage across each resistor can be different.

Since the light bulbs are in series, the current through them is the same.

4. C is correct.

Power = current^2 × resistance

$P = I^2 R$

Double current:

$P_2 = (2I)^2 R$

$P_2 = 4(I^2 R)$

$P_2 = 4P$

Power is quadrupled.

---

5. A is correct.

$$V = IR$$

$$I = V / R$$

$$I = (220 \text{ V}) / (400 \text{ Ω})$$

$$I = 0.55 \text{ A}$$

6. D is correct. A parallel circuit experiences the same potential difference across each resistor.

However, the current through each resistor can be different.

7. C is correct.

Ohm's Law:

$$V = IR$$

$$V = (10 \text{ A}) \cdot (35 \text{ Ω})$$

$$V = 350 \text{ V}$$

8. A is correct. Current remains constant across resistors in series and voltage remains constant across resistors in parallel.

Equivalent resistors of R_2 and R:

$$R_{eq} = R_2 + R$$

$$V = IR_{eq}$$

$$I_2 = V / R_{eq}$$

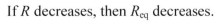

If R decreases, then R_{eq} decreases.

If R_{eq} decreases, then I_2 increases.

Assume a node where I_1 and I_2 start with current I_0

By Kirchhoff's Current Law:

$$I_0 = I_1 + I_2$$

Thus if I_2 increases I_1 decreases to keep I_0 constant.

9. C is correct.

$$V = IR$$

$$I = V / R$$

Ohm's law states that the current between two points is directly proportional to the potential difference between the points.

10. D is correct. Kirchhoff's junction rule states that the sum of all currents coming into a junction is the sum of all currents leaving a junction. This is a statement of conservation of charge because it defines that no charge is created nor destroyed in the circuit.

11. A is correct. Current is constant across resistors connected in series.

12. D is correct. By convention, the direction of electric current is the direction that a positive charge migrates.

Therefore, current flows from a point of high potential to a point of lower potential.

13. D is correct. Magnets provide magnetic forces.

Generators convert mechanical energy into electrical energy, turbines extract energy from fluids (e.g. air and water), and transformers transfer energy between circuits.

14. C is correct.

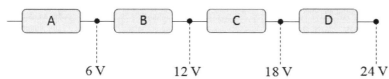

Batteries in series add voltage like resistors in series add resistance.

The resistances of the lights they power are not needed to solve the problem.

15. D is correct. Current is defined as the flow of charge per unit of time:

$$A = C / s$$
$$C = A \cdot s$$

16. B is correct. "In a perfect conductor" and "in the absence of resistance" have the same meanings, and current can flow in conductors of varying resistances.

A semi-perfect conductor has resistance.

17. B is correct.

$$R_1 = \rho L_1 / A_1$$
$$R_2 = \rho(4L_1) / A_2$$
$$R_1 = R_2$$
$$\rho L_1 / A_1 = \rho(4L_1) / A_2$$
$$A_2 = 4A_1$$

$$(\pi / 4)d_2^2 = (\pi / 4) \cdot (4)d_1^2$$

$$d_2^2 = 4d_1^2$$

$$d_2 = 2d_1$$

18. D is correct. The total resistance of a network of series resistors increases as more resistors are added.

$$V = IR$$

An increase in the total resistance results in a decrease in the total current through the network.

19. A is correct. This is a circuit with two resistors in series.

Combine the two resistors into one resistor:

$$R_T = R + R_{int}$$

$$R_T = 0.5 \; \Omega + 0.1 \; \Omega$$

$$R_T = 0.6 \; \Omega$$

Ohm's law:

$$V = IR$$

$$I = V / R$$

$$I = 9 \text{ V} / 0.6 \; \Omega$$

$$I = 15 \text{ A}$$

20. A is correct.

$$\text{Resistance} = \text{Ohms}$$

$$\Omega = \text{V} / \text{A}$$

$$\Omega = [(\text{kg} \cdot \text{m}^2) / (\text{A} \cdot \text{s}^3)] / \text{A}$$

$$\Omega = (\text{kg} \cdot \text{m}^2) / (\text{A}^2 \cdot \text{s}^3)$$

$$\Omega = (\text{kg} \cdot \text{m}^2 \cdot \text{s}^2) / (\text{C}^2 \cdot \text{s}^3)$$

$$\Omega = (\text{kg} \cdot \text{m}^2) / (\text{C}^2 \cdot \text{s}) = \text{kg} \cdot \text{m}^2 / \text{s} \cdot \text{C}^2$$

21. D is correct.

Ohm's Law:

$$V = IR$$

If V is constant, then I and R are inversely proportional.

An increase in R results in a decrease in I.

22. A is correct.

Ohm's law:

$$V = IR$$

Increasing V and decreasing R increases I.

23. C is correct. The total resistance of a network of series resistors increases as more resistors are added to the network.

An increase in the total resistance results in a decrease in the total current through the network.

A decrease in current results in a decrease in the voltage across the original resistor:

$$V = IR$$

24. A is correct. Batteries in series add voltage, and like resistors in series, the same current will flow through each.

25. D is correct.

Calculate resistance:

$$R = \rho L / A$$
$$A = \pi r^2 = (\pi / 4)d^2$$
$$R = [(2.22 \times 10^{-8}\ \Omega\cdot m)\cdot(0.18\ m)] / (\pi / 4)\cdot(0.002\ m)^2$$
$$R = 1.3 \times 10^{-3}\ \Omega$$
$$P = I^2 R$$
$$P = (0.5\ A)^2 \times (1.3 \times 10^{-3}\ \Omega)$$
$$P = 0.32\ mW$$

26. D is correct. Because the material of both wires is the same (copper), the resistivity of both wires is equal.

27. D is correct. Equivalent resistance of parallel resistors:

$$1 / R_{eq1} = (1 / 3\ \Omega) + (1 / 6\ \Omega)$$
$$1 / R_{eq1} = (2 / 6\ \Omega) + (1 / 6\ \Omega)$$
$$R_{eq1} = 2\ \Omega$$

If the 3 Ω resistor burns out, R_{eq} of the parallel resistors become:

$$1 / R_{eq2} = (1 / \infty) + (1 / 6\ \Omega)$$
$$1 / R_{eq2} = 1 / 6\ \Omega$$

$R_{eq2} = 6\ \Omega$

$R_{eq2} > R_{eq1}$

By Ohm's Law:

$V = IR$

$V / R = I$

$V / R_{eq2} < V / R_{eq1}$

$I_2 < I_1$

The current in the 6 Ω resistor decreases.

The current in the 4 Ω resistor cannot go to zero as there is still a voltage source and the circuit is complete.

28. A is correct.

Use definition of one ampere:

1 amp = 1 C/s

Solve:

# of electrons = $(340 \times 10^{-3}\ C\ /\ 1\ s)\cdot(1\ electron\ /\ 1.6 \times 10^{-19}\ C)$

# of electrons = 2.1×10^{18} electrons/s

29. B is correct.

$V = IR$

$R = V / I$

30. D is correct.

Voltage = current × resistance

$V = IR$

$V = (5\ A)\,(15\ \Omega)$

$V = 75\ V$

EELECTROSTATICS – EXPLANATIONS

1. C is correct.

Since charge is quantized, the charge Q must be a whole number (n) times the charge on a single electron:

Charge = # electrons × electron charge

$Q = n(e^-)$

$n = Q / e^-$

$n = (-1 \text{ C}) / (-1.6 \times 10^{-19} \text{ C})$

$n = 6.25 \times 10^{18} \approx 6.3 \times 10^{18}$ electrons

2. C is correct.

Coulomb's law:

$F_1 = kQ_1Q_2 / r^2$

If r is increased by a factor of 4:

$F_e = kQ_1Q_2 / (4r)^2$

$F_e = kQ_1Q_2 / (16r^2)$

$F_e = (1/16)kQ_1Q_2 / r^2$

$F_e = (1/16)F_1$

As the distance increases by a factor of 4, the force decreases by a factor of $4^2 = 16$.

3. D is correct.

Gravitational Force: F_g

$F_g = Gm_1m_2 / r^2$

$F_g = [(6.673 \times 10^{-11} \text{ N·m}^2/\text{kg}^2) \cdot (54{,}000 \text{ kg}) \cdot (51{,}000 \text{ kg})] / (180 \text{ m})^2$

$F_g = 0.18 \text{ N·m}^2 / (32{,}400 \text{ m}^2)$

$F_g = 5.7 \times 10^{-6} \text{ N}$

Electrostatic Force: F_e

$F_e = kQ_1Q_2 / r^2$

$F_e = [(9 \times 10^9 \text{ N·m}^2/\text{C}^2) \cdot (15 \times 10^{-6} \text{ C}) \cdot (11 \times 10^{-6} \text{ C})] / (180 \text{ m})^2$

$F_e = (1.49 \text{ N·m}^2) / (32{,}400 \text{ m}^2)$

$F_e = 4.6 \times 10^{-5} \text{ N}$

Net Force:

$F_{net} = F_g - F_e$

$$F_{net} = (5.7 \times 10^{-6}\,\text{N}) - (4.6 \times 10^{-5}\,\text{N})$$
$$F_{net} = -4 \times 10^{-5}\,\text{N}$$

Because the charges are opposite, subtract F_e from F_g.

Force is expected to be negative since asteroid's charges have the same sign and will repel each other.

4. B is correct.

Newton's Third Law also applies to electrostatic forces.

Newton's Third Law states for every force there is an equal and opposite reaction force:

Electrostatic Force:

$$F_1 = kQ_1Q_2 / r^2$$
$$F_2 = kQ_1Q_2 / r^2$$
$$F_1 = F_2$$

5. D is correct.

$$\text{charge} = \#\ \text{electrons} \times \text{electron charge}$$
$$Q = ne^-$$
$$n = Q / e^-$$
$$n = (-10 \times 10^{-6}\,\text{C}) / (-1.6 \times 10^{-19}\,\text{C})$$
$$n = 6.3 \times 10^{13}\ \text{electrons}$$

6. C is correct.

Coulomb's law:

$$F_e = kQ_1Q_2 / r^2$$

If the separation is halved then r decreases by $\frac{1}{2}$:

$$F_2 = kq_1q_2 / (\tfrac{1}{2}r)^2$$
$$F_2 = 4(kq_1q_2 / r^2)$$
$$F_2 = 4F_e$$

7. D is correct.

Coulomb's law:

$$F = kQ_1Q_2 / r^2$$

Doubling both the charges and distance:

$$F = [k(2Q_1)\cdot(2Q_2)] / (2r)^2$$

$$F = [4k(Q_1) \cdot (Q_2)] / (4r^2)$$
$$F = (4/4)[kQ_1Q_2 / (r^2)]$$
$$F = kQ_1Q_2 / r^2, \text{ remains the same}$$

8. A is correct.

Coulomb's law:

$$F = kQ_1Q_2 / r^2$$

The Coulomb force between opposite charges is attractive.

Since the strength of force is inversely proportional to the square of the separation distance (r^2), the force decreases as the charges are pulled apart.

9. B is correct.

Coulomb's Law:

$$F_1 = kQ_1Q_2 / r^2$$
$$F_2 = kQ_1Q_2 / r^2$$
$$F_1 = F_2$$

Newton's Third Law: the force exerted by one charge on the other has the same magnitude as the force the other exerts on the first.

10. D is correct.

$$F_e = kQ_1Q_2 / r^2$$
$$F_e = (9 \times 10^9 \text{ N·m}^2/\text{C}^2) \cdot (-1.6 \times 10^{-19} \text{ C}) \cdot (-1.6 \times 10^{-19} \text{ C}) / (0.03 \text{ m})^2$$
$$F_e = 2.56 \times 10^{-25} \text{ N}$$

11. C is correct.

Charge = # electrons × electron charge

$$Q = ne^-$$
$$n = Q / e^-$$
$$n = (8 \times 10^{-6} \text{ C}) / (1.6 \times 10^{-19} \text{ C})$$
$$n = 5 \times 10^{13} \text{ electrons}$$

12. A is correct.

An object with a charge can attract another object of opposite charge or a neutral charge.

Like charges cannot attract, but the type of charge does not matter otherwise.

13. D is correct.

$$W = Q\Delta V$$

$$V = kQ / r$$

Consider the charge Q_1 to be fixed and move charge Q_2 from initial distance r_i to final distance r_f.

$$W = Q_2(V_f - V_i)$$

$$W = Q_2[(kQ_1 / r_f) - (kQ_1 / r_i)]$$

$$W = kQ_1Q_2(1 / r_f - 1 / r_i)$$

$$W = (9 \times 10^9 \text{ N·m}^2/\text{C}) \cdot (2.3 \times 10^{-8} \text{ C}) \cdot (2.5 \times 10^{-9} \text{ C}) \cdot [(1 / 0.01 \text{ m}) - (1 / 0.1 \text{ m})]$$

$$W = 4.7 \times 10^{-5} \text{ J}$$

14. D is correct.

Equilibrium:

$$F = kq_1q_2 / r_1^2$$

$$F_{\text{attractive on } q2} = F_{\text{repulsive on } q2}$$

$$kq_1q_2 / r_1^2 = kq_2Q / r_2^2$$

$$q_1 = Qr_1^2 / r_2^2$$

$$q_1 = (7.5 \times 10^{-9} \text{ C}) \cdot (0.2 \text{ m})^2 / (0.1 \text{ m})^2$$

$$q_1 = 30 \times 10^{-9} \text{ C}$$

15. C is correct.

Coulomb's law:

$$F_e = kQ_1Q_2 / r^2$$

$$1 \text{ N} = kQ_1Q_2 / r^2$$

Doubling charges and keeping distance constant:

$$k(2Q_1) \cdot (2Q_2) / r^2 = 4kQ_1Q_2 / r^2$$

$$4kQ_1Q_2 / r^2 = 4F_e$$

$$4F_e = 4(1 \text{ N}) = 4 \text{ N}$$

16. D is correct.

The Na^+ ion is positively charged and attracts the oxygen atom. Oxygen is slightly negative because it is more electronegative than the hydrogen atoms to which it is bonded.

17. C is correct.

Charge = # of electrons × electron charge

$$Q = ne^-$$
$$Q = (30){\cdot}(-1.6 \times 10^{-19}\ C)$$
$$Q = -4.8 \times 10^{-18}\ C$$

18. B is correct.

The repulsive force between two particles is:

$$F = kQ_1Q_2\ /\ r^2$$

As r increases, F decreases

Using $F = ma$, a also decreases

19. C is correct. The Coulomb is the basic unit of electrical charge in the SI unit system and is equal to one ampere per second.

$$1\ C = 1\ A/s$$

20. A is correct.

By the Law of Conservation of Charge, charge cannot be created nor destroyed.

21. B is correct.

Coulomb's Law:

$$F = kQ_1Q_2\ /\ r^2$$

If both charges are doubled,

$$F = k(2Q_1){\cdot}(2Q_2)\ /\ r^2$$
$$F = 4kQ_1Q_2\ /\ r^2$$

F increases by a factor of 4.

22. C is correct. Coulomb's law:

$$F = kQ_1Q_2\ /\ r^2$$
$$Q_1 = Q_2$$

Therefore:

$$Q_1Q_2 = Q^2$$
$$F = kQ^2\ /\ r^2$$

Rearranging:

$$Q^2 = Fr^2 / k$$

$$Q = \sqrt{(Fr^2 / k)}$$

$$Q = \sqrt{[(4 \text{ N}) \cdot (0.01 \text{ m})^2 / (9 \times 10^9 \text{ N·m}^2/\text{C}^2)]}$$

$$Q = 2 \times 10^{-7} \text{ C}$$

23. C is correct.

Coulomb's law:

$$F = kQ_1Q_2 / r^2$$

When each particle has lost ½ its charge:

$$F_2 = k(\tfrac{1}{2}Q_1) \cdot (\tfrac{1}{2}Q_2) / r^2$$

$$F_2 = (\tfrac{1}{4})kQ_1Q_2 / r^2$$

$$F_2 = (\tfrac{1}{4})F$$

F decreases by a factor of ¼

24. A is correct.

$$W = Q\Delta V$$

$$V = kq / r$$

$$W = (kQq) \cdot (1 / r_2 - 1 / r_1)$$

$$W = (kQq) \cdot (1 / 2 \text{ m} - 1 / 6 \text{ m})$$

$$W = (kQq) \cdot (1 / 3 \text{ m})$$

$$W = (9 \times 10^9 \text{ N·m}^2/\text{C}^2) \cdot (3.1 \times 10^{-5} \text{ C}) \cdot (-10^{-6} \text{ C}) / (1 / 3 \text{ m})$$

$$W = -0.093 \text{ J} \approx -0.09 \text{ J}$$

The negative sign indicates that the electric field does the work on charge q.

25. D is correct.

charge = # electrons × electron charge

$$Q = ne^-$$

$$n = Q / e^-$$

$$n = (-600 \times 10^{-9} \text{ C}) / (-1.6 \times 10^{-19} \text{ C})$$

$$n = 3.8 \times 10^{12} \text{ electrons}$$

26. D is correct.

An object that is electrically polarized has had its charge separated into opposites and thus rearrange themselves within distinct regions.

27. D is correct.

Force due to motion:

$F = ma$

$F = (0.001 \text{ kg}) \cdot (440 \text{ m/s}^2)$

$F = 0.44 \text{ N}$

Force due to charge:

$F = kQ_1Q_2 / r^2$

$Q_1 = Q_2$

$Q_1Q_2 = Q^2$

$F = kQ^2 / r^2$

Rearranging:

$Q^2 = Fr^2 / k$

$Q = \sqrt{(Fr^2 / k)}$

$Q = \sqrt{[(0.44 \text{ N}) \cdot (0.02 \text{ m})^2 / (9 \times 10^9 \text{ N} \cdot \text{m}^2/\text{C}^2)]}$

$Q = 1.4 \times 10^{-7} \text{ C} = 140 \text{ nC}$

28. B is correct.

$F = kQ_1Q_2 / r^2$

	Force from +	Force from –
x direction	→	→
y direction	↑	↓

Net force = →

29. B is correct.

Coulomb's law: the strength of the electrostatic force between two point charges.

$F = kQ_1Q_2 / r^2$

$F = [(9 \times 10^9 \text{ N} \cdot \text{m}^2/\text{C}^2) \cdot (+3 \text{ C}) \cdot (-6 \text{ C})] / (0.5 \text{ m})^2$

$F = 1.3 \times 10^{12} \text{ N}$

F is positive to indicate an attractive force.

30. D is correct.

Coulomb's law:

$$F_1 = kQ_1Q_2 / r^2$$
$$F_2 = kQ_1Q_2 / (0.25r)^2$$
$$F_2 = 16kQ_1Q_2 / r^2$$
$$F_2 = 16F_1$$

F increases by a factor of 16,

$$(1 \text{ N}) \cdot (16) = 16 \text{ N}$$

31. C is correct.

$$F_e = kQ_1Q_2 / r^2$$
$$F_e = [(9 \times 10^9 \text{ N·m}^2/\text{C}^2) \cdot (5.1 \times 10^{-9} \text{ C})(2 \times 10^{-9} \text{ C})] / (0.1 \text{ m})^2$$
$$F_e = 9.18 \times 10^{-4} \text{ N}$$

$F_e \sin(60°)$ represents the force from one of the positive 2 nC charges.

Double to find the total force:

$$F_{total} = 2F_e \sin(60°)$$
$$F_{total} = 2(9.18 \times 10^{-4} \text{ N}) \sin(60°)$$
$$F_{total} = 1.6 \times 10^{-3} \text{ N}$$

The sine of the angle is used since only the vertical forces are added because the horizontal forces are equal and opposite and therefore they cancel.

32. D is correct.

Coulomb's law:

$$F_e = kQ_1Q_2 / r^2$$

If r is increased by a factor of 3:

$$F_{new} = kQ_1Q_2 / (3r)^2$$
$$F_{new} = kQ_1Q_2 / (9r^2)$$
$$F_{new} = (1/9)kQ_1Q_2 / r^2$$
$$F_{new} = F_{original} (1/9)$$
$$F_{new} = (1 \text{ N}) \cdot (1/9)$$
$$F_{new} = 0.11 \text{ N}$$

33. D is correct.

$W = kq_1q_2 / r$

$r = \Delta x$

$r = 2 \text{ mm} - (-2 \text{ mm})$

$r = 4 \text{ mm}$

$W = [(9 \times 10^9 \text{ N·m}^2/\text{C}^2)\cdot(4 \times 10^{-6} \text{ C})\cdot(8 \times 10^{-6} \text{ C})] / (4 \times 10^{-3} \text{ m})$

$W = (0.288 \text{ N·m}^2) / (4 \times 10^{-3} \text{ m})$

$W = 72 \text{ J}$

34. D is correct.

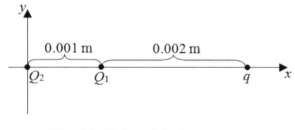

$W = kQq(1 / r - 1 / \infty)$

$W_1 = (kQ_1q) / r_1$

$W_2 = (kQ_2q) / r_2$

$W_{total} = W_1 + W_2$

$W_{total} = kq(Q_1 / r_1 + Q_2 / r_2)$

$W_{total} = (9 \times 10^9 \text{ N·m}^2/\text{C}^2)\cdot(10 \times 10^{-6} \text{ C})\cdot(+6 \text{ μC} / 0.002 \text{ m} + -6 \text{ μC} / 0.003 \text{ m})$

$W_{total} = 90 \text{ J}$

35. B is correct.

Use energy relationship:

$PE_{before} = PE_{after} + KE$

Electrostatic Potential Energy:

$PE = kQq / r$

Solve:

$kQq / r_1 = kQq / r_2 + \frac{1}{2}mv^2$

$\frac{1}{2}mv^2 = kQq(1 / r_1 - 1 / r_2)$

$v^2 = (2kQq / m)\cdot(1 / r_1 - 1 / r_2)$

$v = \sqrt{[(2kQq / m)\cdot(1 / r_1 - 1 / r_2)]}$

$$v = \sqrt{[(2) \cdot (9 \times 10^9 \text{ N} \cdot \text{m}^2/\text{C}^2) \cdot (1.6 \times 10^{-19} \text{ C}) \cdot (1.6 \times 10^{-19} \text{ C}) /}$$
$$(9.1 \times 10^{-31} \text{ kg})] \cdot [(1 / 0.02 \text{ m}) - (1 / 0.05 \text{ m})]$$

$v = 123$ m/s

Note: only the magnitude of the charge is used.

36. A is correct.

1 amp = 1 C/s

# of amps = $(2.3 \times 10^{13}$ electrons / 1)·$(1.6 \times 10^{-19}$ C / 1 electron)·(1 / 15 s)

# of amps = 0.25×10^{-6} amps

# of amps = 0.25 μA

37. B is correct.

1 kW = 1,000 W

1,000 W = 1,000 J/s

1 hr = (60 min)·(60 sec/min)

1 hr = 3,600 s

kW·hr = (1,000 J/s)·(3,600 s)

kW·hr = 3.6×10^3 J

Share your opinion

Your feedback is important because we strive to provide the highest quality prep materials. If you are satisfied with the content of this book, post your review on Amazon, so others can benefit from your experience.

If you have any questions or comments about the material, email us at info@sterling-prep.com and we will resolve any issues to your satisfaction.

To access these and other AP questions online at a special pricing visit:
http://AP.Sterling-Prep.com/bookowner.htm
